Financial Literacy in Today´s Global Market

Edited by Ireneusz Miciuła

Published in London, United Kingdom

Financial Literacy in Today's Global Market
http://dx.doi.org/10.5772/intechopen.111171
Edited by Ireneusz Miciuła

Contributors
Adham Taher Alessa, Ayo Teriba, Bassey Ibor, Ireneusz Miciuła, Jasmina Okičić, Joanita Kataike, Joel Hodroff, Luisa Anderloni, Luyao Zhang, Margret Asiimwe, Meldina Kokorović Jukan, Nadine Strauß, Ornella Moro, Robert Mawenu, Sophie Knowles, Steven Tairu Bello, Sylvester Onyeoma, Thomas Fisher, Vesile Cinceoglu, Willy Rwamparagi Kagarura

First published in London, United Kingdom, 2024 by IntechOpen
IntechOpen is the global imprint of INTECHOPEN LIMITED, registered in England and Wales, registration number: 11086078, 167-169 Great Portland Street, London, W1W 5PF, United Kingdom

British Library Cataloguing-in-Publication Data
A catalogue record for this book is available from the British Library

Additional hard and PDF copies can be obtained from orders@intechopen.com

Financial Literacy in Today's Global Market
Edited by Ireneusz Miciuła
p. cm.
Print ISBN 978-0-85466-422-1
Online ISBN 978-0-85466-421-4
eBook (PDF) ISBN 978-0-85466-423-8

For EU product safety concerns:
IN TECH d.o.o., Prolaz Marije Krucifikse Kozulić 3, 51000 Rijeka, Croatia,
info@intechopen.com or visit our website at intechopen.com.

Meet the editor

Ireneusz Miciuła is an assistant professor at the Institute of Economics and Finance, University of Szczecin, Poland. He is the author of more than 250 scientific and journalistic publications on economics, finance, management, and information technologies. He has participated in numerous international scientific conferences. He received a scholarship from the Human Capital Operational Program and conducted research at the European University Institute, Italy. He is a visiting researcher at many universities in Germany, Czech Republic, Romania, Albania, Greece, and Portugal. He is a member of the *Journal of Economics and Public Finance* and a reviewer for the Polish-U.S. Fulbright Foundation. He is a member of the Polish Finance and Banking Association and Polish Economic Society, as well as an expert at the Polish Agency for Enterprise Development and the Energy Regulatory Office. He is a scientific expert at the Foundation for Polish Science.

Contents

Preface **IX**

Section 1
Financial Education **1**

Chapter 1 **3**
Introductory Chapter: Modern World of Finance
by Ireneusz Miciuła

Chapter 2 **9**
Financial Inclusion and Financial Literacy
by Bassey Ibor

Chapter 3 **23**
The Needs for Financial Literacy in the Fintech Era: Italian Experiences
by Luisa Anderloni and Ornella Moro

Chapter 4 **43**
Financial Inclusion and Digital Financial Literacy: The Case of Microfinance Sector in Bosnia and Herzegovina
by Jasmina Okičić and Meldina Kokorović Jukan

Chapter 5 **69**
Financial Literacy Plus New Purchasing Power, How Ledger Economics Can End Poverty and Promote Continuous Economic Improvement
by Thomas Fisher and Joel Hodroff

Section 2
Global Financial Market **87**

Chapter 6 **89**
Systematic Review of Monetary Policy Effect on Foreign Direct Investment
by Adham Taher Alessa

Chapter 7 **101**
The Fundamentals of Stock Market Investing in the Twenty-First Century
by Steven Tairu Bello

Chapter 8 109
Assessing the Effect of Financial Management Practices on Financial Performance and the Moderating Role of Farm and Farmers' Socioeconomic Characteristics on Dairy Enterprises
by Joanita Kataike, Margret Asiimwe, Robert Mawenu and Willy Rwamparagi Kagarura

Section 3
Financialization and the Financial Future of the World 125

Chapter 9 127
Public Finance in a Digital Economy
by Sylvester Onyeoma

Chapter 10 137
The Role of Reading Economic News in Germany and the UK
by Nadine Strauß, Sophie Knowles and Vesile Cinceoglu

Chapter 11 157
Market Shocks, Financial Literacy, and Net Worth
by Ayo Teriba

Chapter 12 171
Content Analysis of the Financial Literature Over Time in the World
by Luisa Anderloni and Ornella Moro

Chapter 13 193
The Future of Finance: Synthesizing CeFi and DeFi for the Benefit of All
by Luyao Zhang

Preface

Financial Literacy in Today's Global Market is the result of current research by many authors from various academic centers, whose main goal in the presented chapters is to provide knowledge, recommendations, and practical solutions to new challenges within the contemporary processes of financial globalization, financial literacy, and the international market.

It is broadly understood that financial literacy in the global world is one of the most important factors for the intelligent and sustainable development of knowledge-based economies. The global market is a subject of interest in technical and social sciences, associated with the interpenetration of technical, organizational, marketing, social, and psychological processes and phenomena. All these elements are connected with the modern knowledge of the processes taking place in the global world of finance. This is due to the undeniable impact of information technologies and the interdisciplinary nature of the organization of the global financial market on socio-economic development. The selection of topics presented in this book reflects the increasing importance of financial processes, the necessary education regarding the world of finance, and the future global socioeconomic problems resulting from changes in the organization of financial flows. As part of this book's scientific research, special attention was paid to the issues of contemporary foundations of the global finance market based on the development of information technologies and knowledge and education in the discipline of finance. This book indicates that knowledge and technology are the basic factors stimulating socioeconomic development and influencing changes in the global environment, including financial processes that are fundamental in the economy.

Section 1, "Financial Education", includes chapters on financial literacy, solutions in financial education, and optimization of contemporary education of societies. Section 2, "Global Financial Market", presents chapters on the development of the global financial market and case studies of specific countries or international organizations. Section 3, "Financialization and the Financial Future of the World", includes chapters on the development of contemporary financial processes such as financialization, the determination of the future development of the world of finance, and the most important aspects of the world of finance that are waiting to be solved and applied in practice by global financial markets.

We would like to thank all those who contributed to the creation of this publication, especially the authors for their inspiring scientific considerations. As the editor of this monograph, I hope that the presented issues will motivate readers to become interested in the subject matter, which will translate into undertaking their own investigations and developing new solutions to the discussed research problems.

Ireneusz Miciuła
Department of Sustainable Finance and Capital Markets,
Institute of Economics and Finance,
University of Szczecin,
Szczecin, Poland

Section 1

Financial Education

Chapter 1

Introductory Chapter: Modern World of Finance

Ireneusz Miciuła

1. Introduction

Finance is monetary phenomena and processes, or in other words, monetary resources, operations, and legal norms relating to them. Finance is also a social relationship that arises from collecting and spending money. Therefore, the science of finance examines money streams flowing between economic entities during the processes of production, distribution and exchange (consumption), and material accumulation, as well as money resources collected and distributed during these processes [1]. The science of finance studies and explains the economic content of the mentioned monetary phenomena and processes, that is, the connections and dependencies between the flow of money streams and the distribution of its resources and the flow and distribution of resources of products, material and immaterial services, and human labor [2]. The subject of interest in finance is the possibility of using the abovementioned relationships and dependencies to use money to control the planned course of material processes, that is, the production, distribution, and consumption of products and services [3]. The subject of interest in finance is primarily its creation in the banking system, the movement of money – circulation between various economic units and their groups, and "settling" in the form of savings and monetary reserves [4]. Therefore, finance is a field of science that deals with the analysis of how people allocate available financial resources in a given period, or it should be defined as all economic phenomena related to the accumulation and distribution of monetary resources, which can be defined as economic relations resulting from the movement of money, with collecting and spending monetary resources [5]. Finance features:

On a macroeconomic scale:

1. Passive: they record in monetary terms what is happening in economic life without influencing its modifications or structure.

2. Active: they implement a specific system of incentives by means of which they influence the course of economic processes.

On a microeconomic scale:

1. Distributive: involves transferring material values between various economic entities using money.

2. Control: involves the use of relationships between the movement of monetary resources and the movement of material value in order to obtain signals about

the course of economic processes from the observation of the course of financial phenomena.

3. Stimulation (motivational): related to the active role of finance in the economy. Its aim is to influence the efficiency of collecting and spending money. For this purpose, it is necessary to use financial incentives that motivate to undertake or conduct activities or activities in exchange for monetary benefits.

It is commonly believed that finance occurs where money is used in economic processes and is usually defined as all phenomena and processes related to the accumulation, flow, division, and expenditure of monetary resources. In connection with this broad definitional analysis, finance should be defined as a "multi-paradigm" economic science, the subject of which is the description, analysis, and assessment of globalization processes, choices, and financial decisions made under conditions of risk by economic units [6]. That is why, scientific discourse on the unified division of scientific fields and disciplines is so important. It is undoubtedly an issue to consider whether, like management sciences, we should also separate the science of finance, which will be a discipline of economic sciences focusing on financial processes. Especially, as nowadays, in some classifications, there is economics and econometrics (although it is more of a research method involving the study of quantitative relationships between economic phenomena and variables), and in others, we have economics and finance as a discipline in the field of social sciences. We can see that even the classification of scientific fields and disciplines requires unification, and this is not easy and unambiguous. Although there is undoubtedly no business, management or economics (globally functioning scientific disciplines) without analysis and conclusions from the results that finance gives directly relating to monetary valuation. Therefore, just as energy is the driving force of the economy, finance is the foundation of all economic activities [7]. In modern times, knowledge and skills in the field of finance should be developed already in primary education [8] especially due to the continuous development of finance as a field that concerns all economic units, and therefore the entire society. Additionally, due to the fact that, apart from the traditional approach, where there is a connection between the monetary sphere of the economy and the real sphere, that is, financial phenomena arising in connection with the production of goods and services that meet human needs, we are dealing with an autonomous approach. This results in a reality in which the sphere of finance exists separately from the real sphere (autonomy of the sphere of finance) and money exists in an abstract (symbolic) dimension, which causes many processes that directly affect entire economies and societies operating on the global market.

2. Financial literacy and the importance of financial education

Financial education is understood as a process enabling the improvement of the low level of financial literacy, that is, knowledge, skills, but also awareness and financial behavior appropriate to the situation. However, due to the dynamic development of the complexity of the financial market, this process requires adaptation to the changing environment. Although financial education has evolved, both in terms of its importance and in relation to the organization and implementation of the entire process, the changes have not kept pace with the multi-faceted development of the global financial market. Additionally, the reason for the lack of financial success in societies in many countries is often considered to be their low level of financial literacy, which often results from insufficient financial education. The abovementioned development and the accompanying increasing complexity of all segments of the financial market require new educational content and forms. Meanwhile, financial education, especially on a larger scale, has not changed much over the years. Innovations in financial education are understood as new or transformed existing solutions in various areas related to the financial education process [9]. Therefore, financial education is an important process that makes it possible to improve the low level of financial awareness in the societies of many countries [10]. Many economic entities (governments, financial institutions, businesses, and households) are interested in improving low levels of literacy due to its impact on both the well-being of society and the economy [11]. This situation means that the importance of financial education continues to grow. In recent years, the number of activities in these areas has increased rapidly [12]. The most important innovations in financial education include solutions for organizing the financial education process, new, extended educational content and a number of new forms of financial education [13]. This confirms its importance among the necessary competences in an economy based on the information society, the development of which is related to information technology.

With globalization and technical progress, the demand for information is growing [14]. It can be transmitted, saved, and processed, but nowadays, information also functions in the virtual world, that is, the Internet space, where it is collected in databases. Its quantity has resulted in the need to solve new problems and search for optimal solutions, which is illustrated by the area of interest in big data. Information is an interdisciplinary, ubiquitous term, in common use and associated with various adjectives, for example, economic, legal, tourist, and financial information. At the same time, financial knowledge is the basis for functioning as an economic entity on the markets of the global economy. Therefore, the consequences of financial illiteracy are fundamental to functioning in social exchange markets. Frauds taking advantage of ignorance in this matter are commonplace, and regulators cannot keep up with changes in the law to properly protect financial market participants, as evidenced by international credit scandals around the world.

Nowadays, running a business or investment activity requires the ability to search, analyze, and use selected information to support decision-making processes. A special role in obtaining information about economic entities is assigned to financial statements, which should provide useful financial information. This is why, financial information is so fundamental in the information society. Especially, as new information technologies are rapidly developing and being used in this field so much so that the world has designated a new area of interest under the term Financial Technology (FinTech).

3. The needs for digital financial literacy in the FinTech (financial technology) era

Digital finance, often referred to as financial technology (FinTech), is the application of digital technologies to financial activities [15]. Consumers and businesses are increasingly using digital financial services. The COVID-19 pandemic has further increased this trend [16]. Digital finance is new financial technologies can facilitate access to financial services and improve the efficiency of the financial system [17]. Digital finance is the delivery of traditional financial services digitally, through devices such as computers, tablets, and smartphones [18]. Digital finance has the potential to make financial services accessible to underserved populations in areas that lacked physical infrastructure for these services [17]. We are currently witnessing the digital transformation of financial services, which additionally increases the need for financial education of entire societies [19].

Digital finance is the term used to describe the impact of new technologies on the financial services industry. It includes a variety of products, applications, processes, and business models that have transformed the traditional way of providing banking and financial services [20]. While technological innovation in finance is not new, investment in new technologies has substantially increased in recent years, and the pace of innovation is exponential [21]. We now interact with our bank using mobile technology. We make payments, transfer money, and make investments using a variety of new tools that were not there few years ago [22]. Artificial intelligence, social networks, machine learning, mobile applications, distributed ledger technology, cloud computing, and big data analytics have given rise to new services and business models by established financial institutions and new market entrants. All these technologies can benefit both consumers and companies by enabling greater access to financial services, offering wider choice and increasing efficiency of operations.

The digital revolution of the financial system along with the development of cryptocurrencies requires changes in financial education and its adaptation to changes introduced in the functioning of global financial markets. Nowadays, scientists, experts, and practitioners are looking for technological solutions and appropriate legal conditions for the most beneficial use of the achievements of the FinTech field. That is why, this monograph presents multi-aspect research on all possible solutions in the field of FinTech, what is the future of finance in today's global markets.

We would like to thank all those who contributed to the creation of this publication, and especially the authors for their inspiring scientific considerations. As the editor of this monograph, I hope that many of the presented issues will motivate the reader to become interested in the subject matter, which will translate into undertaking own investigations and new solutions to the discussed research problems.

Author details

Ireneusz Miciuła
Department of Sustainable Finance and Capital Markets, Institute of Economics and Finance, University of Szczecin, Szczecin, Poland

*Address all correspondence to: irekmic@wp.pl

References

[1] Miciuła I. Współczesne metody i instrumenty zarządzania ryzykiem walutowym w przedsiębiorstwie. Studia i Prace Wydziału Nauk Ekonomicznych i Zarządzania. 2012;**28**:67-80. Available from: https://wneiz.pl/nauka_wneiz/sip/sip28-2012/SiP-28-67.pdf

[2] Cieślukowski M. Nauka o finansach publicznych w świetle paradygmatu zrównoważonego rozwoju. Finanse. 2017;**1**:11-22

[3] Filar D, Łukasiewicz-Kamińska A, Miciuła I, Sobiecki G, Niedzwiecki A, Rakoczy J. Od muszli po Bitmonety. Oblicza pieniądza i systemów walutowych. Warszawa: Texter; 2014

[4] Lusardi A, Mitchell OS, Curto V. Financial literacy among the young. Journal of Consumer Affairs. 2010;**44**(2):358-380

[5] Beck T, Demirgüç-Kunt A, Levine R, Maksimovic V. Financial Structure and Economic Development. Firm, Industry, and Country Evidence, Policy Research Working Paper, Nr 2423. Washington, DC: The World Bank; 2000

[6] Flejterski S, Solarz JK. Komparatystyka finansów. Warszawa: C.H. Beck; 2015

[7] Miciula I, Kadlubek M, Stępień P. Modern methods of business valuation—Case study and new concepts. Sustainability. 2020;**12**:2699. DOI: 10.3390/su12072699

[8] OECD/INFE High Level Principles on National Strategies for Financial Education. 2012. Available from: https://finance.ec.europa.eu/digital-finance_en [Accessed: February 4, 2024]

[9] Lusardi A. Financial Literacy around the World. Pennsylvania, USA: FINRA, Financial Investor Education; 2013

[10] Ferleger L, Lazonick W. Higher Education for an Innovative Economy: Land-Grant Colleges and the Managerial Revolution in America. 2022. Available from: http://www.thebhc.org/publications/BEHprint/v023n1/p0116-p0128.pdf [Accessed: May 22, 2022]

[11] Grifoni A, Messy F. Current Status of National Strategies for Financial Education: A Comparative Analysis and Relevant Practices, OECD Working Papers on Finance, Insurance and Private Pensions, No. 16. Paris, France: OECD Publishing; 2012

[12] Iwanicz-Drozdowska M. Produkty finansowe i edukacja finansowa w Polsce na tle wybranych krajów wysoko rozwiniętych. Warszawa: Raport z badań. SGH; 2009

[13] OECD. International Gateway for Financial Education. 2024. Available from: http://www.financial-education.org/program.php [Accessed: February 1, 2024]

[14] Błażyńska J. Informacja finansowa w społeczeństwie informacyjnym, Zeszyty Naukowe Uniwersytetu Szczecińskiego nr 827, Finanse, Rynki Finansowe, Ubezpieczenia, vol. 69, 2014, Wydawnictwo Naukowe Uniwersytetu Szczecińskiego, Szczecin 157-165. Available from: https://wneiz.pl/nauka_wneiz/frfu/69-2014/FRFU-69-157.pdf

[15] Vasek M, Moore T. There's no free lunch, even using bitcoin: Tracking the popularity and profits of virtual currency scams. In: International Conference on Financial Cryptography and Data Security. Berlin: Springer; 2015. pp. 44-61

[16] Yen K-C, Cheng H-P. Economic policy uncertainty and cryptocurrency

volatility. Finance Research Letters. 2021;**38**:101428

[17] European Commission. 2024. Available from: https://finance.ec.europa.eu/digital-finance_en

[18] Sapuric S, Kokkinaki A. Bitcoin Is Volatile! Isn't that Right? International Conference on Business Information Systems. Cham: Springer; 2014. pp. 255-265

[19] Miciuła I, Kazojć K. The global development of cryptocurrencies. Prace Naukowe Uniwersytetu Ekonomicznego we Wrocławiu. 2019;**63**(2):183-196. Available from: https://journals.ue.wroc.pl/pn/article/view/355

[20] Popkova E, Krivtsov A, Bogoviz A. Digital economy in the 21st century: An introduction to the institutional approach. In: Popkova E, Krivtsov A, Bogoviz içinde A, editors. The Institutional Foundations of the Digital Economy in the 21st Century. Vol. 10. Boston: De Gruyter; 2021

[21] Woebbeking F. Cryptocurrency volatility markets. Digital Finance. 2021;**3**(3):273-298

[22] Kelly M, Hartley F, Dunne C, Looney A, O'Neill J. Improving Financial Capability – A Multi-Stakeholder Approach. Dublin, Ireland: Raport of the National Steering Group on Financial Education; 2009

Chapter 2

Financial Inclusion and Financial Literacy

Bassey Ibor

Abstract

Finance is, unarguably, an integral part of everyday life and living. Therefore, financial literacy is an essential life skill. Little wonder, therefore, it is widely flag high on the economic policy agenda of emerging economies, globally. This imperative is buoyed by unrelenting growth and sophistication of financial services offerings, mobile demographics, as well as global pursuit of policies that expand and strengthen national welfare systems. Financial literacy is a sine qua non for financial inclusion. Financially disadvantaged and vulnerable segments of the society are enabled to actively contribute to national development through the protection, from social and economic shocks, offered by financial inclusion. Most vulnerable is the sizable rural population with limited access to conventional financial institutions or services in most countries of the world. *Financial inclusion (FI) is the process of ensuring access by this segment of society to appropriate financial products and services at an affordable cost in a fair and transparent manner.* This chapter looks at the concept and significance of financial literacy, its derivative, financial inclusion, and how both interplay in deepening inclusive economic development.

Keywords: financial literacy, financial inclusion, finance, financial skills, globalization

1. Introduction

Inclusive and exclusive growth are the two sides of new mantra promoted globally, through which new methods and schemes are adopted to bring the chunk of disadvantaged, vulnerable, and other excluded populations into the fold of finance. The concept and practice of financial inclusion have grown to become the leading light in the overall strategy of nations for inclusive growth. This explains the prominence, it has assumed in public discourse, lately. Inclusive financing delivers financial services affordably to the vulnerable, disadvantaged, and low-income populations. This motivation, in India, led to the introduction of financial inclusion in 2005. Financial inclusion is a top, people empowering, poverty reduction, program of both emerging and established nations, as well as major development agencies. To push toward worldwide financial inclusion, the central banks of nations have introduced and/or supported several initiatives, pointing to ways in which the efforts of governments, in this direction, can be made more fruitful.

Enabling financial inclusion is the primary focus of financial literacy inventiveness. This postulation, drawn from evidence-aided understanding of the critical local conditions, of denial or deprivations that contribute to backwardness or lack of development in remote areas, accords with the findings of [1]. It is also a defining acknowledgment of the benefits and risks inherent in the role of financial inclusion as an effective mitigation tool for such conditions.

Accordingly, the baseline of financial literacy is creating and raising the level of awareness on (i) financial services offerings and conditionalities among the people, stratified into urban, peri-urban and rural areas, (ii) the locations of functional and affordable financial services access or dispensing points, (iii) costs and redress mechanisms when up taking financial services at designated access points, (iv) the nature of utility of the financial/banking services on offer, and (v) available alternative financial inclusion schemes within the financial ecosystem of the particular jurisdiction. Overall, financial literacy aims at increasing the reachability of financial services to the demographically disadvantaged, vulnerable, rural and poor individuals, households, and communities, who are more often financially excluded from the conventional financial offerings.

2. Financial literacy

Global demographics point to many citizens' inadequate understanding of either their financial needs or the financial instruments/products available and how to access them beneficially. Financial literacy is the knowledge of how, where, and when to make nifty decisions with money and near money, including, but not limited to, budgeting, savings, investments, favorable loan terms, credit impact mitigation strategies, and diverse retirement schemes. So, it is the possession of skills, knowledge, and actions that allow individuals make informed decisions regarding money and money derivatives. One measure or evidence that one is financially literate is taking the right steps to the right financial outcomes and not just understanding the facts about money.

2.1 Contextualization of financial literacy

Financial literacy is conceptualized, defined, and pursued on the public policy recognition that financial inclusion connotes all initiatives aimed at keeping formal financial services available, accessible, and affordable to all segments of the population [2]. Therefore, financial literacy enthuses definite lots of the society, traditionally unserved formal financial services as a direct response to their personal attributes and economic conditions. Unarguably, there are three constants in life: change, taxes, and economic recessions. While practitioners concede that personal development may not easily save one from the first two, financial literacy can definitively help circumnavigate the third. The essential core of financial literacy is to learn how to manage finances wisely, plan for the future, make smart financial choices, thrive in uncertain times by wisely exploring investment opportunities, understanding our risk appetites, and taking actions in line with this understanding to secure our future. We are living in a time of great economic uncertainty, and globally, countries are facing the effects of inflation and other challenges. That is why it is essential to prioritize financial literacy: first as a window to financial inclusion and, ultimately, economic inclusion and development.

2.2 Objectives of financial literacy

The overarching philosophy behind financial literacy is providing every household with access information and sufficient education to a suite of modern financial services, including savings, credit, insurance, and payments to make good financial decisions for themselves. Accordingly, financial literacy initiatives must seek to educate all segments of the population to recognize and uptake formal financial services to achieve inclusive economic development. Attainment of high financial literacy success rate must definitely move individuals and small businesses into the financial services net, enabling them to play actively in the domestic economic space, especially as providers of employment opportunities and generators of primary, as well as secondary sources of household income. To be financially literate is to know how to manage your money (how to borrow and save money) responsibly, as well as how and why to invest and plan for retirement.

2.3 The components and rules of financial literacy

The key dimensions of financial literacy are budgeting, saving, managing debt, investing, and managing credit. There are four rules for constructing financial literacy, namely budgeting, expenditure tracking, debt management, and retirement planning. The principles of financial literacy can basically, therefore, be narrowed to three, namely: (i) making and growing earnings beyond the level of spending; (ii) achieving financial success and freedom that makes money work for the financially literate; and (iii) attaining a readiness for the unexpected turn of events, arising from changes in living conditions and/or the quantum of disposable income. This requires literacy on what insurance or other hedging schemes are available against such adverse turns. Accordingly, to halt and reverse financial illiteracy, a person has to commit to the following: (1) Pitch into financial literature, particularly free online newsletters, from trusted sources; (2) Watch or listen to mainstream media financial tele/broadcasts, podcasts, and features; (3) Make a habit of reading personal and general finance books and learning materials; (4) Use social media and online communication search engines and websites wisely; (5) Prepare and retain a budget and a notepad on financial terms and new learnings, working to internalize them; and (6) Routinely engage with a financial professional when all else fails.

Financially literate individuals are "mathematically" and "emotionally" enlightened and able to effectively manage money, understand credit/debt management, assess the need for insurance and indemnification, evaluate various risks and compensations related to savings and investment opportunities, and understand wider ethical considerations, inherent in the choices they make. Countries are increasingly cognizant of the importance of financial literacy and are providing an assortment of financial literacy programs through appropriate information, education, and communication materials. Others are pushing national policies and strategies to coordinate and guide their financial literacy programs to achieve the ultimate outcome of financial inclusion.

2.3.1 Digital financial literacy

Digital financial literacy is the concept of acquiring appropriate IT-based knowledge, skills, confidence, and competencies to safely use digitally delivered financial products and services. Today, almost all financial products and services, as well as information related to them, are offered or at least available online. Digital financial literacy is, without doubt, the nexus between financial literacy and financial inclusion that is the current crave of nations across jurisdictions. For countries with a sizeable rural poor population with limited access to conventional financial institutions or services, embracing digital financial literacy resources can help this dominant population demographic take charge of their finances through digital financial services offerings, thereby improving their economic wellbeing. This will engender support to national monetary policy feasance and contribute to economic development unobtrusively. There is no gainsaying that, without appropriate digital financial literacy resources and the attendant education they convey, many people would shy away from a gamut of financial services and/or live at the heightened risk of fraud or fraud-enabling forces/schemes.

2.4 Benefits of financial literacy

Individual life goals can be realized through financial literacy by borrowing correctly and operating enterprises to survive and grow. Key benefits of financial literacy include knowledgeably creating a budget, planning for retirement, managing debt, and tracking spending. To a nation, it accentuates the acceptance and sustainability of a regime of financial inclusion. It supports financial sector deepening and economic well-being, through the achievement of monetary policy targets, because less people get excluded from main and sub-stream financial systems. Therefore, successful financial literacy must leverage a strong platform for shared values and experiences, based on a twin-track feedback mechanism between the regulators and the regulated. More specifically, direct benefits derivable from successful financial literacy efforts include: (a) improving both the security and social cohesion of individuals and nations; (b) halting and reversing the catastrophic consequences from inequalities between societal cadres (ethnic, racial, or gender lines); (c) validating the government's commitment as the "protector of last resort," thereby reducing the number of the poor and the burden on the tax paying public, ensuring a minimum social security net; (d) empowering people to be more astute about saving and investing; e) protecting the unguarded or unsuspecting citizens from those who prey upon their ignorance, vulnerability, and greed; (f) inculcating lifelong financial skills and habits, necessary to participate sensibly in financial markets, conducing better enabling environment, where reprobate products are forced out of the market-place and confidence is raised; and (g) stimulating quality financial services, thereby contributing meaningfully to national economic growth and development. These findings are corroborated by Johnson [3]. It is to be noted that the effectiveness of financial literacy campaigns can, sometimes, be counteracted by controlling psychological or behavioural traits, such as fear, risk aversion, inertia, and lack of willpower by target citizen groups, although these peter away as financial literacy takes root.

2.5 Essential skills for achieving and maintaining financial literacy

A number of skills (financial and soft) by finance professionals can be isolated as disposing factors for achieving and maintaining financial literacy success.

2.5.1 Finance skills

Finance skills refer to the set of abilities and knowledge to manage financial resources effectively and notably, include inter alia, budgeting, financial analysis, problem-solving, ethics, risk assessment, strategic financial planning, and project management. The possession of these critical skills leads to improved financial decision-making and a better navigation of the prevailing economic landscape to achieve success. For fuller appreciation of the skills explained here and in the following sections, readers are encouraged to seek specific information about each of them individually.

2.5.2 Communication and interpersonal skills

Communication and interpersonal skills are top-notch on the pile of essential skills for financial services providers and discerning users, for a number of reasons. Firstly, finance professionals, routinely, handle complicated financial data to be presented to clients and stakeholders. Therefore, they need to possess the ability to communicate information concisely and in an easily understandable manner to hallmark success. Secondly, the need to work closely with colleagues and clients (service up takers) to achieve shared goals, calls for strong interpersonal skills to establish trust, build and sustain relationships, as well as facilitate effective teamwork. Lastly, the work requires seamless and sensitive interaction with individuals and groups from different cultures and backgrounds, necessitating excellent communication, diversity tolerance, and interpersonal skills.

2.5.3 Problem-solving skills

Decisions about where and how to uptake financial services present challenges (from simple to very complex scenarios) that can significantly impact the success of financial literacy efforts or even financial inclusion coverage. Should such arise, solid problem-solving skills, help identify potential problems before they arise, and evolve frontal hands-on actions and ingenious resolutions to redress the identified challenges. This is because manifest problem-solving skills call to play critical thinking, attention to detail, and a willingness to work collaboratively with colleagues and clients to achieve desired financial literacy outcomes.

2.5.4 Ethical orientation skills

The drive for financial inclusion, through effective financial literacy schemes, requires both provider and user to be ethically oriented and enamoured. The prerequisites for this are high trust, mutual responsibility and accountability, conflict of interests management, and confidentiality. Besides, the motivation for making financially sound and ethically responsible investment decisions, in the management of other people's money, places a burden on regulatory bodies and financial institutions to seek and enforce strict ethical standards and codes, with violations not lightly treated. Society and financial services vendors must clarify their ethical guidelines, unambiguously, so that service up takers know what is expected of them when using a preferred service offering, selected access points or tools, and what the consequences are if improperly used.

2.5.5 Accounting skills

This set of skills enables accurate and effective analysis of financial data and helps in evaluating financial performance, identifying trends, forecasting future performance, financial planning, managing financial exposures, and achieving regulatory compliance requirements draws in accounting skills, even at the sublime level.

2.5.6 Tactical financial planning skills

Similar to problem-solving skills in resolving financial challenges faced by businesses, tactical financial planning enables skill-holders navigate economic uncertainties to create a roadmap for financial performance, stability, and growth. This set of skills positions one to make informed decisions, to effectively allocate resources, recognize potential financial risks and opportunities, and ably evolve strategies to mitigate or capitalize on them.

2.5.7 Reporting skills

Beyond the analysis of financial data, reporting results to stakeholders in an easy-to-understand manner is crucial in making informed investment and financial service up taking decisions. Closely related to accounting skills and working knowledge of financial analysis tools and techniques, such as ratio analysis and trend analysis, suitable reporting skills eases understanding, interpretation, and use (the main end point of financial literacy) of the analyzed financial data.

2.5.8 Analytical skills

Possessing and demonstrating relevant analytical skills is critical in identifying trends, risks, and opportunities associated with financial services offerings, including the pedigree of the financial services provider data and posturing, to determine whether to take up or disengage a service.

2.5.9 Project management skills

Procuring the skills of planning and budgeting, analyzing financial data, making informed decisions about resource allocation as well as effective project management, helps further financial literacy. This involves the skill to improve the overall financial performance objectives by delivering projects (such as achieving national financial inclusion) on time, within budget, and with good quality outcomes.

2.5.10 Digital/soft skills

Possession of excellent computer (digital/soft) skills to unravel vast financial documentation, several financial analysis software manifestations, as well as digital financial data organization is sine qua non for delivering cutting-edge financial services.

2.5.11 Vulnerability or threat analysis skills

Whether at the strategic, tactical, or rudimentary level, possessing demonstrable quantitative and qualitative threat analysis skills emboldens one's ability to identify, evaluate, and prioritize inherent risks, and develop mitigation or avoidance strategies for long-term success. These skills include, but not limited to, mathematical and statistical risk probability and impact models, expert judgment, and subjective assessment (from reference of peers who have used the product/service) for risks that are difficult to quantify.

3. What is financial inclusion?

Financial inclusion is the process of ensuring unambiguous and non-discriminatory uptake of appropriate financial services, but particularly by those groups that are usually underserved and financially excluded, who currently only have access to basic financial products. This must be at an affordable cost, in a fair, transparent, ethically sound, and dignifying manner. Financial inclusion is viewed as the ability to access and use basic financial services in a manner that is reasonably convenient, reliable, and flexible. Financial inclusion depicts an ecosystem of sustainable, relevant, cost-effective, and meaningful financial services for the financially underserved population, especially rural dwellers. That is, financial inclusion is measured by the adequate, safe, convenient, and affordable range of financial services taken up by citizens, particularly, the low-income, vulnerable, rural, and undocumented person groups. Accordingly, financial inclusion is measured by the proportion of the general population that has this access.

3.1 Contextualization of financial inclusion

As a result of the increasing policy interest in financial inclusion, globally, countries are pursuing policies to strengthen to ensure that all populations excluded from financial services are reached and served [4]. Financial inclusion has been identified, globally, as a major channel for speeding up economic development through its impact on the growth and development of micro, small, and medium enterprises (MSMEs) and other business collectives. This is in recognition, by the central banks of nations that access to microfinance is critical to the survival and growth of MSMEs operators. The contextualization is, therefore, that financial inclusion is to draw the unbanked population into the formal financial system, positioning them to access the whole gamut of financial services that meet their needs at an affordable cost. Financial inclusion, construed as access to financial services, varies widely in concepts across the globe in recognition of jurisdictional peculiarities.

3.2 Why is financial inclusion important?

Financial inclusion is important for a number of reasons, namely:

i. Facilitation of ease of access to appropriate financial instruments, which is construed as the “per Mille” availability of service branches or access points.

ii. Uplifting of the financial conditions and improving the general standard of living.

iii. Improved efficiency of the financial intermediation process, as well as deepening the financial system, wholistically.

iv. Inclusion reduces income disparity by motivating the excluded to join in and invest in physical assets and self-education.

v. Impacts development, invariably aiding poverty reduction, and long-term economic growth.

vi. Engineers credit expansion and the accommodation of relatively unregulated segments of the financial ecosystem, with the caveat that capacity must be built deliberately in this direction;

vii. Offers incremental complementary solutions that tackle poverty, promoting inclusive development and addressing the sustainable development goals (SDGs) targets;

viii. Ensures that economic growth performance is inclusive and sustained, and

ix. Enhances the effectiveness of monetary and fiscal policies of government.

At the long range, access to financial and nonfinancial banking services (roughly called business development services) are crucial ingredients in realizing the potentials of micro, small enterprises in creating jobs, restraining poverty, and spurring economic growth. Aduda and Kalunda [5] promotes mainstream viewpoint that financial inclusion is an unmistaken prerequisite for economic growth and development as a result of its ability to enhance capital creation, finance sector saving, bolster requisite intermediation, and by implication, investment. According to the general theory of entrepreneurship, the abilities to identify and tap the opportunities provided by external business environments to start up or improve businesses differ across individuals and depend on the individuals' abilities to access information and inclination to act upon the information in terms of risks. The theory promotes entrepreneurial opportunity discovery, evaluation, and utilization to exploit and predicts individual attributes made up of psychological and demographic factors, such as gender. In this context, access to quality and affordable financial services and products may help people, especially women and vulnerable groups to exploit available business opportunities. This is the nexus between financial literacy and financial inclusion.

3.3 Objectives of financial inclusion

The level of access to quality financial is one major driver of economic growth, meaning the objective is to create linkages that make usage of cheap, convenient, and dignifying. Another objective is to position people to diversify or increase household income streams and improve asset loss recovery. Further, it sets out to bring disadvantaged and vulnerable sections of the society within the ambit of formalized and standardized services at an affordable cost. Finally, financial inclusion is a bold step toward inclusive economic development by hyping on the indicators of availability, awareness, affordability, adequacy, and accessibility.

3.4 Drivers of enabling policies

This section discusses issues, factors, and economic and demographic scenarios that have created the global pressure for financial inclusion.

3.4.1 What pushes nations to prioritize financial inclusion

A number of factors are responsible for the crave for financial inclusion, across jurisdictions, and they include, but not limited to:

- Globalization: Globalization refers to the shift toward a more integrated and interdependent world economy, along with the merging of distinct and separate national markets into one huge global marketplace. Globalization is real and some dare say, irreversible. Hitherto, recognized geographical boundaries are rapidly collapsing in meaning, relevance, and influence because more and more businesses are competing globally, leveraging technology. As we know it, sovereign control is diminishing faster than the speed of light. Harmonized trading and financial platforms have been, or are being, agreed upon and promoted by governments, regional blocks, and cross-border institutions. The derived effect of globalization is the enormous opportunities presented to internationally responsive nations, through the complex structures and systems of cross-border organizations and the multiple markets servicing them. The world has become a global village with no boundaries to constrain free economic interactions and communication, unprecedentedly, altering the way business with competition is conducted, in the global marketplace. All companies want to sell their goods to everyone, everywhere on the globe. Globalization has provided the impetus for the crave for financial inclusion and, hence the following provide the motivation for financial literacy initiatives:

- Need for inclusive economic growth and development;

- Enhance the effectiveness of monetary policy implementation [6];

- Dictates of national policy, dictated by cross-border affinities and leanings;

- The patriotic feeling of not being left behind, or isolated in the global market place;

- Growing global practice and need to take advantage of technological advancements in the delivery of financial services with decongested banking halls; and

- Nationalistic concerns for the survival and growth of micro, small and medium enterprises (MSMEs)

3.4.2 Challenges of financial inclusion/reasons for financial exclusion

Major reasons for financial exclusion are:

3.4.2.1 High cost of providing and utilizing financial services

This is a disincentive both to the service provider and service user. To the service provider, the cost of setting up of branches/access points may be considered unduly high and not advantageous in perceived low business areas. On the other hand, the poor and rural populations may be demotivated by high access costs on enabling infrastructure, minimum account balance requirements, transaction times, fixed charges on credit and debit cards, loan processing charges, fraud risks, etc. These inhibitions and made worse by high administrative costs, high collateral requirements, and lack of experience within financial intermediaries on the niceties of delivering appropriate services. Most micro, small, and medium enterprises (MSMEs), particularly persons financially excluded who may have their growth numbed.

3.4.2.2 Non price barriers

These barriers arise from stipulations requiring documents of proof regarding personal identity, which most people down the societal ladder generally do not have; thus, justifying their exclusion [7]. Both natural barriers, such as rough terrains and man-made barriers, such as hostile financial services delivery interfaces and limited bank branches or service access points, are factors contributing to financial exclusion. Globally, cost and infrastructure failures make accessing services demotivating.

3.4.3 Types of financial exclusion

From the discussions so far six types of financial exclusion can be established distinguishably, namely:

i. Physical access exclusion: Where exclusion is brought about when local bank branches or nonbank financial service provider offices are closed or demobilized (in response to internal pressures) and service seekers lack reliable, affordable means to reach alternatives.

ii. Access exclusion: Provider's risk evaluation of the current or potential user(s) necessitates access restrictions, resulting in such people being denied a product or service because they are perceived to be highly risky propositions.

iii. Condition exclusion: Here, products or services are rendered inaccessible to those who cannot meet up with conditionalities attached to their offering.

iv. Price exclusion: This is when products are availed at prices, which are unaffordable by the potential and willing up takers;

v. Marketing exclusion: Occurs, where sales and marketing activities are deliberately targeted at some groups, segments, or areas to the exclusion of others;

vi. Self-exclusion: This is situation, where individuals exclude themselves from seeking and utilizing financial products and services for personal reasons, including fear of failure, fear of temptation, or lack of awareness. In certain climes, the pressure to keep a low profile to avoid being targeted by bandits, terrorists, kidnappers, etc. has promoted self-exclusion;

vii. Absence of a market delivery model: Regulators and implementers (such as banks), are yet to resolve a single financial inclusion delivery model, which is most suitable, sustainable, and scalable, globally; so, invariably exclusion occurs anyway.

viii. Dysfunctional financial infrastructure: The unpunctual functionality of the dispensing financial infrastructure curtails uptake, impacting scalability of initiatives [8].

ix. Digital/physical connectivity: Regular connectivity failures and delays in resolving associated consumer complaints accentuate financial exclusion.

Studies have shown that, whereas financial inclusion positively and significantly impacts the operations and growth of entrepreneurship, challenges of distance impinge on how fast and effectively services are accessed in certain jurisdictions [9].

3.5 Pillars of financial inclusion

Financial inclusion assures easy access to financial services by creating equivalent opportunities, which enable the disadvantaged and vulnerable sections of the society, economically and socially excluded, to join together better into the financial system, able to appropriate financial products and services at an affordable cost in a fair and transparent manner. Such enrolment empowers them to actively contribute to national development and protect against socioeconomic shocks. Accordingly, financial inclusion advocacy must actualize deliberate efforts to stand on five ennobling pillars. These are:

Pillar 1: Physical and spatial dispersion of financial services access points to more rural areas and promote access;

Pillar 2: Improve number and functionality of disposing infrastructure;

Pillar 3: Digitize payments, as of primacy, across the country;

Pillar 4: Energize consumer protection framework with strong feedback and enforcement mechanisms; and.

Pillar 5: Uplift financial conditions and improve the standard of living of the poor and the disadvantaged, supported with a veritable accountability, monitoring and evaluation backbone.

Financial inclusion is a significant issue in most developing countries as most marginalized populations, especially women, lack access to essential financial services such as insurance and bank credit, largely due to their smaller size, informality, and concentration in heavily affected sectors. Women entrepreneurs across the globe, who are financially excluded face several constraints and fail due to a lack of access to affordable and quality financial products and services. But their exclusion is due to a number of factors, such as lack of traditional collateral, insufficient financial information, and prevalence of discriminatory property rights. It is noteworthy that women's financial inclusion aids in combatting social marginalization, reducing poverty, and achieving entrepreneurial goals. Increasing women's accessibility, affordability, and utilization of financial services will, therefore, go a long way toward reducing the gender gap in entrepreneurship, as well as promoting the women empowerment and gender equality and linked to enhanced entrepreneurial performance, success, and viability of women-led businesses [10]. Globally, financial inclusion plays a key role in addressing gender inequalities. In many nations, financial inclusion has been central to development policy-making and it has been documented that promoting financial inclusion has been instrumental in achieving the Vision 2030 Agenda for most developing African countries and in achieving the sustainable development goal (SDG) number five on gender equality and women empowerment.

3.6 Financial literacy to financial inclusion

An assessment of financial literacy programs points to the fact that a set of principles and good practices exist for prosecuting and improving financial learning and awareness, to promote financial inclusion. This includes, but not limited to:

i. Promotion of unbiased, fair, and coordinated financial education;

ii. Early commencement of school-based financial training actively supported by all financial institutions to encourage accountability and responsibility;

iii. Financial education should be clearly distinguished from commercial advertising and codes of conduct for the marketing staff of financial institutions should be developed to maintain this distinction;

iv. Deliberate encouragement of clients of financial institutions to understand service information and their potential consequences of their taken up the service and the remedies available in case of service malfunction;

v. Literacy narrowly focuses on important life enhancing issues on which financial inclusion is hinged;

vi. Programs be oriented toward "personalized" financial capacity building and empowerment on specific groups;

vii. Future retirees should be targeted with literacy information, education, and communication that raises their awareness and capability;

viii. Finally, literacy campaigns should include early warning systems on high-risk or vulnerable aspects issues of concern to service up takers (such as fraud).

4. Summary and conclusion

Financial inclusion requires that financial literacy activities direct specific population usually excluded from the official financial sector either because of their knowledge/awareness. However, distance to financial services access points and infrastructural deficiency could challenge how fast and effectively financial literacy initiatives scale up access to financial services by the poor and vulnerable populations, as well as micro, small, and medium-scale enterprises. National policies are motivated by the realization that several nonfinancial personal circumstances such as lack of education, inadequate technical skills, poor access to markets, lack of information, and unreliable infrastructure constrain individuals and businesses. These inhibiting factors are overcome by massive sustained financial literacy campaigns, leading to improved productivity, market access, and profitability. It avails needed knowledge for quality decision-making on the complexities of the world of finance. Ample practice and commitment are prerequisites for acquiring these skills, assured of a plethora of resources to help improve financial literacy. Accordingly, governments must initiate and sustain deliberate efforts to improve public infrastructure to promote financial inclusion, while financial sector regulators should evolve policies, which require financial services providers to spread to more areas, particularly the rural locations, where the poor and most excluded are found. This will overcome the identified challenges of distance, cost, and access and must follow a clear scalable roadmap expanding financial services access points to unbanked and underserved areas. The digitization of payments across the country should be prioritized, including a consumer complaints/protection framework, to increase financial inclusion in any given jurisdiction. It goes without saying that individuals and households must be availed the tools to cope with the increasingly complex world of financial instruments and offerings and assume more responsibility for their retirement security in the face of solvency-threatening pressures on public and private pensions.

Author details

Bassey Ibor
Department of Banking and Finance, University of Calabar, Calabar, Nigeria

*Address all correspondence to: basseyibor@yahoo.co.uk

References

[1] Jacob R. Financial inclusion among rural people with special reference to Kattappana. International Education and Research Journal. 2017;**3**(4):83-84

[2] Triki T, Faye I. Financial Inclusion in Africa. Tunisia: African Development Bank Group; 2013

[3] Johnson DJ. Importance of financial literacy in the global economy. In: Keynote Address to the Financial Education Summit; 12 December; Kuala Lumpur: OECD; 2005

[4] Damayanti SM, Murtaqi I, Pradana HA. The importance of financial literacy in global economic era. The Business and Management Review. 2018;**9**(3):435-441

[5] Aduda J, Kalunda E. Financial inclusion and financial sector stability with reference to Kenya: A review of literature. Journal of Applied Finance & Banking. 2012, 2012;**2**(6):95-120. ISSN: 1792-6580

[6] Khan SR. Fighting Poverty with Microcredit: Experience of the Grameen Bank and Other Programmes in Bangladesh. Washington DC: World Bank; 2011

[7] Ibor B, Offiong A, Mendie E. Financial inclusion and performance of micro, small and medium scale Enterprises in Nigeria. International Journal of Research Granthaalayah. 2017;**5**(3):104-122. DOI: 10.5281/zenodo.439557

[8] Islam N. Impact of financial inclusion on the women SME entrepreneurs in Bangladesh. Social Science Review Quarterly. 2020;**1**(1):14-26

[9] Shane SA. A General Theory of Entrepreneurship: The Individual-Opportunity Nexus. Vol. 20. Northampton, MA: Edward Elgar Publishing; 2003

[10] World Bank. Financial Inclusion. 2020. Available from: https://www.worldbank.org/en/topic/financialinclusion/overview#1

Chapter 3

The Needs for Financial Literacy in the Fintech Era: Italian Experiences

Luisa Anderloni and Ornella Moro

Abstract

The issue of financial literacy has been increasingly examined in Italy. It derived from the focus on overindebtedness and the threats posed by loan sharks. As paradoxical as it may seem, the overindebtedness risk is particularly high among the unbanked — households and micro/small businesses—because of their difficulties in having access to formal bank credit. Overindebtedness, usury, and the absence of connections with banks are all symptoms of a difficulty in relating appropriately to the banking system linked in part to inadequate levels of financial literacy. In the same way, the low propensity to insure has probably to do with a low understanding of the insurance process. This makes the unbanked/uninsured households and small enterprises, particularly vulnerable to risk. This paper aims to analyze the current situation of financial literacy in Italy, taking into account the vulnerability of some segments of the population and the inadequacies on the supply side. Surveys over time have shown a low level of financial literacy in Italy compared with advanced economies. A number of initiatives have been taken to attempt to improve financial literacy, especially among the young and more vulnerable. This chapter aims at presenting these initiatives and making a preliminary evaluation of them.

Keywords: financial literacy, household finance, financial constraint, overindebtedness, Italian financial market

1. Introduction

The attention to the issue of financial literacy (FL) has developed in Italy in parallel with the attention paid to the phenomenon of overindebtedness of households and to the risk of falling into the trap of loan sharks. Furthermore, as paradoxical as it may seem, because of the occurrence of unbanked people and of difficulties in accessing bank credit by households, micro, and small businesses.

The phenomena of overindebtedness of households and the absence of banking relations, as well as usury, are all signs of a difficulty in relating appropriately to the banking system and are latent symptoms of an inadequate level of financial literacy.

Financial literacy issues were then increased by the stimulus of the context of what was once the European Economic Community (Commission of European Union).

This awareness then developed both in the academia and in consumer associations and then attract the attention of the supervisory and control bodies on the financial markets and later of financial intermediaries that then guided its promotion with multiple initiatives.

Furthermore, we should mention the low propensity to insurance in the Italian market, which, on the one hand, denotes a lower familiarity with insurance processes and, on the other hand, makes families more vulnerable to the occurrence of unexpected events.

Historically in Italy, such phenomena and their negative consequences are more serious than in other countries. They therefore deserve an in-depth analysis.

The chapter is structured as follows: Section 2 illustrates various phenomena that denote a need for financial literacy, Section 3 analyses the level of financial literacy in Italy that is still low compared to other advanced economies, Section 4 illustrates the main initiatives undertaken to improve financial literacy in the country, and Sections 5 gives final remarks.

2. The framework of financial literacy needs in Italy

As mentioned earlier, there are three main phenomena contributing to awareness of financial literacy's development: overindebtedness, risk of falling into the trap of loan sharks, and risk of being financially excluded.

As far as overindebtedness is concerned, Italy is a country that has historically recorded a high propensity to household savings, with a limited recourse to debt. At national level, household debt has a structurally lower impact on the disposable income than in comparable advanced economies in Europe and the US (**Figures 1** and **2**).

Households' debt was used, in Italy, almost exclusively for mortgage loans, with very little use of consumer credit, at least until the 1990s. Later, consumer credit has grown at an accelerated pace. However, the percentage of households using it is still lower than in other developed economies as it is less than 15% in recent years. In general, the percentage of households that resort to debt — for mortgages, consumption, or business—is below 30% (**Figure 3**).

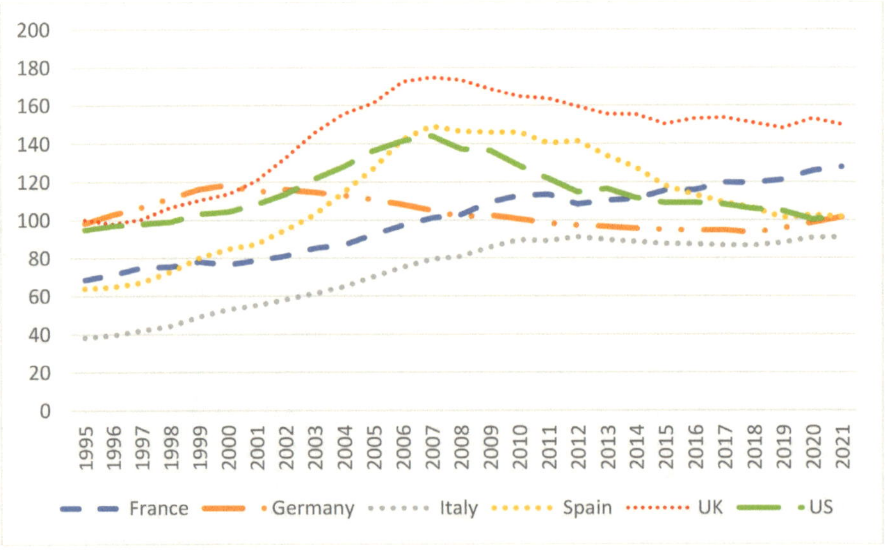

Figure 1.
Households debt on total income %—Source: OECD. https://data.oecd.org/hha/household-debt.html.

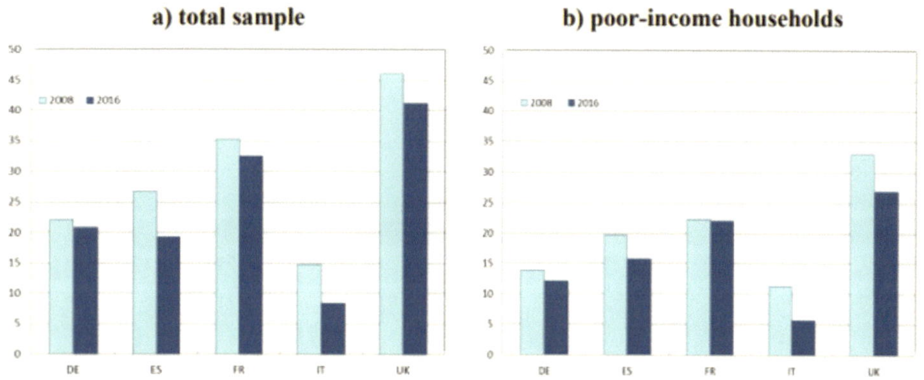

Source: EU-SILC dataset.
Share of total households in the left panel (Table 1, first row) and on poor-income households in the right panel (Table 1, second row).

Figure 2.
Households with consumer credit and incidence of poor-income households (percentage). Source: Magri et al. [1] and EU SILC (2008 and 2016).

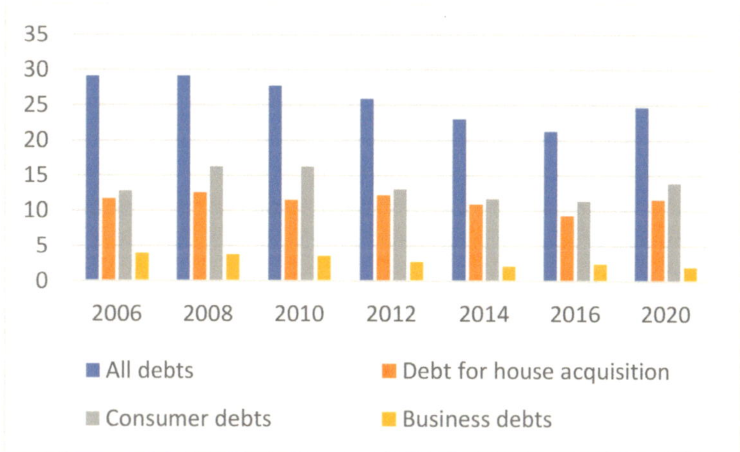

Figure 3.
Proportion of indebted households distinguished reason of indebtedness—Source: Bank of Italy.

However, in Italy, despite a low incidence of indebtedness, there is a segment of the indebted population at risk of contracting debts that it cannot cope with because of low- and uncertain-income flows and also a low level of financial literacy. The latter makes the problems more serious because it makes individuals less aware of the risks of overindebtedness and makes individuals less able to take appropriate and timely action to get out of this situation (**Figure 2**).

According to a study on the definition and measures of overindebtedness of households in Italy, the share of overindebted families — the estimate on 2010 data—would indicate average values ranging from 1.2 to 6.2% of the population, but with 29.8% feeling some economic distress [2]. Obviously, the figures are higher for particular groups: 30–50 years old, self-employed, lowest income quintile, and geographical location (South and Islands).

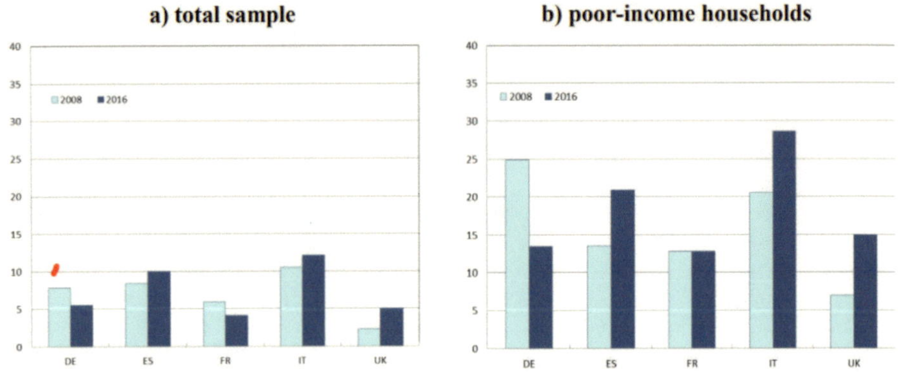

Source: EU-SILC dataset.
Share of total households in the left panel (Table 2, first row) and on poor-income households in the right panel (Table 2, second row).

Figure 4.
Households in arrears on consumer credit repayments – (percentages of households with consumer credit). Source: Magri et al. [1] and EU SILC (2008 and 2016).

In addition, the aftermath of the crisis and the slower rate of economic recovery have also had a major impact on households' capacity to discharge their obligations. Italy has the highest proportion of households in arrears (12%), especially in the poor-income groups (29%) (**Figure 4**) [1].

The situation is made significantly worse by the lack of accessible support financial and social services to help those affected [3]. Social workers themselves do not have the financial skills to spot and support those in need.

As a sign of the belated perception of the seriousness of household financial vulnerability, the Bank of Italy mentioned the issue for the first time in 2020 in its Annual Report.

From then on, the authorities' concerns have been rising, especially as regards the "Buy Now Pay Later" practice spread, which clearly exposed those most vulnerable tempted by consumer goods to even more overindebtedness[1].

It is well-known that the excessive accumulation of debts together with precarious jobs causes a deterioration in households' social and economic well-being, thus leading in the long run to social exclusion and poverty.

Exclusion from the official credit market due to low creditworthiness or even overindebtedness can push people to find a "solution" to their difficulties by having recourse to usury. The attention to this phenomenon in Italy exploded in 1995 following tragic news events. By its nature usury is hidden. So no statistics are available about how widespread the practice is in the country. Moreover, particularly in Italy, there is a strong connection between usury and criminal activities, such as extortions and racketing.

Only in 1996 in Italy has usury been treated definitely as illegal. Procedures were then introduced to restructure consumer debts[2]. Such procedures aim at making it easier to cope with the situation and avoid entering a dangerous debt spiral [4].

---

[1] See Bank of Italy, October 28th, 2022, Communication on "Buy Now Pay Later" schemes "(BNPL)". This form of credit is not specifically regulated and therefore the applicable regulatory framework and associated protections depend on the specific design of the operation.

[2] See Law n. 108/1996 defining the offense of usury and establishing a Fund, through which victims of usury can obtain a loan commensurate with the usurious interests and the damages deriving from them, without interest, to be returned within 10 years.

Since no data are available, a proxi is offered by the data on the contributions to the anti-usury fund provided by the Court of Auditors that document not only a growing fund allocation to deal with the issue but also a growing number of beneficiaries (**Table 1**) [6].

The victims are not always aware that they have fallen into loan sharks' traps. Sometimes, transactions are intrinsically connected to slightly illegal moves (such as tax evasion, involvement of straw men, use of cash in transactions, and so on). This discourages the victims from lodging a complaint and refer to the court.

Regarding the phenomenon of financial exclusion, it should be noted that Italy has in the past recorded a large number of underbanked or unbanked people [7, 8]. The international comparison —- dating back to 2003—reveals the seriousness of the situation (**Figures 5** and **6**).

Overindebted persons who experienced severe incidents of repayment are often excluded by the official credit markets and payment networks: a complex relationship exists between overindebtedness and financial exclusion [10–12].

Not to forget that the absence of banking relations means the exclusive use of cash as a means of payment and a total lack to financial and experience.

In recent years, the diffusion of accounts operated only by cards—without the possibility to take credit or withdraw sums in excess of available funds and equipped with bank details—has reduced the number of formally unbanked people. But price policies and restrictions on the provision of credit to vulnerable people still make it

Year	2008	2009	2010	2011	2012	2013	2014	2015	2016	2017	2018	2019	2020	2021
Amount of contributions to the anti-usury Fund (Euro millions)	69.07	23.6	12.86	11.64	6.75	70.00	32.27	21.35	15.44	26.85	18.89	24.24	32.67	30.04
N. of beneficiaries	n.a.	n.a.	4828	3786	3436	2964	2929	2695	2178	2260	2025	1993	1443	n.a.

Table 1.
State contribution to the anti-usury fund—Source: Italian Ministry of Economics and Finance [5].

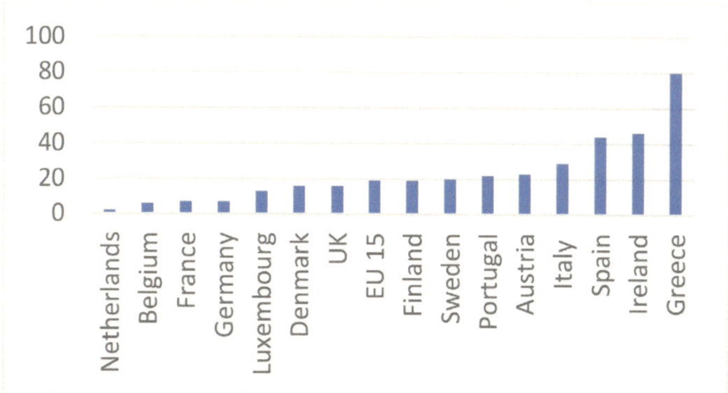

Figure 5.
People without a current account which comes with a payment card or chequebook (%) – Source: Eurobarometer [9].

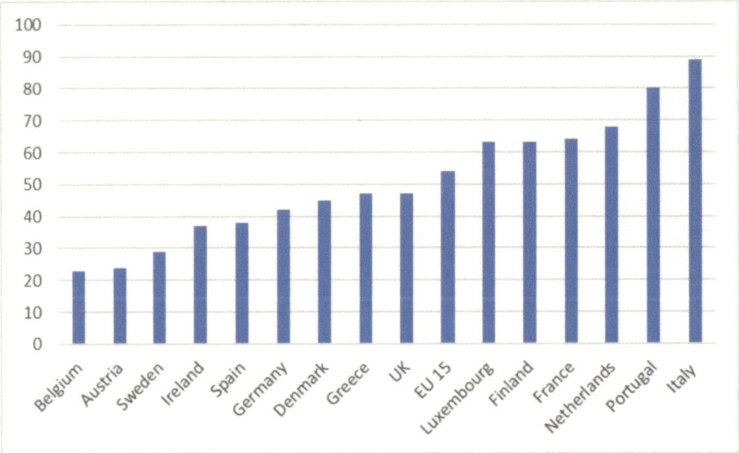

Figure 6.
Persons without a deposit account, which pays interest but has not payment card or chequebook (%)—Source: Eurobarometer [9].

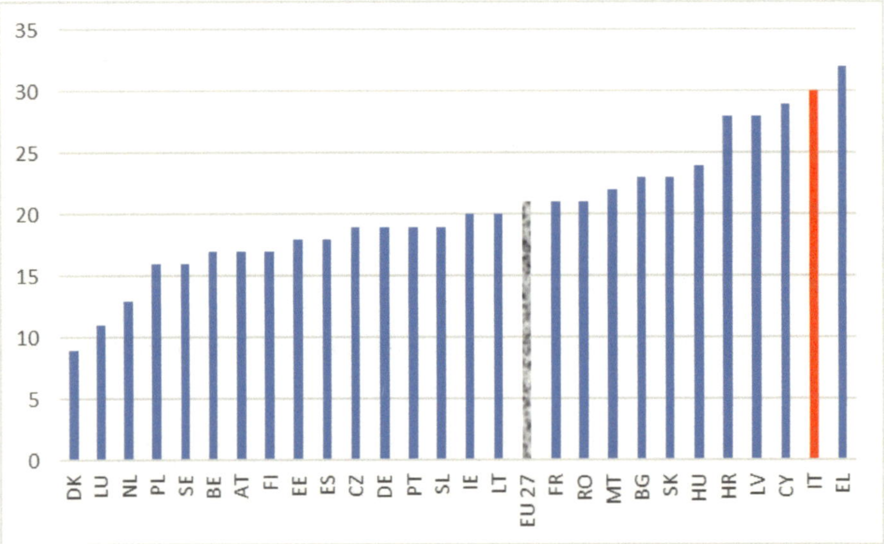

Figure 7.
Use of financial instruments: Lack of possession of financial instruments other than bank accounts or deposits. Source: Eurobarometer [13].

difficult for segments of the population to access banking and financial services that meet their needs.

If enlarging the range of financial products beyond current or savings account, (i.e., private pensions or retirement products, life insurance, nonlife insurance, mortgage or home loan, other consumer loans, investment products, and crypto-securities), Italy still comes last or nearly among the EU 27 countries, just behind Greece, with 21% of the sample not having owned such financial product in the last 2 years (**Figure** 7).

Finally, we should mention as weakness the low insurance coverage of the Italian population in the nonlife sector, although the insurance statistics in Italy are inflated by the obligation of having a motor vehicle liability insurance. Excluding the latter, insurance premiums in Italy as regards health, life, and nonlife represent 1.1% of GDP in Italy versus 3% in France and Belgium, 2% in Spain, and 1.8% in Germany.

The risks associated with sub-insurance are particularly significant when considering, for example, the specific geographical features of the country. Italy is one of the European countries most exposed to seismic and flood risk, and at the same time is a country in which the most important share of wealth is invested in real estate. Nevertheless, only 52% of the houses are covered by fire risk and only 4.9% by catastrophic risk, while about 80% of the housing stock is exposed to both.

A recent survey [14] has shown that, although there is a strong perception and awareness of exposure to risks, not all those who are aware of taking a risk say they want to insure themselves (for various reasons, including other life priorities, or lack of resources). In fact, the data shows that 45% of those who claim to feel exposed, do not have any type of coverage.

All this is symptomatic of poor levels of financial literacy and low experience in the management of sound banking relations [15].

3. The level of financial literacy in Italy

Numerous studies and surveys document over time a low level of financial literacy *in Italy* [16], still currently lower than the European Union average and other advanced countries (**Figure 8**).

The low values of the financial knowledge score contribute to this positioning (**Figure 9**). And, on the front of the financial behavior score, which considers the behaviors while choosing products by keeping track of expenses and striving to achieve financial goals, behaviors are even less virtuous (**Figure 10**).

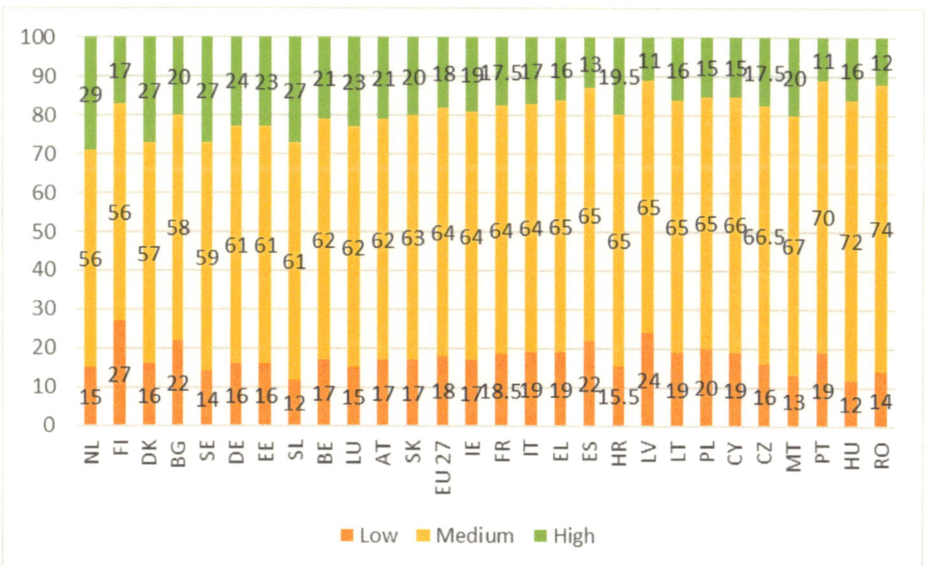

Figure 8.
Overall financial literacy score, distribution % per level—Source: Eurobarometer [17].

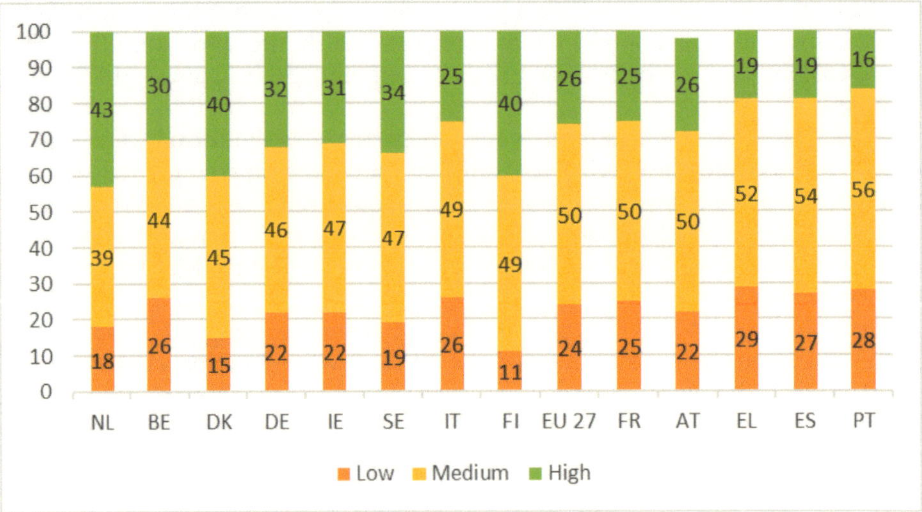

Figure 9.
Financial knowledge score, distribution % per score level—Source: Eurobarometer [17].

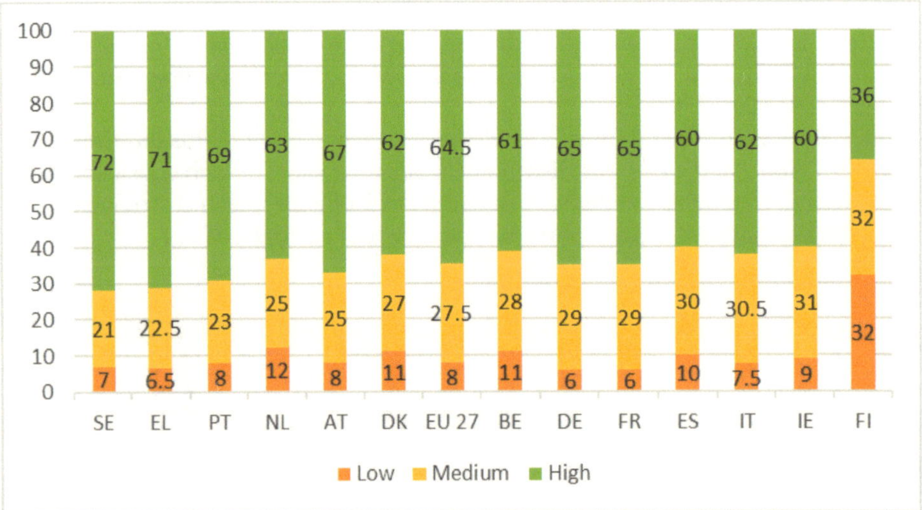

Figure 10.
Financial behavior score, distribuzione % per livelli—Source: Eurobarometer [17].

As for young people, at the international level, the PISA sample survey on financial literacy for 15-year-olds notes that Italian students reach a score of 476[3], which is in the group of countries whose mean scores are above the OECD mean [18–20].

It should be noted that more than 20% of Italian students are at level 1 or below, that is the level in which they display only basic financial literacy skills. Indeed, they can identify common financial products and terms, and interpret information related to basic financial concepts. They can also apply basic single numerical operations,

[3] This score is lower of that of, for example, Portugal and Spain.

such as addition, subtraction, or multiplication, in financial contexts that they are likely to have personally experienced. However, students performing at or below level 1 are not yet able to apply their knowledge to real-life situations involving financial issues and decisions.

Low levels of literacy among the Italian population were also detected by a survey conducted by the Bank of Italy in early 2020 (by Alessio et al. [21])[4] which, on a scale ranging from 1 to 21, gives an average score of 11.2. This value is substantially in line with that observed by a similar survey in 2017 [22]; however, the stability of the literacy index conceals variations in its three components: the level of knowledge is slightly improving (+0.4), while the behavioral and attitude components show −0.2 and −0.1, respectively.

Also, the survey conducted by the Edufin Committee[5] agrees that perceived financial knowledge is—and remains—very low; overall, there are grades below sufficiency, even among those with higher incomes and qualifications [23].

The low level of financial competence also affects those who are self-employed or own or manage entrepreneurial activities; in a country, such as Italy, in which micro- and SMES are the backbone of the economy this raises concerns and highlights the opportunity for improvement.

According to a recent survey, [24] the weighted financial literacy score for micro-entrepreneurs is 2.2 (which corresponds to 70% of the maximum score level); but it should be noted that the share of respondents reaching an adequate level of financial literacy is lower than 40%.

Furthermore, financial literacy shortcomings, in these segments of the population, can only be grasped if we consider that the questions used to define the score are at a very low level of knowledge, behavior, and attitudes.

As we shall see later, there are many initiatives to promote financial literacy that are addressed to this segment of the population, confirming the perceived need for improvement.

Finally, with reference to the different segments mentioned above, adults, young students, self-employed, and small entrepreneurs, the analysis of financial literacy has extended to consider digital literacy. The latter is of increasing importance both in the daily lives of individuals and in the use of financial services because of the growing, and often more convenient, supply of services through digital channels.

4. The initiatives to promote financial literacy in Italy

As noted above, In Italy awareness of financial literacy has been developed behind other advanced economies. As a result, many of the efforts to improve the system have been initiated at a later stage, whereas the shortcomings in financial literacy are more severe.

Banks and consumer associations launched the first initiatives sparingly in conjunction with the introduction of the provisions of banking transparency introduced in Italy in the early 1990s.

Sometimes, these initiatives have also had significant marketing objectives for products and services, as well as promotion of the bank's image.

[4] The survey uses the OECD-INFE methodology.

[5] As to the nature, mission and activity of this committee, see Section 4 below.

From many sides, and especially from the Bank of Italy, the coordination of the various initiatives has been requested to consolidate and increase their impact; the Italian government has supported this request and has taken an institutional role in coordination and promotion.

Below, we illustrate the most important initiatives—inspired also by the OECD guidelines and policies [25–27]—grouping them according to promoter groups, namely the government with different departments, regulation and supervision bodies, and professional and consumer associations, local authorities often coordinate with local agencies, as well as individual financial operators.

4.1 The Italian government and the "Committee for the planning and coordination of financial education activities"

In quite recent times, in 2017, the government with a decree set up a "Committee for the planning and coordination of financial education activities." It received the mission of promoting and coordinating initiatives useful for raising financial, insurance and social security knowledge and skills among the population as to improve everyone's ability to make choices consistent with their own objectives and conditions.

The coordination function is carried out, first of all, through the composition of the 11 members of the committee; they are designated by the competent ministers[6], by the bodies of regulation and supervision over intermediaries and financial markets[7], by the National Council of Consumers and Users (CNCU), and the Supervisory Body and Financial Adviser Register (OCF).

We want to emphasize that the commission's composition is broad and composite to effectively coordinate the activities of all the main players in financial education in the country.

The committee has developed a National Strategy for Financial Education, starting from financial literacy data (in line with what we outlined in the previous section) and from the analysis of the financial educational initiatives so far implemented [28]. The strategy consists of three points: the definition of the vision and mission, the main guidelines for its implementation, and the criteria for the evaluation of the strategy.

The long-term strategy of the nation is very ambitious, creating conditions for everyone to have access to knowledge and financial expertise so that they can build a peaceful and secure future. It considers the need to create an "ecosystem" that promotes coordinated and effective financial, insurance, and social security education initiatives.

Two main lines are used to develop it:

- Large-scale initiatives aimed at a wide audience to promote financial literacy using media and public advertising tools and
- a system of incentives[8] designed to encourage initiatives in specific social groups, coordinated with third parties.

---

[6] Minister of Economy and Finance, the Minister of Education, University and Research, the Minister for Economic Development, and the Minister for Labor and Social Policy.

[7] The Bank of Italy, the National Commission for Companies and the Stock Exchange (CONSOB), the Institute for Insurance Supervision (IVASS) and the Supervisory Commission on Pension Funds (COVIP).

[8] Using—as resources—part of the revenue for sanctions imposed by the Competition and Market Authority.

The strategy is based on criteria of excellence, not to disperse resources in initiatives of poor quality and limited impact, which could prove counterproductive and collaboration because only the coordination of initiatives can produce good results, incisive, and lasting. In particular, the committee aims to encourage collaboration with associations and nonprofit organizations that allow to reach widely large segments of the population, particularly those who are most vulnerable.

Moving from strategy to "national plans," these are clearly operational and outline in a concrete way the main initiatives. They were first implemented for the three-year period 2017–2019 and continued until 2020 due to COVID-19, and then declined annually for the three-year period 2021–2023. These were set, considering priorities toward target groups, as follows:

- 2021: Financial and digital literacy and upskilling for women and young people;
- 2022: Financial and e-skills literacy and upskilling for all adults, including the elderly, to be achieved, where possible, also in the workplace;
- 2023: Financial and digital literacy and upskilling for micro and small enterprises.

Among activities, we can mention various coordination tasks and support to international initiatives such as The Month of the Financial Literacy in October, the Global Money Week, promoted by OCSE, the World Investor Week (WIW), promoted by IOSCO, and many others.

As for the assessment, given that the population's knowledge basis changes slowly over time, the achievement of the aforementioned goals will be assessed over a five-year period and will be based on periodic sample surveys.

It is worth mentioning, among the goals, of the period the following:

- Raising awareness of micro and small enterprises regarding specific issues such as new forms of financing and sustainable investments;
- Raising the awareness of micro and small enterprises on specific issues, such as new forms of financing and sustainable investment;
- Combining financial expertise with digital skills, in view of the opportunities and risks of digital finance and the drive for the digital transformation of the country, impressed by the PNRR and digitization in the payments sector. Indeed, these competences constitute an additional factor of social inclusion and a contribution to strengthening financial resilience.

It also positively broadens the educational perspective by including the objective of raising awareness of sustainability among citizens and businesses, spreading knowledge of environmental issues and challenges, educating about financial choices, insurance, and social security inspired by sustainability canons.

Finally, given the mission of the committee, great emphasis is placed on the need to keep up to date the census of financial education initiatives implemented or planned, including those in the digital field, carried out by the members of the committee and the main stakeholders.

The activity of communication, dissemination of information, and training modules takes place through the portal, created and managed by the committee called "What matters"/"What counts"[9].

4.2 Banking, financial, insurance and pension authorities

Bodies of regulation and supervision on financial intermediaries and markets interpret their market surveillance role not only in terms of efficiency and stability but also in terms of inclusiveness and transparency. Within the scope of their supervisory activity, there is a call to bank to provide explicit information.

All these bodies are engaged in various activities of study and investigation on the phenomenon of financial literacy, thus providing an important contribution to the monitoring of the phenomenon and to the development of policies that are tailored to meet the needs that have been identified[10] [29–34].

They also in their websites created specific sections or portal dedicated to "citizens" (both consumers and micro and small business) with the aim to promote financial literacy and providing dissemination materials[11] with fact sheets and glossaries, FAQs, and implementing consumer protection[12]. They also announce and summarize the program of financial literacy initiatives promoted or jointly realized by each body.

4.2.1 Bank of Italy

It seems that the Bank of Italy is the most active and effective. In its organizational structure, it has established a "customer protection and financial education department." It is divided into three services that include financial education beside supervision of the behavior of intermediaries and individual protection of clients. Within the scope of supervision activity, in the provisions on the organization and management of banks, there is a call to provide explicit information to client in order to make sure that they fully understand what they are buying and their obligation and that the choice meets their needs and are compatible with their financial capability.

It realized multiple initiatives aimed at both the adult population (including those who attend the provincial centers for adult education, women, and vulnerable or disadvantaged people), as well as the young and very young and also micro and small businesses. It adopts a "training of trainers" model, which consists in meetings and collaborations with those (teachers, representatives of associations, and trade unions) interested in acquiring the skills to provide financial training.

This approach has a multiplication effect by which a much larger population is reached than that which can be reached directly by Bank of Italy staff. It also enables to integrate financial education into broader education and offers training initiatives in providing the assistance needed to overcome difficulties and vulnerability.

---

[9] See www.quellocheconta.gov.it

[10] See the long list of studies and surveys indicated, in our bibliography.

[11] These include brochures, news, videos, calculators, games and infographics that make learning fun and practical together with useful tools for everyday choices.

[12] For Bank of Italy see the portal "Economics for everyone" (formerly "What matter") acceding it through the section "Services to the public"; for CONSOB see the section "Financial education"; for IVASS see the section "For Consumers", mainly devoted to consumer protection issues and "#Learn with IVASS", devoted to insurance literacy; and for COVIP see "Social security education".

The Bank of Italy has promoted various initiatives with two target audiences: young people and the adult population.

For young people, the project is named "financial education in schools"[13]. As mentioned above, the Bank of Italy was the first institution, in 2007, to sign a protocol with the Ministry of Education, with the aim of offering schools a structured educational path with economic-financial contents (followed by school projects).

It is worth mentioning that this project is based on the idea of "training the trainers"; the teachers who join the project participate in the training seminars offered by the branches of the Bank of Italy, and subsequently pass the topics on to the students, including them in their own curricular programs or carrying out enhancement projects. Teaching materials are at the teachers' disposal in which the didactic component has been strengthened over time, created with the help of educationalists and teachers, in addition to contents development.

For adult target, Bank of Italy promoted financial education program aimed at small entrepreneurs. It has been realized with the collaboration with two associations of entrepreneurs (Confartigianato and CNA). Overall, around 250 trainers from the two associations were involved who, in turn, reached around 3000 entrepreneurs. Here again, the inspiring idea is that to train the trainers in order to activate a multiplier effect.

4.2.2 CONSOB

Consob offers a wide range of financial education initiatives; it provides training to secondary school teacher who will introduce financial education principles to their pupils. It assists them in choosing resources and tools, as well as in creating assignments and assessments that students will complete. After receiving the necessary training, the teachers will use for their lessons Consob fundamental modules. They cover a variety of subjects with their pupils (links between economics, finance, law, and individual behavior and speculative bubbles and scams that have produced behavioral traps). Additionally, Consob has a comprehensive website devoted to financial education that includes a wealth of information on a variety of topics for both adults (including how to recognize and manage financial scams and financial abusive, information on financial instruments, investment advice, behavioral errors and investments during crises, and the information exchange between client and consultant) and teens (return from planning to savings to investment; sustainable investments, and the digitalization of the investment advice service). It uses several teaching tools, including games, slideshows, brief videos, and financial planner. In addition, it has encouraged discussions and teachings on subjects such as investors' and savers' protection from financial frauds and financial crises through students' dramatic representation of notable financial stories. Consob also organized, with University of Insubria, initiatives of financial education for Italian small and medium-sized enterprises, with the goal to increase understanding of practical instruments and strategies for PMIs' access to quotation on stock markets or with the goal to understand Fintech's opportunities for accessing financial markets.

Furthermore, it yearly publishes a report on the investment choices of Italian households. The 2022 report provides evidence on the financial knowledge, attitudes, and financial choices of Italian investors and also identifies potential alert profiles that may

[13] Since its inception in the 2008–2009 school year, it is estimated that the project has reached over 550,000 students. In the 2021–2022 school year, the project involved around 3000 classes across the country, equal to almost 1 percent of classes in Italy.

emerge to protect them. It has a focus on the impact that current economic dynamics may have on individual financial choices. Among the results of the survey emerges how investors seem increasingly aware of the need to raise their knowledge and skills, and they are ready to examine relevant topics for the most significant financial decisions.

4.2.3 IVASS

In an effort to promote a strong insurance culture throughout Italy and assist its citizens in safeguarding their assets and lives, IVASS has improved its website by adding user-friendly insurance materials devoted both to schools, such as educational and entertaining games, videos, quizzes for learning experiences tailored to every ages, and short video on various insurance subjects (such as health insurance policies, fraudulent online insurance, advanced payments in life policies) useful for adults that have already bought insurance products. Other initiatives devoted to young and adults are IVASS's conference on agricultural and climatic risk, held during the financial education month's initiatives and links, in their institutional webpages, to videos on several digital financial frauds (made by CERTFIN, a public-private cooperative with partners from regulatory authorities, financial associations and banks).

Survey on insurance knowledge and behavior," commissioned from Ivass and conducted by the University of Milan-Bicocca and by Doxa, is the first national effort aimed at measuring Italians' awareness of the necessary safeguards and protective behavior. Ivass will use the findings of the survey to guide initiatives aimed at developing a sustainable insurance culture.

4.2.4 COVIP

COVIP, pursuing the task of disseminating information aimed at improving the knowledge on retirement matters, carried out this activity mainly through its website under the section "for the citizen" and its subsection "social security education" with guides and information sheets.

4.3 Financial intermediaries' associations

The financial intermediaries' associations are not member of the committee for the planning and coordination of financial education activities. The main associations, (mainly ABI representing banks, ASSOFIN for consumer credit and mortgage intermediaries, ANIA for insurance companies, and ASSOFONDIPENSIONI for pension funds' managers) all they participate with initiatives to "The Month of Financial Education" promoted by the committee Edufin and, with greater or lesser emphasis, on their websites deal with financial literacy.

4.3.1 ABI

ABI established FEduF, Foundation for Financial and Savings Education, considered in the broader sense of "education for economic citizenship aware and active, to develop and spread financial and economic knowledge". It is joined by banks (almost all), other associations of banking and financial intermediaries, companies, and nonprofit entities.

It is very active in raising awareness and promoting educational initiatives, as well as designing and implementing innovative tools to disseminate financial education concepts on a large scale (such as educational workshops, theater performances, multimedia, video, and so on). It also represents the member institutions in the dialog and discussion tables on the issue of financial education and promotes the visibility and dissemination of initiatives carried out jointly with the FEduF.

In particular, it collaborates with individual member institutions in order to:

- Create local and national events—dedicated to students, teachers, adults, and businesses—customizable according to the needs of individual banks and institution members;

- Enhance the financial education experience of individual banks in the national and international scenario;

- Intercepts requests for financial education by schools of specific areas to be met by the promotion of initiatives of individual banks operating in the territory.

In catalyzing the initiatives of individual banks and intermediaries, it gives them visibility on its web in the "calendar" section.

The projects are targeted toward both schools (of every order and grade) and adults, promoting a very wide range of initiatives, tailored to the needs of different targets.

4.3.2 ASSOFIN

Assofin in its site within the "consumer" section has a subsection "financial education." The main initiatives implemented are a simulator evaluation of a loan called "Monitorata", the video "the finance precise as at university, easy as on television" and an advertising message "What to do in case of difficulty."

Monitorata is an online service that does not have any commercial intent, but rather offers the essential elements to know and monitor credit capacity through a self-assessment of the financial profile. Its aim is to make it easier to understand whether, given its economic and financial situation, the proportion of funding is sustainable. It aims to familiarize with the elements that contribute to determining the creditworthiness and help to understand the reasons for refusing one or another debt position in a logic of protection from future difficulties and defaults.

The video "Encyclopedia" covers the most common and important terms of use in banking and finance. The videos are simple and concise, with the aim of helping the consumer become aware of the simplest banking and financial transactions.

Finally, "What to do in case of difficulty" is an advertising message created in collaboration with the main consumer associations with the aim of encouraging dialog between intermediaries and customers in difficulty with their financial situation.

4.3.3 ANIA

Through the Ania Consumatori Forum, ANIA has created "IO&irischi," an insurance education initiative aimed at students of Italian schools to promote in the new generations a greater awareness of risk and a culture of its prevention and management.

The initiative aims to develop a more aware approach to risk as an essential factor of life and to make children reflect on the individual and social choices related to it, sensitizing them to the concepts of law, duty, and responsibility.

The project[14] provides an organic kit of free teaching tools easy to use, which allows teachers to develop in the classroom in full autonomy. The course is structured in five modules and offers various teaching tools (teacher guide, didactic-operative cards, set of in-depth focus, tools to involve students in individual and group work, a game magazine with a series of games, tests, and informative pills).

Finally, the material includes an evaluation/certification of skills, prepared on the Oecd-Pisa problem-solving model.

5. Final remarks

The focus on financial literacy in Italy has developed at a slower pace than in other developed economies. In addition, we have highlighted that this is a context where many macroeconomic factors (such as household indebtedness, micro and small business financial fragility, reliance on the usury lending market, presence of un-banked or underbanked and underinsured population) denote poor familiarity with the banking and financial system, and reduced financial literacy among the population.

The adoption of rules on the transparency of banking operations and services in the 1990s was a first stimulus to greater attention by regulatory and supervisory bodies, trade associations, banks, and intermediaries. It also was the trigger for increased awareness among customers about the nature of products and services they were buying, how effective they were in responding to their needs, and whether they were financially and economically compatible with their personal situation. However, despite this delay, there were several follow-up initiatives that had the advantage of being "put into system" involving a plurality of financial institutions, as well as different target segments to create a multiplier effect of the impact. In particular, the government-sponsored Edufin committee, the Bank of Italy, Consob, and ABI have played a significant role in promoting systemic initiatives. Targets were on the one hand students, in cooperation with the Ministry of Education, the school boards, and school managers, and on the other adults, involved through professional associations, nonprofit organizations, and unions. The Bank of Italy's systematic adoption of the "teach to the teacher" model, for instance, has had a positive multiplier effect.

As a weakness, it should be noted that the adult vulnerable population, whose fragility is due to limited literacy in general, to low and stable levels of income—if not even poverty—often associated with social or psychological difficulties, is still not sufficiently involved in financial literacy initiatives, compared to its needs. In order to reach this group with programs cut on their limited basic skills, including their reduced or absent digital literacy, it would be important to promote initiatives of "teach to social workers" so that they could help vulnerable people to cope with economic and financial difficulties and to relate appropriately to financial products and intermediaries.

Another weakness in the Italian system is the lack of awareness and information on social security coverage. As mentioned above, the public pension, historically generous but already decreasing, will barely reach subsistence levels for the future generations, for which, however, it is not just a problem of literacy and awareness: the most pressing issue is the lack of stability in the employment landscape for young

[14] It has been realized with the collaboration of the European Association for Economic Education (AEEE Italy), the involvement of teachers and associations of school heads, as well as scientific advice of the Catholic University of Milan

people entering the workforce. It is hoped that new labor laws will be implemented to provide new generations with more assurance, such as a higher minimum income and other job-related protections such as continuity of working relations, which all leads to the possibility of borrow and plan for retirement.

In conclusion, it should be stressed that financial innovation, technology, and new forms of digitalization are raising the standard of financial expertise that is essential in everyday life.

In addition, there are other literacies complementary to financial literacy from that on basic taxation (in a country where taxation is complex even in very simplified situations) to the digital one that increasingly invests the operation of a simple daily life, to that of cyber security and fraud prevention of various kinds.

It is, therefore, important to note that financial education, in addition to other educations, should be a part of curricular programs at least in the vocational training circuit, where there are multiple criticalities and where curricula and teaching methods need to be thoroughly revised.

The job market of vocational schools is often in craft or commercial self-employment or in microenterprises, and consequently, the development of these skills would also fill those gaps of financial literacy that are observed between micro-entrepreneurs and self-employed. This is especially true for those occupations that may be highly technical but do not lead to the development of other critical skills for a higher social/economic integration.

In addition to the institutional initiatives of financial literacy, it would be beneficial if television and educational programs or investigative journalism could play a more significant role than in the past in promoting financial literacy among the general public.

Author details

Luisa Anderloni[1*] and Ornella Moro[2]

1 Università degli Studi di Milano – University of Milan, Italy

2 Università degli Studi di Sassari – University of Sassari, Italy

*Address all correspondence to: luisa.anderloni@unimi.it

References

[1] Magri S et al. The Expansion of Consumer Credit in Italy and in the Euro Area: What Are the Drivers and the Risks? Questioni di Economia e Finanza - Occasional Paper. Rome: Banca d'Italia; 2019. p. 500

[2] D'Alessio G, Iezzi. Household Overindebtedness: Definition and Measurement with Italian Data, Questioni di Economia e Finanza - Occasional Paper. Rome: Banca d'Italia; 2013. p. 149

[3] Antenucci D, Caldarelli G. Il debt advice per il consumatore. In: Natura, dibattito europeo e implicazioni per l'Italia, Questioni di economia e finanza - Occasional Paper. Banca d'Italia; 2022. p. 740

[4] Anderloni L. Sovraindebitamento delle famiglie e politiche di prevenzione e gestione: alcune esperienze estere e prospettive per l'Italia. In: Porta A, Masciandaro D, editors. L'usura in Italia. Milano: Egea; 1997. pp. 75-122, ISBN 88-238-0399-3

[5] MEF (various years). Fondo per la prevenzione del fenomeno dell'usura Rapporto sulla gestione. Rome: MEF

[6] Corte dei Conti. La prevenzione del fenomeno dell'usura, Deliberazione del 27 giugno 2022. Corte dei Conti; 2022, n. 15/2022/G

[7] Anderloni L et al. In: Anderloni L, Braga MD, Carluccio EM, editors. New Frontiers in Banking Services: Emerging Needs and Tailored Products for Untapped Markets. Berlin: Springer; 2007, ISBN 9783540464976

[8] Anderloni L. Le istanze di social banking negli anni 2000: teoria ed evidenza empirica in Italia. In: Anderloni L, editor. Il social banking in Italia: un fenomeno da esplorare. Milano: Giuffrè; 2003. pp. 3-133. ISBN 8814099715

[9] Eurobarometer. Public Opinion in Europe: Financial Services, Standard Report. Eurobarometer; 2004

[10] Anderloni L, Vandone D. The dimension of over-indebtedness in Italy and the characteristics of the over-indebted households. In: Ferretti F, editor. Comparative Perspectives of Consumer over-Indebtedness: A View from the UK, Germany, Greece, and Italy. The Hague: Eleven International Publishing; 2016. pp. 291-313. ISBN 9789462366732

[11] Anderloni L, Vandone D. Risk of over-indebtedness and behavioural factors. In: Lucarelli C, Brighetti G, editors. Risk Tolerance in Financial Decision Making [a cura di]. Basingstoke: Palgrave Macmillan; 2010. pp. 113-132. ISBN 978-02-3028-113-4

[12] Anderloni L, Vandone D. Households over-Indebtedness in the Economic Literature. Italy: WP DEMM-University of Milan; 2008

[13] Eurobarometer. Retail Financial Services and Product. Report. Flash Eurobarometer 509. European Union; 2022

[14] ANIA–IPSOS. I nuovi bisogni di protezione degli italiani, in ANIA. Rome: ANIA–IPSOS; 2022. Available from: https://www.ania.it/documents/35135/53747/I+nuovi+bisogni+di+protezione+degli+italiani+-+Indagine+ANIA-Ipsos.pdf/b5aefb18-f0bc-7865-e57a-104e42f3cc40?version=1.0&t=1686751770776

[15] Atkinson A, Messy FA. Measuring Financial Literacy: Results of the OECD/

International Network on Financial Education (INFE) Pilot Study, OECD Working Papers on Finance, Insurance and Private Pensions. Paris: OECD iLibrary; 2012. p. 15

[16] Bongini P et al. Financial literacy: Where do we stand? Journal of Financial Management, Markets and Intermediaries. 2015;**3**(1):3-12

[17] Eurobarometer. Monitoring the Level of Financial Literacy in the EU. Report. Flash Eurobarometer 525. European Union; 2023

[18] OECD. Evaluation of National Strategies for Financial Literacy. Paris: OECD; 2022. Available from: https://www.oecd.org/financial/education/evaluation-of-national-strategies-for-financial-literacy.htm

[19] OECD. OECD/INFE 2020 International Survey of Adult Financial Literacy. Paris: OECD; 2020a. Available from: www.oecd.org/financial/education/launchoftheoecdinfeglobalfinancialliteracysurveyreport.htm

[20] OECD. PISA 2018 Results (Volume IV): Are Students Smart about Money? Paris: PISA, OECD Publishing; 2020b. DOI: 10.1787/48ebd1ba-en

[21] D'Alessio G et al. L'alfabetizzazione finanziaria degli italiani: i risultati dell'indagine della Banca d'Italia del 2020, Questioni di economia e finanza - Occasional Paper. Rome: Banca d'Italia; 2020. p. 588

[22] Di Salvatore A et al. Measuring the Financial Literacy of the Adult Population: The Experience of Banca d'Italia, Questioni di Economia e Finanza - Occasional Paper. Rome: Banca d'Italia; 2018. p. 435

[23] Comitato Edufin (various years). Report. Rome: MEF; 2023

[24] D'Ignazio A et al. Micro-entrepreneurs' financial and digital competences during the pandemic in Italy. In: Questioni di economia e finanza - Occasional Paper. Rome: Banca d'Italia; 2022. p. 724

[25] OECD. G20/OECD INFE Policy Guidance on Digitalisation and Financial Literacy. Paris: OECD; 2018

[26] OECD. G20/OECD INFE Report on Adult Financial Literacy in G20 Countries. Paris: OECD; 2017

[27] OECD. OECD/INFE International Survey of Adult Financial Literacy Competencies. Paris: OECD; 2016, Available from: www.oecd.org/finance/OECD-INFE-International-Survey-of-Adult-Financial-Literacy-Competencies.pdf

[28] EDUFIN Committee. Comitato per la programmazione e il coordinamento delle attività di educazione finanziaria, Principali risultati del Censimento delle iniziative di educazione finanziaria, assicurativa e previdenziale realizzate in Italia nel triennio 2015-2017. Rome: MEF; 2018. Available from: www.quellocheconta.gov.it

[29] CONSOB. Rapporto 2022 sulle scelte di investimento delle famiglie italiane. Rome: CONSOB; 2022, ISSN 2465-1974 [online]

[30] De Bonis R et al. Educazione finanziaria: presupposti, politiche ed esperienze della Banca d'Italia, Questioni di economia e finanza - Occasional Paper. Rome: Banca d'Italia; 2022. p. 726

[31] Gallo R et al. Le coperture assicurative contro i rischi operativi delle imprese italiane: alcune evidenze, Note di stabilità finanziaria e vigilanza. Rome: Banca d'Italia; 2022. p. 31

[32] IVASS. Indagine su Conoscenze e comportamenti assicurativi degli

italiani. Rome: IVASS; 2021. Available from: https://www.ivass.it/consumatori/imparaconivass/indagine-conoscenza-assicurativa/indagine_su_conoscenze_comportamenti_assicurativi_degli_italiani.pdf

[33] Lusardi A et al. Financial Literacy, Longevity Literacy, and Retirement Readiness. The 2022 TIIAA-GFLEC Personal Finance Index; 2022

[34] Lamboglia S, Travaglino F. Statistical sources for assessing financial literacy, Questioni di economia e finanza - Occasional Paper. Rome: Banca d'Italia; 2022. p. 725

Chapter 4

Financial Inclusion and Digital Financial Literacy: The Case of Microfinance Sector in Bosnia and Herzegovina

Jasmina Okičić and Meldina Kokorović Jukan

Abstract

This chapter discusses the nexus between financial inclusion and financial literacy, focusing on the microfinance institutions' contribution to increasing of financial literacy and financial inclusion among their clients. The microfinance sector in Bosnia and Herzegovina is perceived as the most well-organized and regulated worldwide. We use it as a case example of how microfinance institutions make changes in the financial system landscape and contribute to the well-being of individuals. During the COVID-19 pandemic, microfinance institutions in Bosnia and Herzegovina organized a series of workshops on digital financial literacy in order to provide their clients with the knowledge related to digital financial products/services used to help their clients better to integrate into the financial system. The chapter provides evidence on digital financial literacy initiatives contributing to financial literacy increase and more frequent usage of digital financial services contributing to greater financial inclusion of individuals. The presented research will contribute to the existing literature in terms of a better understanding of the importance of financial literacy and education in building inclusive financial systems as well as provide evidence of positive practices among financial institutions, namely microfinance institutions in regard to increasing financial literacy.

Keywords: financial inclusion, digital financial literacy, financial health, microfinance sector, Bosnia and Herzegovina

1. Introduction

As one of the preconditions of sustainable economic growth, financial inclusion has been on the policymakers' agenda for more than several decades now. As it is indicated by the World Bank (WB) [1], universal financial inclusion needs to be achieved by 2020, yet countries still struggle to create a financial ecosystem that is accessible to all. According to the latest Global Findex Survey (GFS) from 2021, account ownership around the world increased by 25% in the 10 years spanning 2011 to 2021, from 51% of adults to 76% of adults [2]. From 2017 to 2021, account ownership in developing economies increased by 8%, but still, there are more obstacles to achieving universal financial inclusion in developing economies due to a number of barriers and lower efficiency of the financial system.

More in-depth analysis provides evidences that, besides the standard set of barriers to financial inclusion (financial products/services being too expensive, lack of necessary documentation, availability and trust in financial institutions, insufficient funds, and religious reasons), financial illiteracy is one of the reasons of poor financial inclusion. Through comprehensive cross-country analysis [3] a positive and significant relationship between financial literacy and measures of financial inclusion was found. The financial measure includes having a bank account at a formal financial institution, including mobile money accounts; the proportion of adults in a country that has a debit card; the proportion of respondents that use a bank account to save; and the proportion of adults in a country that use of debit cards. Thus, it can be concluded that raising financial literacy among the general population can be a good way forward to increasing financial inclusion.

Developing countries, among which is Bosnia and Herzegovina (B&H), are putting efforts to improve financial inclusion through improving financial system regulatory and institutional framework, improving banking systems and increasing awareness of the financial health importance. These efforts are coordinated among financial system regulators (central banks and regulatory agencies), financial institutions as well as civil society organizations working on improving financial literacy and financial health among individuals and on a household level. The importance of financial literacy and financial health was even more emphasized during the 2020–2023 COVID-19 pandemic, which profoundly changed people's lives in terms of their spending habits and interaction with financial institutions. Then, more than ever before, financial literacy became crucial for maintaining day-to-day payments during the lockdown. In that respect, financial institutions increased their efforts to provide adequate solutions for their clients to overcome challenges imposed by the pandemic. Most of the financial institutions (banks, insurance companies, and microfinance institutors) created online platforms and new mobile applications to ensure their clients have access to their financial products/services.

This chapter provides insight into the efforts of microfinance institution(s) in B&H to improve (digital) financial literacy of their clients in order to ensure their better financial health which will consequently positively impact the performance of the financial institution itself. As a response to the lockdown, one of the leading microfinance institutions in B&H started the imitative series of workshops to improve digital financial literacy among their clients in order to break down the fear of using digital platforms (online banking) for payments. The intention behind the initiative was to empower clients to use online banking in order to shorten the time needed for the completion of payments (prior to using online banking, clients were forced to stand in lines in banks to complete payments), to ensure more cost-efficient payment (on-line payment are less costly than payment in the bank) and, at that time, to decrease the health risk associated with the COVID-19 infection.

2. Financial inclusion and (digital) financial literacy nexus

The definition of financial inclusion is rather complex. As an antipode to financial inclusion, financial exclusion was the firstly introduced concept and it referred to as the process where the poor and disadvantaged are prevented from accessing the financial system [4] and the inability to access necessary financial services in an appropriate form [5]. Being a rather broad socio-economic concept, the most comprehensive definition of financial inclusion was given by the WB [6] in which financial inclusion means that individuals and businesses have access to useful and affordable financial products and services that meet their needs – transactions, payments, savings, credit, and insurance – delivered in a responsible and sustainable way.

However, as the financial system evolves, financial institutions are embracing digital transformation where financial services and products are mostly digitalized, which directly contributes to greater financial inclusion in general. The findings of the latest WB-GFS from 2021 [2] show that COVID-19 boosted the adoption of digital financial services in developing economies and that mobile money has become an important enabler of financial inclusion (especially in Sub-Saharan Africa). Today, financial inclusion is understood through the ability of financial institutions to provide widely accessible financial services/products using digital technologies. In that sense, in today's academic and practical discourse, the term digital financial inclusion is being used more often and is perceived as the enabler of achieving universal financial inclusion. In respect to defining the concept of digital inclusion, digital financial inclusion, as defined by the WB [7], refers broadly to the usage of digital financial services to advance financial inclusion, i.e., the deployment of digital means to reach the digitally financially excluded and underserved populations with such financial services.

Digital financial inclusion is seen as the fourth stage of the financial revolution after developing microcredit, microfinance, and financial inclusion [8]. From the first microcredit and microfinance products/services (which will be discussed in more detail in the next section), the new financial landscape evolved to boost the inclusion of the adult population into the financial systems. Digital transformation of financial services has significantly increased financial inclusion, but still, the financial landscape counts on the financial institutions such as microfinance organizations to adopt the new technologies and provide digital financial products/ services to the unbanked part of the population.

One of the key barriers to (digital) financial inclusion is a lack of financial and ICT knowledge as reported by [9]. For the past several decades, financial literacy has been the key driver of financial inclusions since a better understanding of basic financial concepts, the usability of financial products/services and their contribution toward financial health and overall financial well-being of individuals is enabling greater involvement in the financial system. To that end, government, non-government organizations, universities, and financial service providers are creating different initiatives and education programs to improve financial literacy with more or less success. However, what research shows [10] is that promoting financial literacy is a way to ensure people live more financially secure lives.

Now, we turn our attention toward understating the microfinance landscape and its contribution to financial inclusion.

3. Microfinance and its contribution toward financial inclusion

Measured by the level of financial products and services ownership and usage, financial inclusion is directly linked to the ability of financial institutions to reach out to each adult individual. In a dominantly bank centric financial system, where commercial banks play the key role in providing bank accounts, credit and debit cards, savings and borrowing offers, individuals are often faced with the situation that they do not meet strict banking rules to be the bank clients or, what are the most usual case, these products and services are too expensive for lower-income groups, especially in developing part of the world. To fill the gap in the financial system and provide products and services to the poorest, the idea of microfinance was born. The following sections discuss the notion of microfinance, the history of microfinance institutions' development, and the characteristics of microfinance institutions.

3.1 The notion of microfinance and microcredit (microloan)

The concept of microfinance has its roots in the 18th-century but microfinance started to develop strongly in the last few decades dominantly in underdeveloped and developing countries. The oldest system of microcrediting and microcredit organizations, the predecessor of today's microfinance institutions, the "Irish Loan Fund" system, was founded in Ireland based on the idea of Jonathan Swift. His idea of lending to poor residents without collateral was accepted very slowly, but in 1840 it became widespread throughout Ireland, with the formation of approximately 300 funds. Those funds were lent to approximately 20% of households in Ireland. The four basic components of Swift's lending scheme were: small loans, weekly repayments, co-signers, but not physical collateral, and a lawsuit in case of inability to collect the loan [11].

The origin of the modern concept of microfinancing and the functioning of modern microcredit organizations is linked to the Grameen Bank from Bangladesh and its founder Muhamed Yunus. Yunus started the fight against poverty in 1974 during the great famine in Bangladesh. He discovered how very small loans (microcredits) can significantly improve the lives of the poorest. At that time, he started a research project on the economy in rural areas. His first loan was USD 27, which he lent out of his own funds to a woman who made bamboo furniture. At that time, traditional banks in Bangladesh were not interested in providing small loans to the poor because of the high risk of debt collection. However, Yunus believed that the poor would pay back their debts if given the chance and that the concept of microcredit could be turned into a profitable business model. The Norwegian Nobel Committee decided in 2006 to award the Nobel Peace Prize to the Grameen Bank from Bangladesh, as well as to its founder, for their efforts in achieving the economic and social empowerment of the poorest by providing the opportunity for a large number of poor people to start entrepreneurial activity through microcredit, which formally awarded the entire microcredit sector in the world for its success in reducing poverty. In the explanation of the Committee, it was pointed out that achieving long-term peace in the world cannot be achieved unless a large population of the poor finds a way to get out of the "circle" of poverty, and microcredit is one of those ways. The same was concluded by [12], "The key to ending extreme poverty is to enable the poorest of the poor to get their foot on the ladder of development. The ladder of development hovers overhead and the poorest of the poor are stuck beneath it. They lack the minimum amount of capital necessary to get a foothold, and therefore need a boost up to the first rung." It was clear that new types of financial institutions with more sensibility toward the poor were needed to evolve.

Interestingly, at that time the concept of microfinance had been perceived as unsustainable by the WB and other international donors and financiers for many years. However, after several decades of successful work by the Grameen Bank, the leaders of the WB admitted that "microcredit programs have breathed energy into the market economy in the countryside and the poorest part of the population in the world. By approaching the fight against poverty from a market point of view, millions of people have been enabled to improve their position with dignity." [13] Joseph Deiss, the Chairman of the General Assembly of the United Nations [14] said in his speech held at the annual assembly of the United Nations on October 13, 2010, that "microfinance is a key instrument for improving the living conditions of poor population." Recognizing microcredit as an effective means of fighting poverty, the WB established the Consultative Group to Assist the Poor (CGAP). CGAP today represents a consortium of over 30 public and private agencies working to improve access to financial services for the poor.

Microfinance is a concept developed from the concept of micro-crediting but in academic literature the term "microfinance" is often identified with the term "microcredit" (or "micro-crediting"), which is wrong. Namely, as already pointed out, Grameen Bank, the forerunner of today's microcredit financial institutions, paved the way for the development of microfinance by approving microloans for the poor. With the development of the bank, i.e., by understanding the needs of the poor for various financial services, the bank's activities expanded and, in addition to microcredit, the bank began to offer a wide range of financial services, from savings to money transfer services. So, microcredits represent only one of the financial products that are found in the wide range of offers of microcredit financial institutions that deal with microfinancing.

Microfinance is a set of different financial services (such as lending and savings), both conventional and digital, intended for those clients who do not have access to conventional financial/banking products and/or services. According to CGAP, microfinance, in a broad sense, refers to the provision/provision of financial services to poor and low-income clients who have limited or no access to conventional banks, while in a narrower sense, microfinance refers to institutions that use new techniques developed in the last 30 years to provide microcredits to informal entrepreneurs, where the range of services of these institutions includes savings, insurance services and money transfer services [15].

Microfinance services are intended for the poorest strata of society, but also for entrepreneurs and small and medium-sized enterprises that do not have the possibility to secure collateral when borrowing funds, do not have stable income, or do not have a credit history. The microfinance project proved to be a successful instrument in solving the financial problems of the low-income population in many parts of the world (e.g., India, Bangladesh, Latin American countries, Bosnia and Herzegovina, etc.).

Owing to the growth in financial technology aided by the widespread adoption of mobile and internet services across the world, the microfinance industry was able to establish a firm standing globally. The global market size for the microfinance industry is estimated to grow by USD 122.46 billion from 2021 to 2026 at a compound annual growth rate (CAGR) of 11.61%. The rapid adoption of technology has been one of the primary contributing factors to the growth of the microfinance sector. Moreover, global development agencies and several governments have been making concerted efforts to alleviate poverty by enabling financial inclusion products, such as micro-credits, to the underserved segment [16].

3.2 The microfinance sector and microcredit organizations

The drivers of the development of the microfinance sector are microcredit financial institutions/organizations. Microcredit organizations can be defined as non-deposit, non-profit, or for-profit organizations, whose main activity is providing microcredit to socially disadvantaged persons with the aim of developing micro-entrepreneurship. These are credit organizations that do not have the character of banks, nor are they established according to bank procedures.

Starting from the given definition, it is possible to distinguish two types of microcredit organizations:

1. non-profit microcredit organizations, which operate as non-governmental organizations (in B&H legislation they are called microcredit foundations), and

2. profit microcredit organizations, which have the status of a financial institution (in B&H legislation they are called microcredit companies).

The microcredit sector, as a rule, develops through the establishment of non-profit microcredit organizations, which grow into for-profit financial institutions through the development of the credit portfolio and expansion of the client base. For-profit microcredit organizations differ from non-profit ones in the way they are regulated, especially in terms of the sources of financing business activities.

For example, according to the Law on Microcredit Organizations of the Federation of B&H (Official Gazette of the Federation of B&H, No. 59/06), a microcredit organization is a non-depository financial organization whose main activity is the granting of microcredits. The microcredit organization performs microcredit activities with the aim of improving the financial position of microcredit users, increasing employment, providing support for the development of entrepreneurship and making a profit. In some countries, as in the case of B&A, microcredit organizations are under the jurisdiction of banking agencies, considering the activity of microcredit.

Microcredits are the most significant financial product that microcredit organizations provide to their clients. The amount of microcredit varies from country to country, as well as from the legal regulations that regulate the activity of microcredit organizations. In B&H, for example, microloans amount to 50,000 KM, which is equivalent to the amount of microloans in the EU of 25,000 EUR.

3.3 An overview of microfinance sector and its contribution toward financial inclusion in Bosnia and Herzegovina

Microcredit organizations in B&H began to develop in the post-war period from 1995 as part of programs implemented in this area with the aim of helping in employment and revitalization of economic activities through the marketing of microcredits. A large number of donors and financiers, primarily the WB, followed by other international organizations, made a significant contribution to the development of this sector by financing the operations of microcredit organizations. Microcredit organizations were created to fill the gap between commercial banks and humanitarian non-governmental institutions to support the development of small businesses and self-employment.

The microcredit sector of B&H has begun to play a significant role in reducing poverty and supporting the development of small and medium-sized entrepreneurship among the socially vulnerable population that does not have the possibility of obtaining financial resources from traditional/conventional banks. According to the Association of Microcredit Financial Institutions in B&H (AMFI) [17], the results achieved in the past 13 years included B&H among the countries with the highest development level in this domain of financial offer, which is often mixed with traditional banking, but the main difference is that the banks serve the wealthiest clients with credit history and collateral, while the microfinance i.e., microcredit organizations serve the clients who do not have collateral and have low income or no income whatsoever.

B&H microcredit organizations are among the leading microfinance institutions in the world, according to the level of transparency in business operations and financial reporting. Forbes' list of the 50 most successful microcredit organizations for 2007 includes five microcredit organizations from B&H [18]. The microcredit sector is one of the few sectors of the B&H economy that has adopted and reached the world business standards that apply in this sector.

The most important microfinance law was adopted in 2006. According to this new regulation framework, former microcredit organizations (originally 35) had to transfer into either microcredit foundations or microcredit companies. According to the mentioned law, microcredit foundations are legally authorized to dispense individual microcredits up to 10,000 BAM in value (5.000 Euros) while microcredit companies are legally authorized to dispense individual microcredits up to 50,000 BAM in value (25.000 Euros). Both types of microcredit organizations are non-deposit-taking financial institutions.

According to the Financial Stability Report for 2021 issued by the Central Bank B&H [19], the operations of the microcredit sector in 2021 were marked by: asset growth, growth of gross loans, and capital increase, accompanied by the decreased value of delayed loans, and profitability growth. At the end of 2021, there were 26 microcredit organizations operating in B&H: 14 microcredit companies and 12 microcredit foundations. At the end of 2021, the total assets of the microcredit sector were higher by 7.8% compared to 2020, while loans increased by 8.2%. Out of the total microcredits amount, 97.4% was extended to individuals and households. The main sectors being financed are the agriculture sector (27.6%), followed by the financing of housing needs (17.4%) and the service sector (11.1%).

4. BH microfinance institutions initiatives for improving financial literacy: The case of digital financial literacy initiative: "Our classorom"

4.1 Initiative description and methodological framework for measuring the efficiency

Microfinance institutions in B&H developed individual approaches toward addressing client's needs. The main reason for their success and the low percentage of non-performing loans is their ability to provide custom-made financial products/services as well as to support their clients in terms of financial education. During the COVID-19 pandemic, one of the biggest microcredit organizations in B&H, MI-BOSPO, organized a series of educations on digital financial literacy for their clients to help them to overcome obstacles posed by the lockdown.

MI-BOSPO became aware of the fact that their clients are exposed to waiting in long lines to complete the payments in commercial banks as well as of long commuting time spent on public transportation in order to pay their monthly loan installments. Sometimes, this waiting and commuting time could take several hours and could pose a health risk as well. This microfinance organization at that time had only one cashier in Tuzla where the microcredit installments could be paid, meaning that the majority of the clients paid installments through commercial banks. With the aim to motivate and support their clients (dominantly women) to use new digital technologies, such as online and mobile banking tools, to ease their business activities and support their family financial needs, MI-BOSPO has identified a need for a structured approach in the digital financial education. To that end, the initiative, called "Our Classroom" was launched in 2020 and 2021. The initiative was designed to raise the level of digital financial literacy among women, and increase the level of their knowledge and skills in digital banking tools, the types of digital services available, the reliability of the tools, and the simplicity and security of use. The main idea behind the initiatives was to assure the safety of their clients by eliminating waiting in long queues, and their health protection during the time of the pandemic, but also help their clients to overcome the prejudices such as internet safety, distrust, fear of something new and virtual, and present the advantages and possibilities given by this method of money transfer. The overall objective was to provide responsible financial services and increase the skills and knowledge of women clients on the use of digital banking tools.

"Our classroom" initiative included a series of tailored educational workshops on the following topics:

- introduction to digital payment channels (electronic banking, mobile banking, credit cards, payment and withdrawal of money at the ATMs),
- advantages and possibilities of internet and mobile tools, applications and services for money transfer and payments,
- internet and mobile security and safety, and
- raising the level of digital literacy, trust, and awareness.

Education was implemented by the independent consultant. To provide better outreach the clients, workshops were organized in 10 towns throughout the whole territory of B&H (Tuzla, Brčko, Bijeljina, Gradačac, Kalesija, Lukavac, Doboj, Zenica, Živinice, Srebrenik, Vlasenica, Banja Luka, Gračanica, Sarajevo, Zavidovići).

To follow the implementation as well as to capture the effects of educational workshops, the Faculty of Economics, University of Tuzla was commissioned to evaluate the level of digital financial literacy of MI-BOSPO clients and their need for education. The comprehensive methodology was developed in order to capture the effects of the initiative. To that end, protocols for collecting base-line and end-line data were developed. The following activities were performed:

- preparation of survey methodology and questionnaires,
- sample calculation of targeted survey participants,
- data collection, and
- data analysis.

For the purpose of understating the level of financial literacy, the incentive to use online banking and the effectiveness of the training in increasing digital financial inclusion, a base-line survey was conducted using the questionnaire prepared for this purpose.

The sample included clients of the microcredit organization MI-BOSPO. The basic sociodemographic features of the respondents are given in **Table 1**, while the geographical distribution sample is given in Appendix I.

The average size of households was 3.72 with a standard deviation of 1.42. At least one household had only one member, and the largest of them had even 9. An average

Sociodemographic characteristics		Frequency	Percentage
The middle	Rural	157	65.1
	Urban	84	34.9
	Total	241	100.0
Residence	FBiH	132	55.0
	RS	104	43.2
	Brčko district	4	1.7
	Total	240	100.0
Marital status	Unmarried	16	6.7
	Married	181	75.4
	Divorced	21	8.7
	Widow	22	9.2
	Total	240	100.0
Education	Unfinished elementary school	1	0.4
	Finished elementary school	47	19.5
	Medium professional qualifications	179	74.3
	Tall professional qualifications	3	1.2
	Master's degree	10	4.1
	Doctorate	1	0.4
	Total	241	100.0
Primary source of income	Pensioner	20	8.3
	Self-employed	168	69.7
	Employed	39	16.2
	Second	14	5.8
	Total	241	100.0
Income level per households	less than 500 BAM	14	7.1
	501 BAM - 1000 BAM	49	24.7
	1001 BAM - 1500 BAM	43	21.7
	1501 BAM - 2000 BAM	42	21.2
	2001 BAM - 2500 BAM	28	14.1
	over 2500 BAM	22	11.1
	Total	198	100.0

Sociodemographic characteristics		Frequency	Percentage
Income from registered business	less than 500 BAM	57	28.6
	501 BAM - 1000 BAM	69	34.7
	1001 BAM - 1500 BAM	26	13.1
	1501 BAM - 2000 BAM	20	10.1
	2001 BAM - 2500 BAM	13	6.5
	over 2500 BAM	14	7.0
	Total	199	100.0
Access to Internet	Yes	225	94.1
	no	14	5.9
	Total	241	100.0

Source: Authors' calculations.

Table 1.
Sociodemographic characteristics of respondents.

number of people included in the business is 2.44 with a standard deviation of 1.71. At least one household only had one member, and the largest them even 15. When it comes to the type of business, mostly the respondent stated that are working in the agriculture sector (40.2%), trade (21.6%), services (32.8%), and production (5.0%) sectors.

At the end of the project, the end-line survey was conducted among the clients who attended education. In total 66 responses were collected in the endline-survey which was sufficient enough to draw conclusions on the efficiency of the initiative.

The following sections provide the analysis of the data collected through base-line and end-line survey.

4.2 Understanding of the current usage level of digital banking products/services

In this section, the research results related to understanding the current usage level of digital products/services by the MI-BOSPO clients are presented. The focus is given to better understanding of the current practices of using financial products in general, both for personal and business use, as well as of the use of Internet and mobile banking services for personal and business needs with the aim to understand the reasons for poor usage of online banking services.

4.2.1 Use of financial products and services for personal and household needs

The frequency of usage of financial product and service for personal and/or needs households are given in **Table 2**.

With further analysis of the use of financial services, it was detected that from the total number of respondents, 37 of them (25.9%), who receive salary in cash, transfer this salary to a bank account, while 106 respondents (74.1%) do not transfer their salary on to the bank account. On the other hand, the respondents who receive their

Characteristics		Frequency	Percentage
Having the opened bank account	yes	197	83.1
	no	40	16.9
	Total	241	100.0
The bank where the account is open	NLB Bank	38	0.20
	New bank	27	0.14
	Raiffeisen bank	20	0.10
	Sberbank	20	0.10
	Unicredit bank	20	0.10
	Other banks	69	35.6
	Total	194	100.0
Knowledge on whether local community stores accept payment cards	yes	166	69.5
	no	40	16.7
	I do not know	33	13.8
	Total	239	100.0
The main way of receiving salary	In cash	146	61.3
	Through the bank account	74	31.1
	In the last 6 months did not receive any income	18	7.6
	Total	238	100.0

Source: Authors' own research.

Table 2.
Usage of financial products and services for personal and needs households.

salaries through the bank account, in 15 cases (20,3%) withdraw the money from the bank account, while 59 respondents (79,7%) do not withdraw the money.

Additionally, the analysis of the payment habits was conducted where respondents were asked to answer which types of payment are using to pay for their bills. The results are provided in the following **Table 3**.

When it comes to payment methods, it can be observed that the respondents mainly pay cash, which shows that the respondents are not utilizing the opportunities of faster payment methods such as online payments through mobile applications and Internet banking.

The payment methods		Frequency	Percentage
Cash payments	yes	233	98.7
	no	3	1.3
	Total	236	100.0
From their bank accounts	yes	67	28.3
	no	170	71.7
	Total	237	100.0

The payment methods		Frequency	Percentage
Using mobile application	yes	19	8.1
	no	217	91.95
	Total	236	100.0
Using computer	yes	10	4.3
	no	225	95.7
	Total	235	100.0

Source: Authors' own research.

Table 3.
The payment methods.

With respect to the business needs of respondents, only 26 of them (11.7%) declared that for the purposes of their own business, they have contracted services of Internet and mobile banking in some of the banks. Big majority of respondents, 197 of them, (88.3%) claim that do not these services for personal use.

4.2.2 Use of internet and mobile banking services for personal and business needs

The majority of respondents (89.9%), declared owning some devices, such as tablets, smart telephones, and computers for personal use. However, as many as 196 of the respondents, or 82.7%, claim that they do not use the Internet and/or mobile banking for their own personal needs and/or for the needs of their own households.

The respondents who confirmed their usage of Internet and mobile banking services for personal use, provided more in-depth information on the purposes of using online banking services. The most commonly used services Internet and/or mobile banking for personal needs and/or needs of households are given in **Table 4**.

In respect to the use of Internet and mobile banking services for business needs, 110 respondents (48.2%) declared that for the purposes of their own business have some type of electronic device, such as a tablet, smartphone, or computer. However, the majority of them (89.4%) claim that they do not use the Internet and/or mobile banking for business needs. Only 24 respondents, or 10.6% of them declared some of the services of Internet and/or mobile banking for business purposes.

Type of Internet and mobile banking services used		Frequency	Percentage
Domestic payments - payment direction and others species accounts	Yes	30	71.4
	No	12	28.6
	Total	42	100.0
Funds transfer on to personal and business accounts	Yes	17	40.5
	No	25	59.5
	Total	42	100.0
Funds transfer between own accounts	Yes	11	26.2
	No	31	73.8
	Total	42	100.0

Type of Internet and mobile banking services used		Frequency	Percentage
Currency conversion	Yes	4	9.5
	No	38	90.5
	Total	42	100.0
Checking the account balance, transaction and credit card debts	Yes	35	83.3
	No	7	16.7
	Total	42	100.0
Overview of all orders, their status, and others information	Yes	28	66.7
	No	14	33.3
	Total	42	100.0
Overview of exchange rates/exchange rates lists	Yes	4	9.5
	No	38	90.5
	Total	42	100.0
Overview of useful contacts in the Bank	Yes	10	23.8
	No	32	76.2
	Total	42	100.0

Source: Authors' own research.

Table 4.
The most commonly used services Internet and/or mobile banking for personal needs and/or needs households.

Type of Internet and mobile banking services used		Frequency	Percentage
Domestic payment – utility bills and other invoices payment	Yes	20	83.3
	No	4	16.7
	Total	24	100.0
Foreign payments	Yes	2	8–7
	No	21	91.3
	Total	23	100.0
Funds transfer between own accounts	Yes	12	54.5
	No	10	45.5
	Total	22	100.0
Currency conversion	Yes	3	14.3
	No	18	85.7
	Total	21	100.0
Two-way communication with the bank	Yes	6	27.3
	No	16	72.7
	Total	22	100.0
Products notice and services banks and special benefits and actions for client's banks	Yes	12	54.5
	No	10	45.5
	Total	22	100.0

Type of Internet and mobile banking services used		Frequency	Percentage
Account balance and transactions overview	Yes	21	95.5
	No	1	4.5
	Total	22	100.0
Payment obligation way paid order	Yes	16	72.7
	No	6	27.3
	Total	22	100.0
Bank statements and payment orders generation and overview	Yes	15	86.4
	No	7	13.6
	Total	22	100.0
Overview of all orders, their status and other information	Yes	19	86.4
	No	3	13.6
	Total	22	100.0
Overview of exchange rates/exchange rates lists	Yes	4	18.2
	No	18	81.8
	Total	22	100.0
Overview of the useful contacts in the Bank	Yes	6	27.3
	No	16	72.7
	Total	22	100.0

Source: Authors' own research.

Table 5.
The most commonly used services of Internet and/or mobile banking for business purposes.

An overview of the most commonly used service for business purposes is given in the **Table 5**.

The main reasons for poor usage of Internet and mobile banking are presented in **Figure 1**.

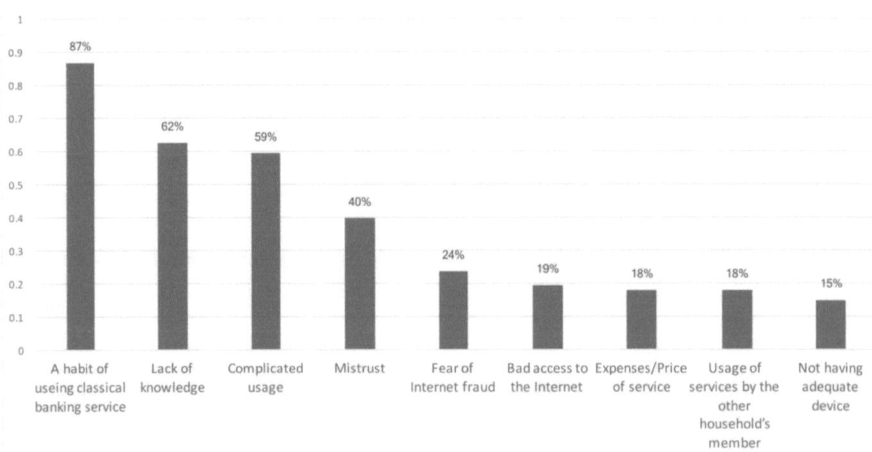

Figure 1.
Reasons for insufficient usage of Internet and mobile banking services. Source: Authors' own research.

Based on the data presented in the previous figure, it can be concluded that the most important barriers to the usage of Internet and mobile banking services are the habit of using classical banking services, lack of knowledge, complicated use, mistrust, and fear of Internet fraud.

4.3 Knowledge regarding the use of Internet and mobile banking services and willingness to participate in education

Assuming that the survey participants do not have adequate knowledge of the use of Internet and mobile banking services, one of the research goals was to establish the level of relevant knowledge on basic financial concepts. For that purpose, a questionnaire consisting of 14 statements was created. The results given in **Table 6** enables a better insight into the knowledge of respondent in regard to the usage of Internet and mobile services banking.

As it can be observed from the previous table, the most dominant answer to all statements is "I don't know" if the statement is true or not. This means that respondents lacked knowledge of basic financial concepts.

Combining the results of the reasons for the poor usage of Internet and mobile banking services with the understating of basic financial concepts, it was clear that more education is needed in order to break down the circle of fear of using online banking services. 65 respondents (27.3%), expressed their willingness to participate in education in which they would gain more theoretical and practical knowledge about Internet and mobile banking. Most of the respondents, i.e., 173 of them, or 72.7%, did

Statement		**Frequency**	**Percentage**
Internet and/or mobile services can be used to check the account balance and payments from and to bank account	True	157	66.8
	False	5	2.1
	I do not know	**73**	**31.1**
	Total	235	100.0
Internet and/or mobile services can be used for debt balance overview, overdue and unpaid installments, interests, costs, and limits on credit and debit cards.	True	122	51.9
	False	5	2.1
	I do not know	**108**	**46.0**
	Total	235	100.0
Internet and/or mobile services can be used for utility bills and other bill payments	True	195	83.0
	False	1	0.4
	I do not know	**39**	**16.6**
	Total	235	100.0
Internet and/or mobile services can be used for payment of utility bills using the option to take of photo of the bill which will automatically translated into the payment request	True	78	33.3
	False	10	4.3
	I do not know	**146**	**62.4**
	Total	234	100.0

Statement		Frequency	Percentage
Internet and/or mobile services can be used for currency conversion	True	44	18.8
	False	12	5.1
	I do not know	**178**	**76.1**
	Total	234	100.0
Internet and/or mobile services can be used to review payments	True	151	64.5
	False	5	2.1
	I do not know	**78**	**33.3**
	Total	234	100.0
Internet and/or mobile services can be used to create templets of payment instructions for future faster payment	True	88	37.6
	False	4	1.7
	I do not know	**242**	**60.7**
	Total	234	100.0
Internet and/or mobile services can have an option to set the future date for the payment	True	34	14.6
	False	15	6.4
	I do not know	**184**	**79.0**
	Total	233	100.0
Internet and/or mobile services can be used for utility bill subscriptions by using e-payments	True	49	20.9
	False	9	3.8
	I do not know	**176**	**75.2**
	Total	234	100.0
Internet and/or mobile services can be used to get information about the Bank	True	116	49.8
	False	3	1.3
	I do not know	**114**	**48.9**
	Total	233	100.0
Internet and/or mobile services can be used to find the closest ATM or branch office	True	121	51.7
	False	3	1.3
	I do not know	**110**	**47.0**
	Total	234	100.0
Internet and/or mobile services can be used for payment of public taxes	True	91	38.9
	False	8	3.4
	I do not know	**135**	57.7
	Total	234	100.0

Statement		Frequency	Percentage
Internet and/or mobile services can be used for bank statement withdrawal Internet and/or mobile services can be used for bank statement withdrawal	True	89	38.0
	False	10	4.3
	I do not know	**135**	**57.7**
	Total	234	100.0
Internet and/or mobile services can be used for bank statement withdrawal	True	57	24.4
	False	12	5.1
	I do not know	**165**	**70.5**
	Total	241	100.0

Source: Authors' own research.

Table 6.
Relationship knowledge – use Internet service and mobile banking.

not express this willingness. The majority of the respondents, 158, or 66.4%, believe that their use of Internet and mobile banking would not change significantly, despite the acquisition of more theoretical and practical knowledge, while 80 respondents, or 33.6%, believed that they would use the Internet and mobile banking more if they gained more theoretical and practical knowledge about it.

4.4 Effects of "our classroom" initiative toward improving knowledge and usage practices of Internet/mobile banking

The results of knowledge self-assessment with respect to usage of Internet and/or mobile banking services after the education within "Our classroom" are presented in **Figure 2**.

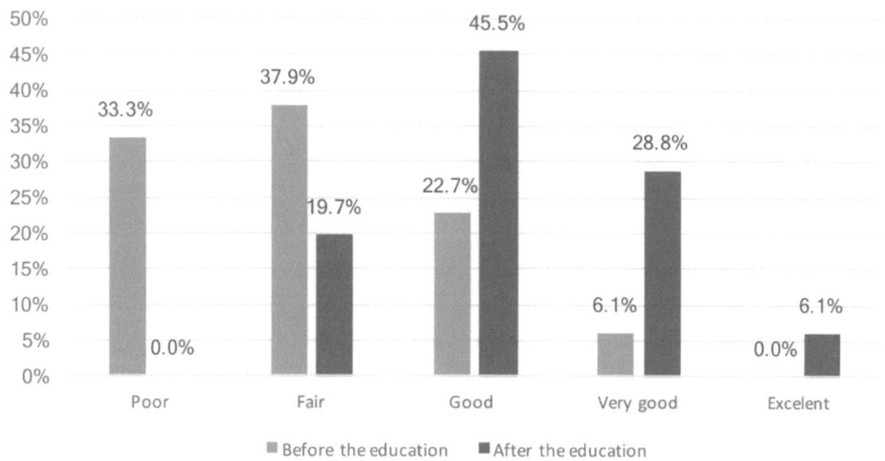

Figure 2.
Knowledge self-assessment with respect to usage of Internet and/or mobile banking services. Source: Authors' own research.

As it can be observed, participation in education improved the level of self-assessed knowledge with respect to the usage of the Internet and/or mobile banking services. Prior to the education, the majority of respondent assessed their knowledge as poor (33,3%) or fair (37,9%), while after the education it can be observed that the level of knowledge significantly increased. More than 45% of respondents assessed their knowledge as good, 28,8% as very good, and 6,1% as excellent. It can be concluded that education improved the self-assessed knowledge among participants since none of the respondents assessed their knowledge as poor after the completion of the education.

Self-assessment of the level of Internet and/or mobile services usage prior to education in contrast to after the education is presented in **Figure 3**.

Based on the self-assessment of Internet and/or mobile services usage frequency before and after education, it can be concluded that education had a positive impact on the intention to use online banking services. While more than 72% of the respondents reported that never used Internet and/or mobile services prior to education, only 19,7% of them reported that they do not intend to use it in the future. On the other hand, 27,3% of respondents declared the intention to use the service occasionally, and 31,8% of them that they will use the Internet and/or mobile services frequently.

In order to gain a more in-depth understanding of the knowledge increase after the education, respondents were asked to answer whether some statements regarding the usage of Internet and mobile services are correct. The results of this assessment are given in **Table 7**.

Based on the results presented in the previous table, it can be concluded that participation in education contributed toward a better understanding of the basic financial concepts among participants. The majority of responders answered correctly to the proposed statements, while the percentage of the answer "I don't know" is in a range from 2 to 23%.

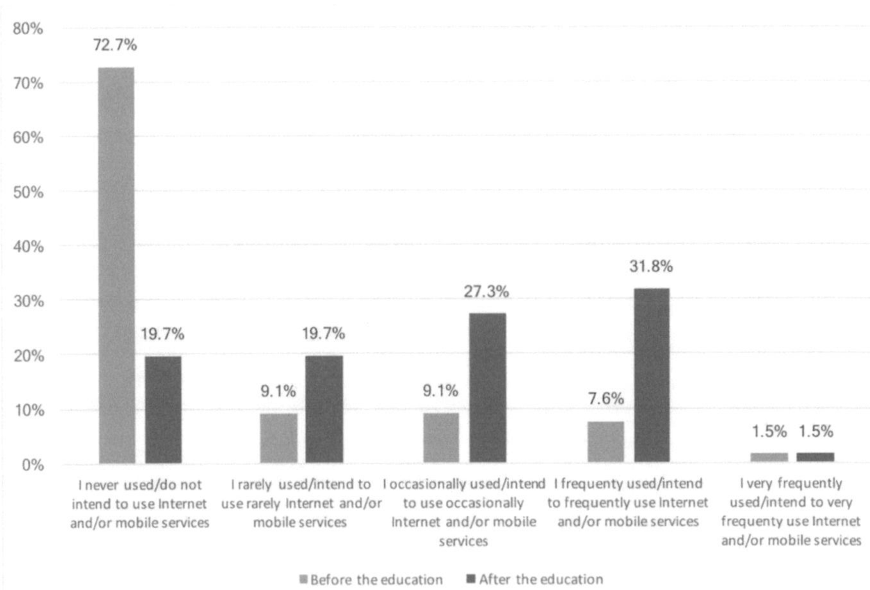

Figure 3.
Self-assessment of Internet and/or mobile services usage frequency. Source: Authors' own research.

Statement	True (%)	False (%)	I do not know (%)
I am more confident and have less fear with respect to Internet payment after the education	81	9	9
I completed at least one transaction using the Internet or mobile banking services after the education	32	68	0
As a result of the education I know how to check my account balance using online banking	45	55	0
As a result of the education I know how to file a request for online banking services	44	47	9
Internet and/or mobile services can be used for payment of utility and other bills	100	0	0
Internet and/or mobile services can be used for payment of utility bills using the option to take of photo of the bill which will automatically translated into the payment request	94	0	6
Internet and/or mobile services can be used for currency conversion	77	0	23
Internet and/or mobile services can be used for an overview of completed payments	89	0	11
Internet and/or mobile services have the option to create templets of payment instructions for future faster payment	91	0	9
Internet and/or mobile services can have an option to set the future date for the payment	80	0	20
Internet and/or mobile services can be used for utility bill subscriptions by using e-payments	85	0	15
Internet and/or mobile services can be used to obtain information about the bank	98	0	2
Internet and/or mobile services can be used to find the closest ATM or branch office	97	0	3
Internet and/or mobile services can be used for payment of public taxes	79	0	21
Internet and/or mobile services can be used for bank statement withdrawal	88	0	12
Internet and/or mobile services can be used for foreign payments	88	0	12

Source: Authors' own research.

Table 7.
Attitudes and knowledge toward using Internet and/or mobile services after education.

It has to be emphasized that participation in education also contributed toward the increase of the confidence and trust among participants to use the Internet and/or mobile services. More than 81% of respondents confirmed that their trust and confidence were increased as a result of education.

5. Conclusions

Digital transformation as the concept of digital technology use in business practices, is profoundly integrated in today's everyday life. The need for digital transformation was even more obvious during the COVID-19 pandemic. As a result of the lockdown, most of the day-to-day activities and business operations were transferred into the online world. The financial sector, like any other service sector, had to adapt and offer their clients products and services that are available online and do not require that client has to come to the bank or any other financial institution.

During the lockdown period, many financial institutions in B&H faced the problem of reaching their clients and adequately addressing their needs, despite the fact that most of the financial institutions initiated digital transformation of their businesses and were already offering Internet and mobile services to their clients.

Needs assessment conducted by MI-BOSPO provided an insight into their clients' level of usage of Internet and mobile banking services, level of knowledge (financial literacy), and confirmed the need and readiness of their clients to participate in education to increase their level of financial literacy and improve their habits of using the Internet and mobile banking service. As a result of the needs assessment among MI-BOSPO clients, "Our classroom" initiative was introduced. The initiative envisaged the organization of tailored education workshops, based on the needs assessment research conducted prior to workshop organization, where clients would gain a better understanding of the key financial concepts and practical aspects of using the Internet and mobile banking.

As a result of "Our classroom" initiative, valuable insights into financial inclusion and literacy were gained. An interesting finding is that there are around 19% of clients do not have bank accounts which is the primary indicator of financial inclusion. The clients are mostly receiving cash payments which further dissimulated them to have bank accounts. Those who own a bank account rarely use Internet and mobile banking services. Only 14,5% of clients use these services for personal affairs, while just 10% for business purposes, proving that digital financial inclusion is even lower than the overall financial inclusion measured by bank account ownership. The research conducted prior to workshops provided an insight into a better understanding of the low digital financial inclusion through a better understating of the factors contributing to poor usage of Internet and mobile banking services. The research showed that the main reasons for avoiding online banking services are (1) the habit of using classical banking services, (2) lack of knowledge, (3) complicated use, (4) mistrust and (5) fear of Internet fraud. Besides the habit of using classical banking services, all other four barriers to using online banking are related to poor financial literacy. More in-depth analysis showed that the majority of clients did not have knowledge of the basic financial concepts.

"Our classroom" initiative resulted in the positive change toward increase of (digital) financial literacy and (digital) financial inclusion. Endline research showed that initiative contributed toward:

1. improvement of the level of self-assessed knowledge with respect to usage of Internet and/or mobile banking services, since none of the respondents assessed their knowledge as poor after the completion of the education. More than 45% of respondents assessed their knowledge as good, 28.8% as very good, and 6.1% as excellent.

2. increased intention to use online banking services among clients. While more than 72% of the respondents reported that never used Internet and/or mobile services prior to education, only 19.7% of them reported that do not intend to use it in the future. 27.3% of respondents declared that they have the intention to use

the service occasionally, and 31.8% of them that they will use the Internet and/or mobile services frequently.

3. a better understanding of the basic financial concepts among participants. The majority of responders answered correctly to the proposed statements, while the percentage of the answer "I don't know" is in a range from 2 to 23%.

4. increase of the confidence and trust among participants to use the Internet and/ or mobile services. More than 81% of respondents confirmed that their trust and confidence were increased as a result of education.

Acknowledgements

Authors would like to express their gratitude toward the microcredit foundation MI-BOSPO from Tuzla, Bosnia and Herzegovina for initiating the "Our classroom" initiative and recognizing the importance of the scientific approach toward measuring the effects of these efforts. The authors would like to thank personally to Mr. Safet Husić, CEO at MI-BOSPO, Ms. Azra Berilo, HR manager at MI-BOSPO and Ms. Dragana Lukić, marketing manager at MI-BOSPO.

Conflict of interest

The authors declare no conflict of interest.

A. Appendix

See **Table 8**.

Municipality/City	Frequency	Percentage
Banja Luka	1	0.4
Bijeljina	30	12.4
Bratunac	5	2.1
Brčko	4	1.7
Čelinac	1	0.4
Derventa	1	0.4
Doboj	8	3.3
Donji Žabari	1	0.4
Gračanica	1	0.4
Gradačac	20	8.3
Ilidža	4	1.7

Municipality/City	Frequency	Percentage
Janja	7	2.9
Jelah	2	0.8
Kakanj	4	1.7
Kalesija	21	8.7
Kladanj	1	0.4
Kostajnica	1	0.4
Laktaši	1	0.4
Lepenica	2	0.8
Lukavac	4	1.7
Milići	1	0.4
Miljanovci	1	0.4
Modriča	2	0.8
Novi Grad	2	0.8
Odžak	8	3.3
Prnjavor	10	4.1
Puračić	1	0.4
Sapna	3	1.2
Sarajevo	13	5.4
Srebrenik	8	3.3
Teslić	4	1.7
Tešanj	3	1.2
Travnik	2	0.8
Tuzla	17	7.1
Ugljevik	4	1.7
Visoko	5	2.1
Vlasenica	10	4.1
Vogošća	2	0.8
Zavidovi	6	2.5
Zenica	2	0.8
Zvornik	6	2.5
Žepče	2	0.8
Živinice	10	4.1
Total	241	100.0

Source: Authors' calculations.

Table 8.
Geographical distribution of the sample.

Author details

Jasmina Okičić and Meldina Kokorović Jukan*
Faculty of Economics, University of Tuzla, Tuzla, Bosnia and Herzegovina

*Address all correspondence to: meldina.kokorovic@untz.ba

References

[1] World Bank. UFA2020 Overview: Universal Financial Access by 2020. World Bank. 2018. Available from: https://www.worldbank.org/en/topic/financialinclusion/brief/achieving-universal-financial-access-by-2020 [Accessed: August 22, 2023]

[2] Demirgüç-Kunt A, Klapper L, Singer D, Ansar ST. Global Findex Database 2021: Financial Inclusion, Digital Payments, and Resilience in the Age of COVID-19. Washington, DC: World Bank; 2022. DOI: 10.1596/978-1-4648-1897-4

[3] Grohmann A, Klühs T, Menkhoff L. Does financial literacy improve financial inclusion? Cross country evidence (September 2017). DIW Berlin Discussion Paper No. 1682. 2017. 10.2139/ssrn.3034178

[4] Leyshon A, Thrift N. Financial exclusion and the shifting boundaries of the Financial system. Environment and Planning A: Economy and Space. 1996; **28**(7):1150-1156. DOI: 10.1068/a281150

[5] Sinclair PS. Financial Exclusion: An Introductory Survey. Edinburgh: Centre for Research in Socially Inclusive Services (CRISIS), Heriot-Watt University; 2021

[6] World Bank. Overview. World Bank [Internet]. 2022. Available from: https://www.worldbank.org/en/topic/financialinclusion/ [Accessed: August 22, 2023]

[7] World Bank. Digital financial inclusion. World Bank. 2022. Available from: https://www.worldbank.org/en/topic/financialinclusion/publication/digital-financial-inclusion [Accessed: August 22, 2023]

[8] Lauer K, Lyman T. Digital Financial inclusion: Implications for customers, regulators, supervisors, and standard-setting bodies. In: Consultative Group to Assist the Poor (CGAP) Brief; Consultative Group to Assist the Poor (CGAP). Washington, DC, USA; 2015

[9] Anakpo G, Xhate Z, Mishi S. The policies, practices, and challenges of digital Financial inclusion for sustainable development: The case of the developing economy. FinTech. 2023;**2**(2):327-343. DOI: 10.3390/fintech2020019

[10] Lusardi A, Mitchell OS. The importance of financial literacy: Opening a new field. NBER Working Papers 31145. National Bureau of Economic Research, Inc. 2023

[11] Hollis A, Sweetman AC. Competition and institutional development: The Irish loan funds through three centuries. Economic History. 1997;**1997**:9704003

[12] Sachs J. The End of Poverty: How We Can Make It Happen in Our Lifetime. UK: Penguin; 2005

[13] Yunus M, Jolis A. Banker to the Poor: micro-Lending and the Battle against World Poverty. New York, NY: Public Affairs; 2003

[14] Dreiss J. Statement of H.E. Mr. Joseph Deiss, President of the 65th Session of the General Assembly, at the 29th Plenary Meeting: Follow-up to the International Year of Microcredit. 2010. Available from: https://www.un.org/en/ga/president/65/pdf/statements/20101013-microcredit.pdf [Accessed: August 10, 2023]

[15] Rosenberg R, Gonzalez A, Narain S. The new moneylenders: Are the poor being exploited by high microcredit interest rates?. Occasional Paper, No. 15. 2009. Available from:

https://www.cgap.org/sites/default/files/CGAP-Occasional-Paper-The-New-Moneylenders-Are-the-Poor-Being-Exploited-by-High-Microcredit-Interest-Rates-Feb-2009.pdf [Accessed: June 24, 2023]

[16] PwC. Next-gen microfinance: The role of digital technology [Internet]. 2023. Available from: https://www.pwc.in/assets/pdfs/consulting/financial-services/fintech/publications/next-gen-microfinance-the-role-of-digital-technology.pdf [Accessed: July 23, 2023]

[17] AMFI. About us [Internet]. 2023. Available from: https://amfi.ba/en/about-us/ [Accessed: July 20, 2023]

[18] Forbes. The 50 Top Microfinance Institutions [Internet]. 2007. Available from: https://www.forbes.com/2007/12/20/microfinance-philanthropy-credit-biz-cz_ms_1220microfinance_table.html?sh=7ca2e295b292 [Accessed: August 04, 2023]

[19] CBBiH. Financial stability report for 2021 [Internet]. 2023. Central bank of Bosnia and Herzegovina. 2023. Available from: https://www.cbbh.ba/Content/Archive/575 [Accessed: July 20, 2023]

Chapter 5

Financial Literacy Plus New Purchasing Power, How Ledger Economics Can End Poverty and Promote Continuous Economic Improvement

Thomas Fisher and Joel Hodroff

Abstract

Financial Literacy plus new purchasing power can drive rapid and environmentally sustainable, local-to-global, economic development. Historically, new technologies promote new forms of money and commerce that usher in new economic eras. This chapter is for leaders and innovators in financial services and sustainable economic development. It reveals an emerging era of sustainable prosperity for all. The world can now eradicate centuries-old poverty and inequality at the pace of mobile apps and social media. The funding for this paradigm shift is a next-generation financial instrument and not higher taxes, deeper debt, or redistribution of wealth schemes. The chapter introduces the first token-less ledger currency that is distributed through a public Business-Community Wealth Ledger (BCWL). Dual Currency transactions integrate fiat currencies with wealth-backed ledger currencies, monetizing and mobilizing currently underutilized business resources and increasing profits for participating businesses.

Keywords: financial literacy, ledger economics, ledger dollars, dual-currency pricing, underutilized assets

1. Introduction

The global banking and credit union industry is one of the most powerful industries on the planet. While often blamed for global economic inequality or economic disasters, such as the 2008 global economic downturn, global banking—with the right tools and a profit motive—can rapidly fund and deliver economic solutions of enormous magnitude. At present, banks and credit unions demonstrate their good intentions through their foundations and charitable giving; their support to entrepreneurial start-ups; their volunteer, wellness, ESG, and green teams; their investments in community economic development; and more. But the large-scale programs that target the unbanked primarily center today on teaching financial literacy. These financial-literacy programs operate far below their potential to raise-up individuals, and do not transform the poverty facing economically disadvantaged families and communities. Unfortunately, financial Literacy does not give people the purchasing power needed to improve their standard of living and quality of life nor to send their children to better schools and colleges.

2. The modern economic context

Such material scarcity should be a relic of the past. Today, food is an abundant renewable resource. Education and healthcare are also abundant renewable resources. Everything digital from music and videos to online games and educational content is virtually infinite. The technologies, labor skills, global economic infrastructure, and renewable resources needed to rapidly provide affordable housing on a global scale are all abundantly available. All these resources can be deployed across the globe even more rapidly than when the world mobilized for World War II in only a few years—over 75 years ago—with none of today's global economic infrastructure. The United States went from the end of the Depression to full war preparedness in a mere 14 months, without sending the population to trade schools or colleges. Everything needed was achieved through on-the-job training [1]. A modern day commercial example is how the Sharing Economy, using modern technologies, created millions of jobs and billions of dollars of new wealth in only a couple of years by mobilizing the modest underutilized resources of an empty room in someone's home or an idle car and driver (**Figure 1**).

We have become accustomed to living with massive, underutilized wealth side-by-side with massive unmet needs in the US and across the world. Grocery store aisles, full of groceries, are empty of customers more than they are full. College desks are empty more than they are full. Restaurants, movie theaters, fitness clubs, shopping malls, car dealerships, stadiums, and more are all empty more than they are full—all side-by-side with unmet needs for these very products and services by families and communities. This makes no sense. Because of this abundance, individuals, families, and communities across-the-globe no longer need to endure poverty, hunger, poor health, lack of quality housing and education, nor other reflections of poverty that are an outdated inheritance from the past. The same is true of the glaring disparities in wealth and opportunities that plague communities and nations everywhere. Equity is no longer a matter of taking from some and giving to others. That is a fearful myth that holds back progress for the entire human race.

The challenge and the opportunity lie in creating new economic efficiency to produce and distribute needed goods and services from within the massive underutilized

Figure 1.
Continuous economic improvement.

productive capacity found across the private, public, and nonprofit sectors alike. Achieving the United Nations Sustainable Development Goals (SDGs) by 2030 will no longer be a challenge if we mobilize around a common vision and deploy a new cooperative financial instrument. Our powerful, global free-enterprise system, combined with social entrepreneurial business models, can rapidly carry the entire human family into a twenty-first century of human cooperation and sustainable prosperity.

What has been the hold up? Poverty–and its unwelcome offspring including crime, inequality, poor health, discouragement, and class warfare–only persists because economics and commerce confuse the separate, but distinct, roles of money and wealth. Money is only one essential tool of wealth creation. Other essential tools include technology, infrastructure, human skill and creativity, planning and design, as well as materials and energy. Producing and distributing wealth is the objective of commerce. Wealth is reflected in both a nation's standard of living and its quality of life. While money should merely be a tool of wealth creation, money has sadly become the master of wealth creation [2]. While money was once based upon scarce commodities such as gold and silver coins or precious stones, money is today largely electronic debits and credits in computers, seen as bank accounts and stock portfolios. Yet we fail to grasp how money is running the show in the modern world and driving the economic booms and busts that still plague our economies.

3. Exchange-token money versus wealth

Money has historically played several roles in modern economies as "a unit of account, a medium of exchange, a store of value, and a standard of deferred payment" [3]. Yet, as a unit of account, money constantly changes value. Today a loaf of bread might cost $3.00, but because of inflation, it may cost $5.00 down the road or because of recession/depression it may one-day cost $1.00. Money's changing value is like declaring that a foot is 12 inches long today, yet may be 15 inches long tomorrow or 9 inches long next month. So money, as tokens of exchange, fail as reliable units of measure.

Similarly, exchange-token money fails as a store of value. Consider the 2008 economic crash, when nothing of real value "disappeared," Yet when valuations fell, the US Federal Reserve declared that trillions of dollars in wealth had disappeared [4]. Valuations represent the price (measured in money) that someone's stock, company or home would likely fetch in the market. On the other hand, not the tiniest bit of real wealth disappeared in 2008: technology; infrastructure; human skill, knowledge, and creativity; products and services; materials and energy... all still existed throughout the economic crash.

The distinction between money and wealth helps us to understand the failure of cryptocurrencies to advance meaningful economic development or to solve any of today's social, economic, and environmental problems. Cryptocurrencies are fundamentally new tokens riding on a new ledger (the blockchain), and they represent a next generation of money speculation. Why bother to produce needed goods and services if you can quickly and easily make money through speculation? In fact, cryptocurrencies are much like poker chips. A person buys them with dollars hoping to cash them out for far more dollars: not a great value to society compared to building companies that produce products and services that people need.

This confusion between money and wealth also explains how the economy can grow to many times the wealth that it once contained, and yet six gigantic economic sectors–private; public; nonprofit; cooperative; sharing economy and social impact investing–have not solved the many social, economic, and environmental problems that have all arisen since the post-World War II economic boom. In fact, in the 1950's, it was common for a single head of household working a 40-hour week to buy a house, a car, put food on the table, and pay for a college education for the children [5].

In contrast, today, two working parents, even working overtime, might struggle to be middle-class, with their children leaving college saddled with enormous financial debt. Instead of advances in the factors of production creating an ever-higher quality of life across-the-board, societies are operating at a mere fraction of their true potential, while underutilized productive capacity is a major segment of the economy [6]. Unfortunately, businesses often downsize and fail (the so-called "creative destruction" feature of free enterprise), while there are still extensive unmet needs for these very products and services in the United States and across the globe. This is the price we pay because economics confuses money (the tool) with wealth (the very products, services, infrastructures, community amenities, etc.) that determines the quality of life for families and communities.

Modern exchange-token economies fail to distribute abundant wealth, which languishes everywhere today as underutilized productive capacity, because win-lose competition over money makes wealth appear to be scarce. Instead of encouraging and supporting people to contribute to society efficiently (at every level of skill), purchasing power is distributed through the eyedropper of paychecks. This inefficiency can be addressed by a social entrepreneurial innovation that combines financial literacy with new purchasing power, creating a next generation of currency that monetizes our abundant excess capacity.

Every new economic era produces new organizational forms for individuals, families, and communities to achieve more of their potential. In the modern era, we have created a global economy that, while it has generated massive material and monetary wealth, remains in many ways both inefficient and inequitable. While a mere 12% of the global population is Caucasian, that cohort controls over 85% of the monetary wealth in the world [7]. Considerable efforts by banks, credit unions, and other financial institutions seeking to promote financial literacy fail to address wealth and power inequities. Most financial-literacy programs do not provide economically disadvantaged populations, especially communities of color, with the economic resources they need to rise out of poverty. By operating within today's traditional token-money-centered economic paradigm, these programs fail to tackle poverty at its economic roots. The time has come to develop a new economic language—a new financial literacy—around equity that raises the standard of living and quality of life across-the-board for families and communities without relying on higher taxes, deeper debt, or redistribution of wealth schemes.

4. Introducing economic ledgers to supplement exchange-tokens

This chapter introduces a new model of financial literacy, the engine of which combines traditional bank-based financial literacy programs for the unbanked with a new form of enhanced purchasing power called "Ledger Dollars (L$)" [8]. The source of this new purchasing power is a business innovation and wealth distribution system termed "Ledger Economics." With the decline in use of physical cash and the increasing use of digital debit and credit cards has come a growing recognition of the difference between money, a unit of exchange, and wealth, the goods and services, knowledge and skills, family and community values that surround us. We often call people with a lot of money "wealthy" and those with little money "poor." Yet we also recognize that there are many other forms of wealth—wealth of human knowledge, lived experiences, social connections, self-knowledge, community cohesiveness, environmental resources—all of which exist abundantly around us. These kinds of wealth are all multiplied when they are shared and diminished when they are not.

The distinction between money and wealth is like the difference between a photograph of a place and the place itself (or understanding that a map is not the terrain). Akin to a photograph, money is a useful abstraction of reality and a valuable tool that we can exchange when we need to, but also like a photograph, money cannot capture nor substitute for all the unseen wealth of a place. A place and its people may lack money, but they may not be poor if they have a lot of family and friend relationships, social and cultural traditions, natural resources, and practical knowledge and skills. Nor does any "non-cash" wealth disappear during economic downtowns or pandemics. People may lose jobs or money, but they lose none of their knowledge and capability, which can continue to grow if they choose.

The distinction between money and wealth is particularly relevant given the inequities that the COVID-19 pandemic revealed. While many people struggled to make ends meet during the pandemic, and while communities of color suffered higher rates of infection and death than most white communities, we also saw the emergence of global protests against police brutality on the part of many people, of all races, in many communities: urban, suburban, and rural [9]. While economic inequality increased in many countries during the pandemic, so too did collective action and the community wealth that aggregated community assets represent. Many people lost paychecks during the pandemic, but they discovered dormant purpose and pursued their passions.

The pandemic also showed how much a focus on money rather than wealth has created an enormous amount of excess capacity, wasted resources, and under-used assets of all kinds. It took the closure of most stores and offices during the pandemic and the shift on the part of many people to e-commerce and telecommuting to show how much competitive duplication of goods and services existed in the traditional economy, how much time we wasted going from one place to another, and how much under-utilized space existed all around us. That duplicate effort, wasted time, and excess space did not just represent the normal cost of doing business. They are the result of confusing money and wealth, as we chased money while over-producing. Chasing money in this way also puts downward pressure on profits, wages and people's purchasing power, and misses the fact that there is a tremendous amount of untapped wealth in the world, side-by-side with unmet need.

We continue to compete for money without monetizing or measuring our wealth, a paradox that the pandemic revealed. The pandemic forced us all to depend upon those with whom we quarantined and to seek help from and to help others, drawing upon familial and social connections as well as the aid of communities. The pandemic, in other words, accelerated a shift not only from a cash-based to a debit- and credit-card-based economy, but also from competition over money to an appreciation of the multiple forms of wealth in our communities and among ourselves.

This, in turn, suggests a new way to think about financial literacy. Rather than thinking about it in terms of money, we should think about it more broadly in terms of available wealth. When one of America's most under-appreciated economic thinkers, Henry David Thoreau, went to Walden Pond, he did so to imagine a new kind of economy in which "the cost of a thing is the amount of ... life which is required to be exchanged for it, immediately or in the long run" [10]. He argued in the first chapter of *Walden,* that we focus too often on "political economy"—on the cash-based economy that drives our daily lives—and pay little or no attention to "the economy of living," which is time based: the amount of life's experiences we have to exchange in order to purchase something. In the modern world, we have been blinded to the reality that technology should be shortening the workweek for everyone. Instead, it has primarily been speeding up the pace at which, and the amount of time that, people spend chasing money.

During the pandemic, with many people having less money because of layoffs, furloughs, or pay cuts, the cash economy sometimes seemed like our enemy, a threat to our homes and families. At the same time, we had to learn to be economical in how we lived: reducing our expenditures, eliminating inessentials, and stewarding what we had. While the political economy that drives our legislatures and stock markets seemed increasingly disconnected from our lives, the economy of living, as Thoreau called it, defined the deposits and withdrawals of our day-to-day struggles.

What possibilities does Thoreau's economy of living offer in terms of financial literacy? It might mean that we learn to put a price on what every moment in our life meant to us and to evaluate the cost of everything in terms of the time it would require us to give it up. Would we really assess our time in terms of some wage that someone else has decided to offer us or would we, instead, demand a wage commensurate with the real value that our life has for each of us? Much more is possible through continuous economic improvement where every advance in technology and human capabilities raises the quality of life, shortens working hours, and reduces damage to the natural world.

The contemplation of one's own death that occurs during a pandemic can make such questions more urgent. Money comes and goes, but time is all we have, and Thoreau's economy of living provides a measure of what is the most important of our scarce assets: our own individual lives. Some people may be fine with wasting that asset, frittering their lives away in details, as Thoreau said, or making a living working long hours that keep us away from our families and, in many cases, contribute questionable value to society. But with a novel virus reminding us that we are mere mortals, weighing the cost of things according to the time we must give up in return for them may be the basis for a post-pandemic economy worthy of what we all just went through. Modern ledger theory views wealth as an abundant renewable resource as opposed to the scarcity mentality that surrounds money: there is rarely enough money to do all the things that make life rewarding, but we are surrounded by almost inexhaustible amounts of wealth.

5. Challenges in the modern economy

A dual currency ledger-based economic system may address some of the more perverse aspects of the modern economy. The US healthcare system profits off illness and receives relatively little financial gain by promoting wellness [11]. A heart attack is a major economic event, while people quitting smoking lowers the gross domestic product. The pandemic showed how health disparities continue among those who lack sufficient purchasing power to lead healthier lives. Many employers track and reward their employees for wellness activities, programs proven to reduce healthcare costs, absenteeism, Worker's Compensation Insurance, and disability claims. But those savings mostly occur at the edges of the system, benefiting those already employed, while most health disparities occur along ethnic and racial lines, regardless of employment status. Nor do these wellness programs address the systemic cause of so much ill health in a country like the US, with a food system awash in sugar, salt, and fat, in a physical environment that leads many people to engage in a lot of sedentary behavior. The stress of modern life also drives many family members to alcohol and drug abuse, which are major obstacles to good health.

Transforming health and wellness in our society requires changes in the underlying economics that drive them. That might have seemed impossible prior to the pandemic, but we saw how quickly and profoundly so many things changed in 2020. Why cannot we also change the economy, which is just another designed system and one with numerous perverse outcomes, as our healthcare system shows? What if the ledgers with which we track wellness activities went further and paid people to lead healthier lives in a currency that extends people's purchasing power with merchants who have excess capacity in their establishments? Imagine using excess capacity in the pharmaceutical industry to provide affordable medications for seniors, producing and distributing needed medications profitably but at reasonable costs. Medications are a perfect example where the marginal cost of production for an additional quantity of products is a tiny fraction of the initial production costs [12].

These ideas extend beyond the healthcare system and wellness programs. The monetization of business's underutilized productive capacity impacts every area of work and community life. Imagine workplaces where everyone cooperates to maximize productive efficiency. Instead of win-lose competition over money, visualize an economy where everyone collaborates to rise together. Imagine an economy where advances in technology and other factors of wealth production create "Continuous Economic Improvement (CEI)," defined as an ever-higher quality of life, with ever shorter working hours, and ever less damage to the natural environment.

Most nonprofits utilize volunteers to do the work these organizations do in the world, while often lacking funding to pay for that labor. At the same time, most businesses could use more customers, who have many choices for where they spend their limited funds, and most people could use more goods and services that they do not have enough money to purchase. These three entities occupy the same communities, with money/purchasing power or cash being the only missing ingredient for both merchants and families to each get more of what they want. Meanwhile, an enormous amount of wealth that exists in every community goes unleveraged and unmonetized.

That misalignment of purchasing power and available goods and services undermines the potential for CEI. As a society, we continuously improve our personal and community wealth: our technology and infrastructure, our knowledge and skills, and our personal and social networks. And we continuously upgrade our access to the abundant ecosystem services that nature provides us: solar, wind and geothermal energy, forests and row crops, carbon sinks and our oxygen supply. We have never solved the boom-and-bust cycles in our economy because we do not see the relationship to competitive, money-centered economics versus cooperative people- and planet-centered economics. In contrast, we should expect and make sure that our economy provides an ever-improving standard of living and quality of life, with ever-shorter working hours for everyone and ever less damage to the environment.

Instead of holding down production to the level of available purchasing power–while periodically downsizing much of the economy's productive capacity–CEI would raise the purchasing power for individuals, families, and communities to match society's ever-increasing productive capacity. This model of cooperative efficiency would not raise employer labor costs, increase taxes, or deepen debt. Instead, it would leverage society's current untapped wealth without requiring government subsidies or redistribution of wealth schemes. It would quickly demonstrate that business innovation and the profit motive are far more effective than left-versus-right politics or labor-versus-management battles at solving today's daunting social, economic, and environmental challenges.

6. A community ledger precedent

An early exposition of this idea was put forth when the psychologist B.F. Skinner wrote a book published in 1948 as *Walden Two,* a utopian novel that seeks to imagine a better world for all [13]. Skinner describes a ledger-based system in the book's eighth chapter. The community ledger tracks everyone's contribution, and everyone freely accesses all the food, shelter, clothing, healthcare and, in particular, leisure, including time in nature, all mainstays of their community life.

Walden Two elevates the notion of everyone contributing to the common good so that everyone enjoys a high quality of life. Skinner wrote about labor credits for the work that people do, with each credit representing an hour of community work, and with more credits per hour for unpleasant jobs and fewer credits for desirable ones. It was a simple formula for applying the rules of supply and demand to labor instead of only to the pricing of products and services. All the community and individual needs were met with everyone in the community working a mere 4 hours per day.

In contrast, our current pricing model, based on the supply of desired goods and services in the face of consumer demand, is extremely inefficient. Masses of desirable goods and services are not distributed where they are needed for lack of purchasing power (money!) in the hands of customers/families. While *Walden Two* depicted a utopian community apart from the world around it, its ledger-currency model could coexist, complement, and help solve the intractable problems facing our mainstream fiat currency economies. Rather than replace money, Ledger Dollars (L$) could enhance people's purchasing power and address the paradox of people having needed skills, communities having unmet needs, businesses having underutilized capacity and countless people and businesses being short on what is required to maximize their contributions to the whole.

7. How a ledger economy would work

How would such an economy work in the real world, as opposed to a novel? Employers would continue to pay their employees in cash, but workers might also receive L$ as a supplement to their paychecks—for their wellness achievements or their volunteer activities. Alternatively, an employer with an excess amount of goods or services might offer, as an employee benefit, L$ with which to buy down the business's excess capacity. Employees would redeem their L$, which would then be taken off the books.

There are three everyday business practices that already monetize and distribute enormous amounts of underutilized business capacity.

- The Sharing Economy, utilizes cash transactions combined with new technologies to leverage underutilized assets, be they an empty apartment, an unfilled car seat, or idle workers.

- Employee-benefit programs represent a noncash example, making a business's excess goods and services available to employees at little or no cost.

- A ledger-currency example is loyalty rewards programs, in which benefits to loyal customers are tracked in a ledger, with points being issued, redeemed, and then taken off the books.

In today's economy, all three examples of monetizing excess capacity are competitive business models benefiting one company against their competitors. We introduce a cooperative network where pooled excess capacity benefits all companies, all employees, all families, and all communities.

Businesses could redeem the Ledger Dollars (L$) of one another's employees in the same way. Let us say a person earned L$ for doing valuable work in a community—mentoring children in the local school, helping a community group clean up a vacant lot, or taking care of elderly parents. Merchants with excess capacity—mostly empty grocery aisles, unfilled restaurant seats, unused equipment, unsold merchandise—could offer those at reduced cash prices by accepting purchases partly in cash and partly in Ledger Dollars, which would move their merchandise or utilize their services while also reducing the costs to their customers and benefiting the communities within which they exist. Businesses would, in other words, accept a combination of cash and Ledger Dollars, monetizing their excess capacity and increasing the purchasing power of employees, volunteers, students, retired people, the unemployed and stay at home parents everywhere.

Monetizing wealth through an additional ledger currency would expand the capacity of the public and non-profit sectors as well. A city, for example, could credit its residents for contributions of time or insights they provide to planning processes or committee assignments. Or a nonprofit could credit volunteers for their contributions to the mission of the organization or the aid they provide. These sectors would not only expand their impact, but also engage more people in their work by recognizing and compensating for that effort. It would literally return us to the origin of the word "economy" with roots in the Greek words for "household management," and to the original connotation of the word, involving ideas of thrift and frugality. Instead of wasting the talent and good intentions of the people in a place, a ledger economy would fully utilize the physical, social, and natural assets of a community.

Everything we need to make such a system work already exists. There are digital ledgers aplenty on the Internet, most of them downloadable for free. It only needs agreement among the public, private, and non-profit sectors, each looking to either attract more customers, aid more citizens, or expand people's purchasing power. And once available, a second currency would require little coaxing of people to participate: who would not want recognition and compensation for the voluntary, unpaid work they already do to further a mission they believe in or to take care of those for whom they feel responsible? While many people might say that they do not do this work for the money, most would welcome being rewarded in a way that would also extend their ability to purchase what they need or know that they are helping others who currently lack the financial resources to afford what they need.

All it takes is openness to the idea that the economy is a designed system and money a human creation, both of which are not working well for large numbers of people in the US and across the globe. We cannot just do more of what is not working well: looking for more money to do what win-lose competition over money is failing to accomplish in economic development. In the modern economy, the more money that goes into circulation (from whatever source), the more competitive duplication is created. Instead, we can re-imagine how to make our economy work for more people, in more equitable and environmentally sustainable ways. Indeed, solving the issues of equity and sustainability lies at the heart of why we need to uplevel the current economy using twenty-first century technologies and renewable resources.

Governments and foundations have historically sought to address inequities through fiscal means—taxation and subsidies—or philanthropic ones—gifts and grants. But those monetary methods miss the mark by assuming that we can eliminate inequities with more cash, perpetuating the idea that people without money need charity. Instead, the less cash a community has, the more it relies on non-monetary workarounds, be they familial, social, cultural, or spiritual. Examples include bartering between community members (watch my kids and I'll give you vegetables from my garden); 12-Step groups to address addiction, rather than the expensive healthcare system; volunteer programs to feed the hungry such as Second Harvest and the Humanity Alliance; the sharing economy, which offers less expensive rides and places to stay than the traditional economy; In-kind donations from established businesses and more. All of these are creative workarounds for how the cash economy is underserving many individuals, families, and communities. Non-cash commerce is often far more relational, in contrast with the primarily transactional nature of money-based commerce, and L$ enhance that relation-based wealth and enable many more people to stretch currently limited cash resources.

That suggests an economy operating at a different scale than the traditional one that is based on national currencies. Ledger Dollars operate less like national currencies and more like popular loyalty rewards programs, which are a business-issued currencies backed by each business's available products and services. But unlike loyalty rewards, which reward consumer spending, so that whoever already has the most money now also gets the most rewards, L$ reward far more than spending. Economic ledgers can better match the production of goods and services with business, employee, customer, family, and community wants and needs. National currencies are blunt instruments to address economic inequity, as traditional money chases the highest rate of return. At the same time interest and dividends bring ever more money to those who have the most money. Ledger Dollars encourage a more level economic playing field through more careful and equitable production and distribution of real wealth without any old-fashioned redistribution of wealth schemes. Lastly, national currencies encourage consumerism to promote economic growth, which has negative social and environmental consequences. In contrast, Ledger Dollars promote a higher quality of life by engaging everyone in greater economic efficiency and voluntary sharing of currently idle resources. This approach promotes an ever-higher quality of life without promoting consumer culture. In a post-pandemic world, weary of the physical idleness and social isolation that COVID-19 caused, a new, more equitable and less wasteful economy is just the cure many people are looking for.

None of this means that money is unimportant. During and after the pandemic, many people lost jobs and livelihoods, faced bankruptcy or eviction, and exhausted checking and savings accounts. In response, many governments came to people's aid, distributing financial resources. Instead, a ledger-based, digital economy helps people and communities leverage untapped wealth and lets businesses market their excess capacity in ways that use the talents, skills, and knowledge of people leveraging assets currently going to waste. Ledgers may seem boring; who wants to talk about accounting protocols and financial transactions? And ledgers may appear an unlikely basis upon which to build a new economic model. But they address the challenges of money-centered economics and commerce. Unlike our money economy, ledgers do not crash or suffer inflation, recession or depression; they do not support artificial scarcity or money hoarding, and they do not lend themselves to speculation or theft. Moreover, ledgers help us to measure not just the exchange of cash, but to account for other forms of capital that we have not tallied before.

Ledger economics also gives youth incentives to be entrepreneurial. Universities could accept L$ towards tuition, books, meals, and student housing as part of a Ledger-Dollars program that helps students subsidize their college educations. For example, Fernando and Melissa earn L$ during their freshman and sophomore school years by working part-time in a local community nonprofit organization that is part of the program. The two of them purchase clothes, school supplies and other necessities at the university's store in a combination of US Dollars and Ledger Dollars. Seeing the potential of this cash-like financial incentive, Fernando and Melissa, upon graduation, set up their own non-profit organization to build alliances of institutions, merchants, and community organizations to participate expand the reach and impact of the Ledger Dollar system.

Ledger economics could lead to an explosion of creativity and resources and spawn a cooperative, win-win attitude in the community. Consider how after World War II, the United States led 28 nations in the Marshal Plan to rebuild Europe and Japan. Imagine a twenty-first century Peace Corps funded by Ledger Dollars many times more impactful than today's efforts, or a twenty-first century GI Bill for Youth, where 2 years of domestic or international service work could fund a full-ride college education in Ledger Dollars, because college campuses are awash in empty college desks, empty dorm rooms, and empty cafeterias. Also, imagine what such a mobilization of youth during Covid-19 might have done to take the incredible burden off of our First Responders.

Many businesses, especially restaurants, which were among those most negatively impacted by the COVID-19 pandemic, may be ready for innovation. On the one hand, the pandemic revealed the excess capacity of restaurants, as their dining rooms remained closed, and those that stayed in business had to develop new delivery models, like take-out, drive-through, and home-delivery options. On the other hand, the pandemic also showed how to leverage excess capacity to reduce food costs for families. Some restaurants developed hybrid models in which they delivered components of meals that people could prepare at home, using the distributed network of kitchens in customers' homes. In this way, consumers became producers of the food they ate, using the underutilized capacity of their own kitchens to their advantage [14].

Such innovations tapped a rarely recognized and under-utilized asset in virtually every community: the unleveraged talent and skill of ordinary people. Traditional economists tend to separate producers and consumers, employees and customers, even though, obviously, most consumers need to produce –i.e. work—to buy what they need. That division between producer and consumer leads to the paradox of companies reducing production costs by laying off employees, while also trying to increase consumer spending, including by those just laid off employees. This is one of the greatest lessons of the pandemic: in a global economy that measures wealth in terms of the amount of money one has or controls, it overlooks other forms of wealth that rarely get measured and monetized, and that have far greater value than anything money can buy. The father of capitalism, Adam Smith, recognized this as the paradox of value [15]. He asked why we value diamonds, which we do not need, and do not value water, which we cannot live without. From a monetary point of view, the answer is obvious. Diamonds are rare, so people who want them will pay more money for them than they will for water, which—in Adam Smith's time and place—was widely available. But from a value point of view, his paradox is not obvious. Water is more valuable than diamonds and will always be so because of the essential role it plays in keeping us—and every plant and animal on the planet—alive.

The same paradox exists in our conflation of money and wealth. By tapping excess capacity that surrounds us and increasing purchasing power by rewarding people for socially beneficial activities, we increase everyone's quality of life through an equitable economic system that recognizes the under-valued wealth that exists in every one of us and everywhere around us. That represents a new—and truer—form of financial literacy. Continuous economic improvement based on tapping the excess capacity that is all around us and increasing purchasing power by rewarding people for socially beneficial activities raises the standard of living and improves our quality of life without taking any money or resources away from anyone. This approach can provide rapid, profitable, equitable, and ecologically sustainable economic development wherever people seek to embrace it. Meanwhile, the end of the grow-or-die business imperative opens the door for efficiency and cooperation to replace growth and money-competition as the engines of economic progress.

8. Beyond left versus right

Traditional, competitive, money-centered economics and commerce rests upon the now outdated notion of scarcity, pitting people, communities and nations against one another in a battle for money and domination. A significant challenge to solving our economic problems is the current left-versus-right polarization and stalemate. This status quo prevents us from working together on needed solutions and keeps us from seeing the inherited but now outdated roots of our social, economic and environmental challenges. Ledger economics can counter that polarization by uniting companies, communities, universities, political organizations, and government agencies in a common strategy for progress.

Imagine a Business-Community Wealth Ledger (BCWL) that leverages excess business capacity and promotes continuous economic and community improvements. For Conservatives and Libertarians, the BCWL is 100% voluntary and self-funding. It is business-led, market-based and profit-driven. It respects private property. For Liberals, radicals, greens and socialists the BCWL provides economic development resources that are immediate and not trickle down (**Figure 2**).

The BCWL is an example of Ledger Economics, which builds upon the success of our free enterprise system and improves upon it, much the way that electronic banking and ecommerce have been improvements to old-fashioned paper currency and banking. Ledger Economics brings new opportunities to address social, economic, and environmental challenges. It also will likely bring new challenges that traditionally accompany paradigm-shifting innovations. Ledger Economics does not rely on exchange tokens, such as coins, paper currency or electronic debits and credits in computers, all of which circulate. Ledger Dollars are issued, redeemed, and taken off the books, like loyalty rewards. When Merchants redeem loyalty rewards, they do not use them to pay employees, vendors, or taxes. Ledgers can also account for dual currency sales, in which businesses accept both US$ and L$, as an alternative to the traditional discounting of goods and services, which puts downward pressure on profits and wages. Merchants profit in US$ from dual currency sales, while at the same time, pooling their underutilized capacity into a public asset, mobilizing rather than wasting underutilized business/community wealth (**Figure 3**).

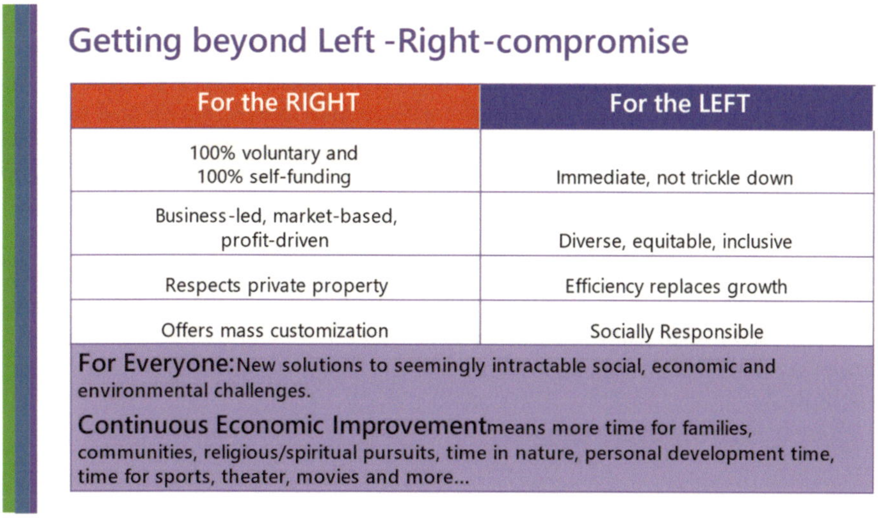

Figure 2.
Beyond left versus right.

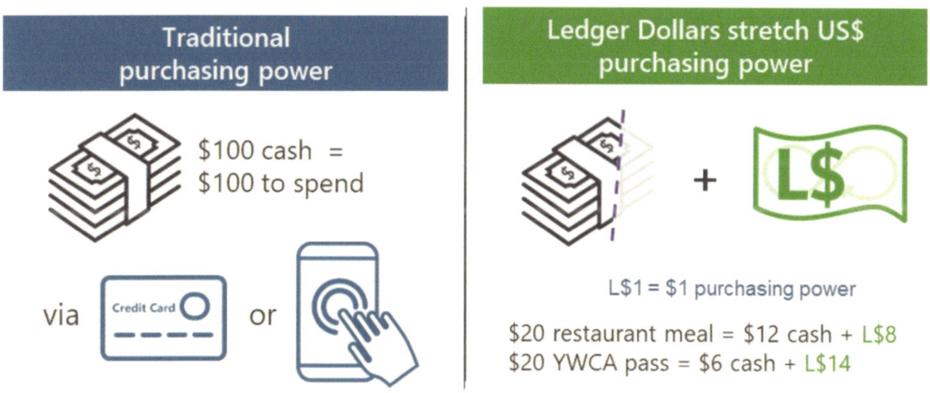

Figure 3.
Ledger dollars versus traditional purchases.

Merchants contract with the BCWL, using ratios and restrictions based upon their marginal cost of production. When discounting, merchants accept fewer dollars to increase sales, resulting in downward pressure on profits and wages. In contrast, a new financial instrument such as the Business Community Wealth Ledger, backed by today's underutilized business capacity, increases purchasing power for employees, families, and communities. Like the Internet, the BCWL would live in the Commons, owned by no-one and managed by protocol rather than politics. Also like the Internet, the BCWL supports mass customization rather than government control. Once a person or a company follows the Internet protocol, they can engage in myriad options. They can do e-commerce, they can engage in charity, and they can have complete freedom of speech and association. As well, they can be for or against guns, drugs, abortions, hunting or veganism. This could be a significant step towards a truly inclusive and equitable, free-enterprise economics, where people all have growing resources to live by their own values.

Merchants sign dual-currency contracts with the BCWL to accept L$ along with US dollars for their goods and services, enjoying cash profits, plus free employee benefits. Members would sign up with the BCWL and receive L$ for their rewardable activities, looking online for the merchants who are part of the system and where they can spend their L$. Community organizations, such as non-profits and school districts, would serve as Sponsors and report to the BCWL the rewardable Member activities. Schools sponsor students; employers sponsor employees; community organizations sponsor volunteers, religious organizations sponsor members; the government sponsors Social Security recipients, public assistance recipients, the unemployed and so forth. Upon receiving the reports of Sponsors, the BCWL would make L$ deposits into member accounts. When L$ are redeemed by Merchants, they would be taken off the books like loyalty rewards, and not circulate like traditional (token) money.

With such a system, everyone wins.

- Merchants profit from increased sales and free employee benefits.
- Members prosper from expanded purchasing power.
- Sponsors benefit from the incentive people have to volunteer or contribute to their communities.

At the same time, disparities would close through new economic efficiencies:

- Leaders gain effective tools to address historic challenges.
- Workplaces become centers of innovation, learning and contribution.
- Families and communities receive newfound wealth that reflects the true value of what they have to offer (**Figure 4**).

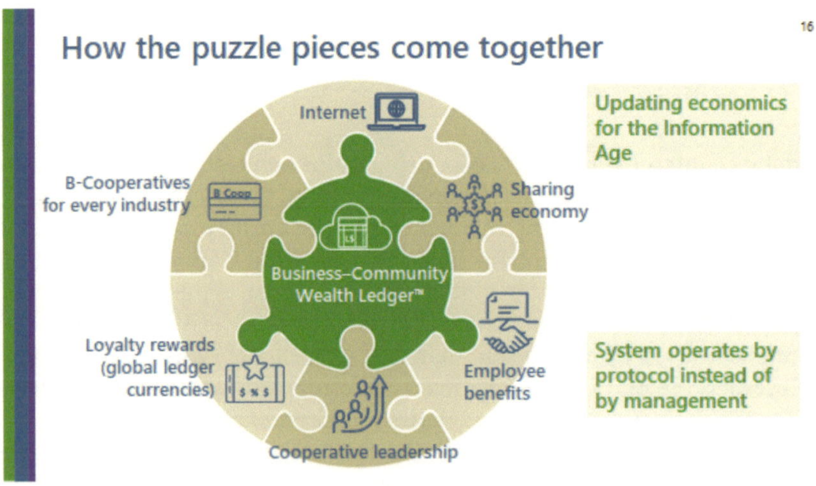

Figure 4.
Business-community wealth ledger.

9. Introducing B-cooperatives

The sharing economy, employee benefits, and loyalty rewards are all established ways to capture and distribute underutilized business capacity. We propose another economic innovation that we term "B-Cooperatives." Today's B-Corporations balance profit with purpose, benefiting communities and the environment as well as their shareholders. Our proposed B-Cooperatives extend that idea beyond individual companies to entire industries, bringing companies together, voluntarily, so that the progress historically lost through competition over money is addressed through free-enterprise cooperation.

The Visa system is an example of the power of industry-wide cooperation. Faced with multiple, competing credit-cards from virtually every bank, Visa created a cooperative association in 1958 using a single industry standard for credit cards, entirely operated by protocol. This brought workability and profitability to the then beleaguered credit-card industry through: (a) a new financial instrument, (b) a new payments platform, and (c) a new cooperative network of banks. The same cooperative framework can be applied to the emerging ledger economy. Rather than multiple competing ledgers, a cooperative association—akin to Visa and the Internet—can define a single industry standard, a universal economic ledger, operated by protocol. This would increase the level of cooperation and participation among Merchants, expand the options and buying power of Members, and grow the amount of community participation and volunteerism among Sponsors and Members.

10. Conclusion

Ledger economics would ultimately move the global economy away from win-lose competition over money and towards more efficient win-win economic cooperation. This would benefit individuals, families, and communities everywhere. It would also answer the historic challenge posed by visionary futurist and inventor R. Buckminster Fuller to the world decades ago: "How do we make the world work for 100% of humanity, in the shortest possible time, through spontaneous cooperation, without ecological offense or the disadvantage of anyone?" [16].

Acknowledgements

The authors would like to express their appreciation to Chris Brooks and Larry Walker for their valuable contributions as reviewers of this work.

Author details

Thomas Fisher[1*] and Joel Hodroff[2]

1 University of Minnesota, USA

2 Scryp, United States

*Address all correspondence to: tfisher@umn.edu

References

[1] Koistinen PAC. Mobilizing the world war II economy: Labor and the industrial-military Alliance. Pacific Historical Review. 1973;**42**(4):443-478. DOI: 10.2307/3638133

[2] Watts A. Wealth versus money. In: Does it Matter? Essays on Man's Relationship to Materiality. Novato, California: New World Library; 1971

[3] Shapiro D, McDonald D, Greenlaw S. Principles of Economics, 3rd ed. Houston: Rice University, Open Stax; 2022

[4] Weinberg J. The great recession and its aftermath. Federal Reserve History, Federal Reserve Bank, Washington D.C; 2013

[5] Johnson DS, Rogers JM, Tan L. A century of family budgets in the United States. Monthly Labor Review. 2001;**124**(5):28-45

[6] Board of Governors of the Federal Reserve System Industrial Production and Capacity Utilization—G.17, Federal Reserve Bank, Washington D.C; 2023

[7] Global Wealth Report 2023, Leading Perspectives to Navigate the Future, Credit Suisse AG, UBS; 15 June 2023

[8] Fisher T, Hodroff J. From money-Centered to People- and Planet-Centered Ledger Economics: Leveraging the Hidden Wealth of Underutilized Productive Capacity. London: Intech Open; 2021 Available from: https://www.intechopen.com/chapters/75019

[9] Fisher T. Space, Structures and Design in a Post-Pandemic World. London: Routledge; 2022. pp. 17-22

[10] Thoreau HD. Walden. New York: Random House; 2000. Chapter 1

[11] Shmerling R. "Is our Healthcare System Broken?" Harvard Health Publishing. Harvard University: Cambridge; 2021. Available from: https://www.health.harvard.edu/blog/is-our-healthcare-system-broken-202107132542

[12] Tuovila A. Marginal Cost Meaning, Formula, and Examples. New York: Investopedia; 2023

[13] Skinner BF. Walden Two. Hackett: Indianapolis; 1948

[14] Duncan N. Life after COVID: Welcome to the World of Hybrid Restaurants. Charlotte, North Carolina: FSR Magazine; Apr 2022

[15] Smith A. The Wealth of Nations. Amsterdam: MetaLibri; 2007. p. 26

[16] Cape J. Buckminster Fuller Reader Penguin Books. New York; 1972

Section 2

Global Financial Market

Chapter 6

Systematic Review of Monetary Policy Effect on Foreign Direct Investment

Adham Taher Alessa

Abstract

This chapter aims to survey researchers' efforts in the literature on monetary policy and foreign direct investment (FDI), mapping the research landscape into a coherent taxonomy and identifying the policy's fundamental characteristics. The survey, conducted in January 2018, presents an updated and state-of-the-art discussion on monetary policy and FDI research, with a specific focus on economic indicators rather than other factors like economic determinants, prosperity, integration, and growth in different countries. The survey searched for articles on monetary policy and FDI in four major databases: Science Direct, EBSCO host, Emerald Insight, and Web of Science (WoS). After filtering for duplicates and relevance, 137 papers were included in the final set. The findings indicate active and diverse research on monetary policy and FDI, making the survey a valuable resource for scholars seeking to explore available research options and gaps in this field.

Keywords: monetary policy, foreign direct investment, money supply, systematic review, science direct, EBSCO host, emerald insight, web of science

1. Introduction

The foreign direct investment (FDI) is considered as one of the most important element to achieve the greatest level of growth and development in the developed and developing economy because of the role it plays in the economy of the host country [1]. According to [2] FDI has grown exponentially as a major form of international capital transfer over the past decade. Between 1980 and 1990, global FDI flows which can be defined as the cross-border outlay for acquisition corporate control or expansion of productive assets which almost tripled as compared to the size of FDI previous decade. It has become a major form of international borrowing for Japan and the United States as the largest lender and the borrower in the world, respectively. Direct investment has increased more rapidly later in the European countries. The host country provides an appropriate climate for foreign direct investment through economic policies that aim to attract a larger amount of foreign direct investment. Among these policies, monetary policy is one of the most important policies that can be used to attract foreign direct investment to the host country [3].

Monetary policy aims to ensure that the money supply is at a compatible level with the real income growth target, so that non-inflationary growth will be guaranteed [4]. Thus, the role of monetary policy in foreign direct investment aims to reduce the interest rate and required reserve on Commercial Banks in the host country and through the control on money supply approaches that can affect the size attraction [3].

The main objective of this paper is to systematically review the literature concerning the impact of monetary policy on the FDI. As such, mapping the research landscape form the literature into a coherent taxonomy, finding out along the way few features that characterize this emerging line of research.

2. Systematic review protocol

This section presents the systematic review protocol used in this paper which specifically includes the keywords selection method, information sources, study selection, section search, inclusion and eligibility criteria, and the data collection process. The review search was conducted from 2008 to 2018.

The most important keywords in the scope of this paper are "Monetary policy and FDI" which consider all monetary policy-related areas, including the economic growth, economic prosperity, economic integration, monetary policy tools, economic determinants, economic liberalization, capital flow, and the economic environment.

This paper chooses four digital databases to conduct the search for target articles. These databases are the EBSCO host, Science Direct, Emerald insight, and Web of Science (WoS) service. The rationale behind this selection is to cover both economic and financial literacy and provide a broader view of researchers' efforts in a wide but relevant range of disciplines. The host academic institutions worldwide depend on this database as their core resource of scholarly information covering Academic Search Premier, Business Source Elite, and E-Journals which offer access to science, technical and economic journal articles indexing cross-disciplinary research in sciences, social sciences, economical, arts and humanities.

The process of study depends on searching the literature sources, followed by two repetitions of checking and filtering. The first repetitions excluded the duplicates and irrelevant papers by scanning the titles and abstracts, while the second iteration filtered the articles after a thorough full-text reading of the screened articles from the sources.

The search was conducted at the begging of 2018, in Science Direct, EBSCO host, Emerald insight, and Web of Science (WoS) databases via their search boxes used mixed keywords that contains "Monetary policy", "Money Supply", and "Foreign Direct Investment" in different variations, combined by the "OR" operator. The exact query text is shown at the top of **Figure 1**. The systematic review protocol further used the options in each search engine to exclude book chapters and other types of reports other than journal and conference articles that determines directly the stability of the economy. Is considered those venues the most probable to include up-to-date and proper scientific works relevant to this survey on the trend in economic environment, economic determinants, and economic liberalization.

Every article that met the criteria listed in **Figure 1** was included in the review. Setting an initial target of mapping the space of research on the economic

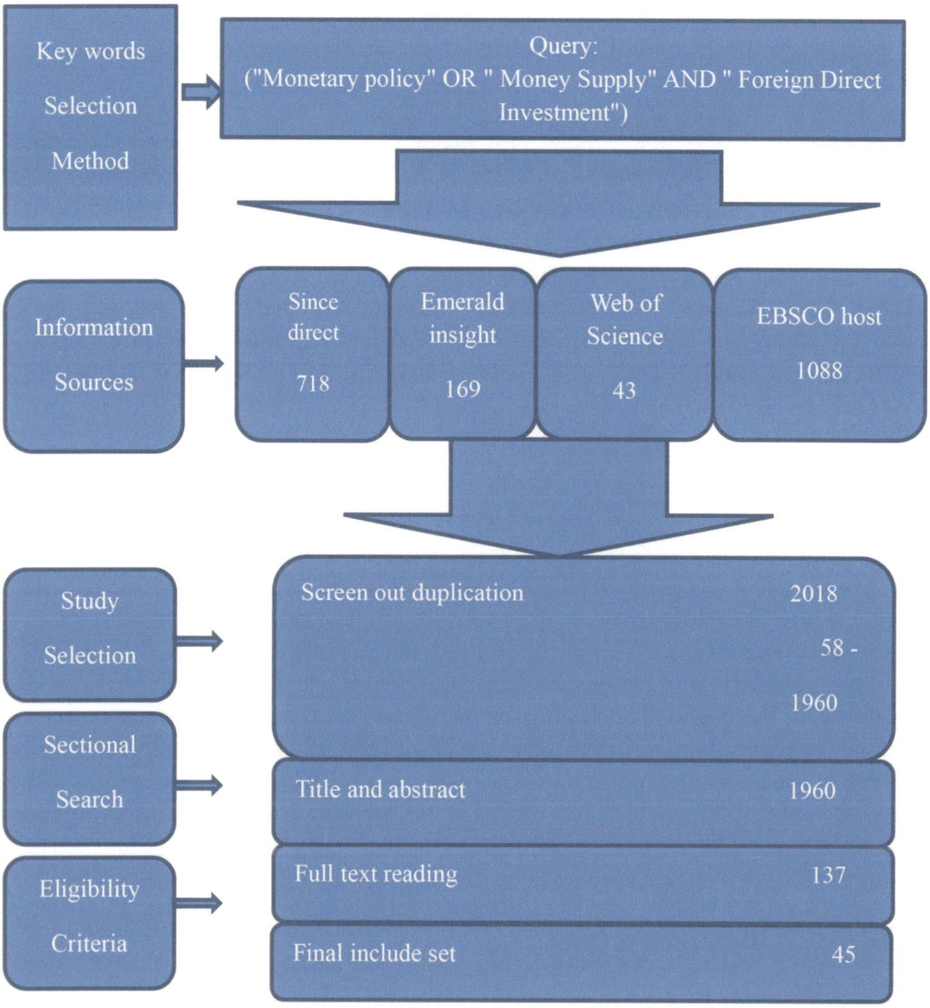

Figure 1.
Systematic review process.

environment, economic determinants and economic liberalization. After the initial removal of duplicate articles, papers were excluded in both iterations of screening and filtering if they did not fulfill the eligibility criteria. Examples of exclusion reasons include; first, the paper is non-English; secondly the papers that dealt with other economic topics such as oil price, cost management, and Commercial Banking; and thirdly the target is the monetary policy rather than other economic policies.

The inclusion criteria that have been used in the systematic review are as follows. Firstly, the paper is an English journal or conference article. Secondly, the main focus is the monetary policy and FDI, in either one or more of the following:

i. Surveying or reviewing the new trend of monetary policy and the foreign investment fields through FDI.

ii. The article that used the most frequent model to analyze the data.

iii. The article interest is in economic growth, economic prosperity, economic determinants, economic environment, economic integration and economic liberalization.

In order to facilitate further steps, a full list of all included articles, with their corresponding initial categories, was compiled from the various sources into a single EXCEL file. Full-text readings were performed and resulted in a large collection of highlights and comments on the surveyed works, as well as in a running classification of the papers into a refined taxonomy. All comments were saved followed by the process of tabulation, summarization, and description of the main findings. Sets of all relevant information including the full list of articles, their respective source databases, purposes, summary and description tables, and review sources. Were also recorded and saved.

3. Results

The initial query search resulted in 2018 articles where 43 articles are from Web of Science database, 718 articles are from Science Direct, 169 articles are from Emerald insight, and 1088 articles are from EBSCO host. Fifty-eight articles were duplicates among the four library databases. After scanning for the titles and abstracts, 1960 more articles were excluded, resulting in 137 articles. Full-text reading excluded 92 articles, leaving forty-five articles in the final included set. Those papers were read thoroughly for the purpose of finding a general map for the conducted research on this topic. These studies were divided according to the statistical model. It was found that 36% of the previous studies used the OLS model, 20% used ARDL model, 17.8% used VAR model, 17.8% used GMM model, and 8% used other models. The summary of the statistical model is show in **Figure 2** below.

4. Systematic literature survey

Based on the result of the study the most frequently used models are OLS and ARDL. As such, this section focused on the literature pertaining to these models.

4.1 OLS model literature

Soufan [5] survey the causal relationship between gross domestic product (GDP) and money supply (MS) in Jordan. In order to determine the direction of the

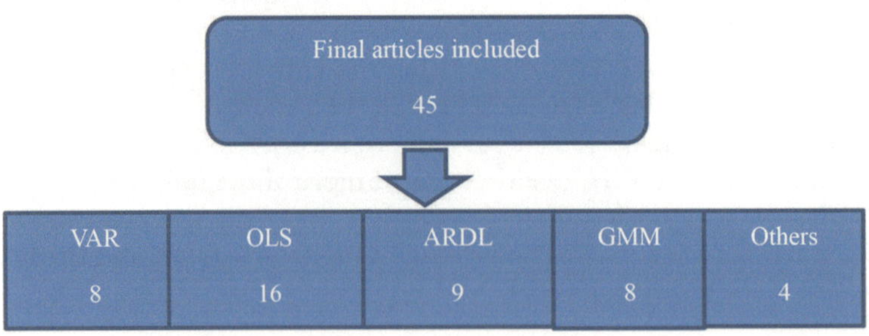

Figure 2.
Summary of statistical model used in previous studies.

relationship, the study use Granger causality test between the two variables during the period from 1978 until 2010. The result of this study shows that there is a causal relationship between the money supply and the gross domestic product, and the direction of this relation as from money supply to the gross domestic product, not vice versa. Therefore, the study concludes that there changes in the money supply in Jordan explain the causality changes in the gross domestic product and not vice versa.

Omanwa [6] studied on the factors that determine the Foreign Direct Investment (FDI) inflows particularly into the Kenyan economy for the period from 1996 to 2009 using annual data and utilize the OLS model to analyze its data. The main result of this article shows that the most significant factors in attracting FDI inflows into Kenya were the size of the market and the level of openness of the economy.

Cavallari and d'Addona [7] investigate the role of output fluctuations and exchange rate volatility in driving the United State (US) FDIs. The study used annual FDI flows from the US to 46 OECD countries from 1982 to 2009. They used panel estimator with random effects and corrected for heteroscedasticity in the residuals of the OLS model using Wooldridge test. The main finding of this paper is significant to the economic prosperity where the elasticity of production foreign investment is more elastic than in the economic recession. Therefore, an increase in exchange rate volatility, on the other hand, has a strong deterrent effect on the US foreign investments.

Mandeep and Renu [8] study the determinants of foreign direct investment in India, by using annual data for the period from 1990 to 2010. The study uses the Augmented Dickey–Fuller (ADF) test and Co-integration analysis to analyzing the variables. The main finding of this paper shows that the determinants of FDI differ from one country to another country depend on other incentives available in the country. The result indicates that trade openness; foreign exchange reserves, GDP and long-term debt have positive impact on FDI, while negative impacts of inflation and exchange rate on FDI have been noticed.

Elfakhani and Mackie [9] examine the main drivers which can explain the relative success of BRIC countries (Brazil, Russia, India, and China). Collectively and individually, in attracting foreign direct investment (FDI). The data over the full sampling period are from 1980 to 2008 and the analysis it by using GLM regression model. Social variables such as high population growth and educated labor and political variables account for 40% and 7% of the variance of FDI inflows to income, respectively. However, the result shows no significance relationship for economic variables. Interestingly, for a sub-period from 1999 to 2008, the importance of financial determinants such as large GDP economy, favorable net trade balance, controlled currency risk and sovereign debt risk drive inward FDI of 44% of the variance. The finding of this paper also shows that decreased in net FDI inflows on all financial, social and political variables through the analyzed period from 1980 to 2008, and the block regression concludes that the social variables account for 40% of the change in net inward FDI, followed by political variables which composes of 7%.

Abbes et al. [10] analyze the relationship between FDI and economic growth. The dataset consists of cross-country observations for 65 countries over the period of 1980 to 2010 periods. This study uses the FMOLS and DOLS to analyze its data. The result shows that the causal relationship between FDI and economic growth does not exist.

Sambhary and Rasheed [11] examine the influence of economic freedom on foreign direct investment (FDI) in 95 countries, over a six-year period from 1995 to 2000 using the generalized least square (GLS) model to analyze its data. The main finding of this paper indicates that in order to attract FDI, the best thing a government can do is to reduce its interference in the economy while, at the same time, protecting property rights and controlling the corruption.

Loris and Mary-Françoise [12] examines the impact of FDI inflows on industrialization in African countries. This paper used annual data for 49 countries over the period of 1980 to 2009. They analyze the data with autocorrelation and heteroskedasticity tests. The main finding of this study shows that the FDI inflows did not have a significant impact on the countries' industrialization.

Boateng et al. [13] examine the government policy implications on FDI inflows in Norway. The paper used quarterly data from 1986 to 2009 and use Fully Modified OLS (FMOLS) to analyze the data. The main results show that money supply, inflation, unemployment and interest rate have significant negative results. Meanwhile the real GDP, sector GDP, exchange rate, and trade openness have a positive and significant impact on FDI inflows.

Hartwell and Michael [14] examine the presence of foreign financial institutions that helped to shape a better business environment over the long-run in emerging markets. The paper used annual country-level data on foreign bank entry and macroeconomic variables for approximately 107 developed and emerging countries for the period 1983–2012. The study used panel fully modified OLS model (PFMOLS) and panel dynamic ordinary least square (PDOLS) to analyze the data. The finding shows that the incursion of foreign banks in emerging markets has a positive effect on the broader business environment.

Lucke and Eichler [15] examine the determinants of bilateral FDI stocks, focusing on institutional and cultural factors. This study used panel data of 55 OECD countries from 1980 to 1997. The OLS results show that a devaluation of the home currency would lead to a decrease in foreign direct investment.

ChamTamsir [16] investigate the relationship between monetary integration, foreign direct investment (FDI) and trade in the West Africa particularly on the second monetary zone on FDI flows to zone member countries. The paper use Ordinary Least Squares (OLS) and fully-modified OLS (FMOLS) models to analyzing the data with annual time series spanning from 1980 to 2013. The finding shows that monetary integration positively enhances FDI inflows; it also revealed that monetary integration enhance trade; and FDI and trade are complementary.

Leoveanu [17] study the possible influence of the monetary policy decisions on ale flow of foreign direct investment in Romania for the period 2003 to 2014. They use an econometric analysis namely the Granger causality test to investigate the relationship between these variables. The result of this study show that the selected variables can be successfully used in the calibration of monetary policy decisions with the purpose to attract foreign investment in the country.

Alqalawi et al. [18] examine the effect of main monetary policy tools in Jordan on price and output level. The study used yearly data from Jordanian monetary sector that cover the period between 1993 until 2013 and use OLS model. The main result of this study indicates that monetary policy can maintain the value of money, considering that the value of money is the opposite of the general level of prices. In addition, it is found that inflation was partially imported, and imported inflation was lower than non-imported inflation due to the increased money supply.

Boateng et al. [19] examine the trends, patterns and the impact of cultural and home country macroeconomic influences, on Chinese cross-border mergers and acquisitions (CBM&A) as foreign entry strategy. The period of study was from 1998 to 2011 and the study use ordinary least squares model (OLSs). The result of this study suggests that CBM&A as a preferred mode of market entry provides a means for obtaining strategic resources to develop competitive advantages for the Chinese emerging market firms, and all independent variables play an important role in explaining the trends of CBM&A outflows by the Chinese firms.

Hermann et al. [20] analyze the relationship between central bank independence (CBI) and uncertainties of inflation by including the phenomena of exchange rates and foreign capital flows. There is two specific aim of this investigation. The first aim is to see whether uncertainty of inflation induces volatility of exchange rates, and vice versa, under differing degrees of CBI. Another aim is to explore whether the dynamics of the former relationship influence foreign capital flows in turn. The study was conducted 22 emerging countries through the period from 1968 to 2013 by using Granger causality. The results of the tests for high and low CBI country subgroups show interesting differences. For the high CBI countries, an uncertainty of inflation and uncertainty of exchange rates indicates that there is no causal relationship between them. However, a weak link runs from FDI to uncertainties of inflation in the long run. For the low CBI countries, there is strong evidence of causal links running from uncertainties of inflation to uncertainties of exchange rates on the one hand and to FDI flows on the other. In addition, there is an indication of a bi-directional causal link between FDI flows and exchange rates for these countries.

4.2 ARDL model literature

Bekhet and Matar [21] examine the short- and long-term equilibrium relationship between the stock price index (SPI) and the macroeconomic variables in Jordan. The study used annual data from 1978 to 2010 and analyzes it by using ARDL model. The main result of this paper shows that the ARDL approach indicate the existence of the long-term equilibrium relationship between the SPI and macroeconomic variables.

Shahbaz and Mafizur [22] explore the relationship between exports, financial development and economic growth in the case of Pakistan for the period of 1991 to 2012. The quarterly data for these periods were analyze using ARDL model. The results of this paper show the long-run co integration relation between exports, economic growth and financial development in case of Pakistan, that economic growth and financial development spur exports growth in Pakistan and Granger causality analysis reveals feedback hypothesis that exists between financial development and economic growth, financial development and exports and exports and economic growth.

Mugableh [23] investigates the relationships between FDI inflows and their determinants in Malaysia using annual time-series data from 1977 to 2012. The analysis using ARDL model shows that decreasing the consumer price index in Malaysia increases the value of FDI inflow and stabilizes the macroeconomic and financial environments. Furthermore, appreciation of exchange rates depresses the flow of FDI into Malaysia due to their negative effects on exports. Increases in output values stimulate the flow of FDI into Malaysia. The growth of gross domestic product in the host country improves the macroeconomic environment, which invites overseas investors. Finally, increasing the broadest money supply raises the domestic market capitalization of listed corporations, which induces international corporations' confidence in the Malaysian financial system.

Bekhet and Al-Smadi [24] estimate the equilibrium relationships and to detect the directions of causality among Jordanian FDI inflows and their determinants.

This paper uses the ARDL model to study the time seize data for the period from 1978 to 2012. The main results of this paper identify that there are long-run and short-run relationships among FDI and its determinants. Moreover, the Granger causality test recommends a deferent causal relationship among FDI and their determinants.

Lee [25] examines the short-run and long-run dynamic relationships between exchange rates and foreign direct investment (FDI) in Korea. Monthly data retrieved from the Bank of Korea from January 1999 to March 2012 are used. The main result using ARDL model shows evidence of a structural break from the global financial crisis of 2007–2009 shock to FDI flows in Korea.

Sunde [26] investigated economic growth as a function of foreign direct investment and exports in South Africa. The study uses annual data for the period from 1990 to 2014 and analyze it by using ARDL model to identify the long run relationship among the variables. The results confirmed co-integration between economic growth, foreign direct investment, and exports. This implies that economic growth, foreign direct investment, and exports move in the same direction trending upwards. On the other hand, the Granger causality (VECM) analysis for the short run relationship found unidirectional causality between economic growth and foreign direct investment running from foreign direct investment to economic growth, unidirectional causality between foreign direct investment and exports running from foreign direct investment to exports and bi-directional causality between economic growth and exports.

Durmaz [27] examine the determinants of foreign direct investment and concentrate on the linkage between democracy and foreign direct investment in Turkey. The data are from 1977 to 2011 and are using ARDL model. The findings show that, in the long run, FDI inflows have spillover effects on Turkey's economy. Determinants such as improved freedom with better political rights and more civil liberties in the country will have structured a stable government with better policies and institutions. This paper satisfies the established need to study the democracy and FDI inflows link, which is necessary for an emerging market such as Turkey.

Mamunur et al. [28] investigate the determinants of FDI in the top 15 most competitive countries in the Asia Pacific region. This study used a time series and cross-sectional data from 2000 to 2013, by using ARDL model. The result of this paper indicates that FDI inflow is related positively to domestic market size, trade openness, and political stability, and inversely related to the inflation rate. Meanwhile GDP, openness, and political stability exhibit a significant long-run relationship with the FDI inflows.

5. Conclusion

This literature review aims to present updated and state-of-the-art discussion on the research about monetary policy and FDI and to highlight research trends in this area. This systematic review differs from previous reviews, due to focuses on evaluating the impact of monetary policy on FDI by using economic indicators only, and show the relationship between monetary policy and FDI, rather than on the economic determinants, economic prosperity, economic integration, economic growth, and the economic environment of developing and economically developed countries.

Furthermore, the study proposes taxonomy of related literature. Developing the taxonomy of literature in a research area, particularly, has several benefits. Taxonomy of published works organizes publications. A new researcher in monetary policy criteria, may discovered a large number of papers on the subject without any kind of structure and may fail to obtain an overview of this area. One of the advantages of this study is different papers could be review or examine to identify the tools and methods used in examine the relationship between monetary policy with FDI. Taxonomy of the related literature, as shown in **Figure 2**, could systematize these different studies and activities into a meaningful, manageable and coherent layout. The structure introduced by the taxonomy provides a researcher with important insights into the subject in one way through the utilize model.

Author details

Adham Taher Alessa
Fakulti Ekonomi dan Muamalat, Universiti Sains Islam Malaysia (USIM), Nilai, Negeri Sembilan, Malaysia

*Address all correspondence to: adham.phd@gmail.com

References

[1] Adams S. Can foreign direct investment (FDI) help to promote growth in Africa? African Journal of Business Management. 2009;**3**(5):178

[2] Ren S, Hao Y, Wu H. The role of outward foreign direct investment (OFDI) on green total factor energy efficiency: Does institutional quality matters? Evidence from China. Resources Policy. 2022;**76**:102587

[3] Olweny T, Chiluwe M. The effect of monetary policy on private sector investment in Kenya. Journal of Applied Finance and Banking. 2012;**2**(2):239

[4] Precious C, Makhetha-Kosi P. Impact of monetary policy on economic growth: A case study of South Africa. Mediterranean Journal of Social Sciences. 2014;**5**(15):76

[5] Soufan T. The causal relationship between monetary policy and economic growth in Jordan during the period 1978-2010. Interdisciplinary Journal of Contemporary Research in Business. 2013;**5**(8):56-67

[6] Omanwa SM. Determinants of FDI in Kenya: An empirical study. Vilakshan: The XIMB. Journal of Management. 2013;**10**(1):30-38

[7] Cavallari L, d'Addona S. Business cycle determinants of US foreign direct investments. Applied Economics Letters. 2013;**20**(10):966-970

[8] Mandeep K, Renu S. Determinants of foreign direct investment in India: An empirical analysis. Decision. 2013;**40**(1-2):57-67

[9] Elfakhani S, Mackie W. An analysis of net FDI drivers in BRIC countries. Competitiveness Review. 2015;**25**(1):98-132

[10] Abbes SM, Belmokaddem M, GuellilMohammed S, Yassine ZG. Causal interactions between FDI, and economic growth: Evidence from dynamic panel co-integration, Procedia Economics and Finance. 2015;**23**:276-290

[11] Sambhary RB, Rasheed AA. Does economic freedom in host countries lead to increased foreign direct investment? Competitiveness Review. 2015;**25**(1):2-24

[12] Loris G-DS, Mary-Françoise R. Foreign direct investment inflows and the industrialization of African countries. World Development. 2015;**74**:43-57

[13] Boateng A, Xiuping H, Shaista N, Junjie W. Examining the determinants of inward FDI: Evidence from Norway. Economic Modelling. 2015;**47**:118-127

[14] Hartwell CA, Michael B. A helping hand: Examining the effect of foreign banks on the business environment. International Journal of Emerging Markets. 2015;**10**(4):875-895

[15] Lucke N, Eichler S. Foreign direct investment: The role of institutional and cultural determinants. Applied Economics. 2016;**48**(11):935-956

[16] ChamTamsir. Does monetary integration lead to an increase in FDI flows? An empirical investigation from the West African Monetary Zone (WAMZ). Borsa Istanbul Review. 2016;**16**(1):9-20

[17] Leoveanu VM. The Relationship between Monetary Policy and Foreign Direct Investment in Romania during

2003-2014. International Business Information Management Association (IBIMA); 2016;**28**

[18] Alqalawi UR, Ahmad A, Rasha I. The Influence of Indirect Monetary Tools on Price and Output: The Case of Jordan (1993-2013). 2017

[19] Boateng A, Min D, Yan W, Chengqi W, Mohammad A. Explaining the surge in M&A as an entry mode: Home country and cultural influences. International Marketing Review. 2017;**34**(1):87-108

[20] Hermann S-A, Chandana C, Serapio B. Foreign capital flows, uncertainties of exchange rates and central Bank Independence: Implications for emerging economies. Atlantic Economic Journal. 2017;**45**(4):485-496

[21] Bekhet HA, Matar A. Co-integration and causality analysis between stock market prices and their determinates in Jordan. Economic Modelling. 2013;**35**:508-514

[22] Shahbaz M, Mafizur RM. Exports, financial development and economic growth in Pakistan. International Journal of Development Issues. 2014;**13**(2):155-170

[23] Mugableh MI. Time series analysis of inward foreign direct investment function in Malaysia. Procedia-Social and Behavioral Sciences. 2015;**172**:679-685

[24] Bekhet HA, Al-Smadi RW. Determinants of Jordanian foreign direct investment inflows: Bounds testing approach. Economic Modelling. 2015;**46**:27-35

[25] Lee JW. Dynamic relationships between exchange rates and foreign direct investment: Empirical evidence from Korea. Asian Economic Journal. 2015;**29**(1):73-90

[26] Sunde T. Foreign direct investment, exports and economic growth: ADRL and causality analysis for South Africa. Research in International Business and Finance. 2017;**41**:434-444

[27] Durmaz N. Foreign direct investments, democracy, and economic growth in Turkey. International Journal of Social Economics. 2017;**44**(2):232-252

[28] Mamunur R, Hui LX, Jye WS. Political stability and FDI in the most competitive Asia Pacific countries. Journal of Financial Economic Policy. 2017;**9**(02):140-155

Chapter 7

The Fundamentals of Stock Market Investing in the Twenty-First Century

Steven Tairu Bello

Abstract

This chapter discusses the fundamentals of stock marketing investing in the twenty-first century. In a nutshell, this chapter seeks to provide a fundamental understanding of stock market investing to interested laypersons across the world. It examines the various issues of critical importance in stock market investing. It dissects the experience of beginners, the most vulnerable participants in the stock market, and equips them with some knowledge cushion. It discusses several strategies for managing the various pitfalls inherent in stock market investing. Finally, it discussed the revolutionary impact of technology on stock market investing.

Keywords: beginners, fundamentals, investments, pitfalls, stock market, revolution, strategies, technology

1. Introduction

This chapter delves into the basics of investing in the stock market during the twenty-first century. It seeks to give a basic comprehension of stock market investing to individuals worldwide who are interested in stock market investment. The chapter covers various crucial aspects of stock market investing and offers guidance for beginners, who are often at risk in making stock investment decisions. It provides strategies for navigating the challenges in the stock market. In addition, it explores the transformative role of technology in the world of stock market investing in the twenty-first century.

2. What is stock market investing?

To properly understand the concept of stock market investing, it is important to have a good grasp of what the stock market is. The stock market is the market for trading or making investments in stocks. It is sometimes referred to as the equity market and is a pool of financial organizations where regular buying and selling of shares and securities occur [1]. Therefore, simply stated, stock market investing is a process of buying and selling stocks or buying and selling ownership in a company, as purchasing the stock of a corporation entitles an investor to own part of the corporation, with money-making or money-loss potential.

Stock market investing is closely associated with stock market forecasting, as investors naturally have the tendency to want to forecast the movement of the market when investing. Stock market forecasting is an attempt to predict the future value of an individual stock, a particular sector, or the market as a whole (Capital.com, 2023)[1]. These forecasts generally use fundamental or technical analysis to determine the direction of a stock, a sector, or the market. Fundamental and technical analysis are two major schools of thought for researching the movement of stock prices in the market, yet they are at opposite ends of the spectrum [2]. Further discussion will be provided on fundamental and technical strategies later in this chapter. To predict the movement of the market, an investor must be adequately informed. Accurate stock market models can equip investors with the information they need to make productive decisions [1], but inexperienced investors might lack the expertise of engaging such pieces of information to their advantage.

3. Stock market strategies for beginners

Strategies for stock market investing are becoming increasingly complex as advanced technology and new analytical tools become available in the stock market. For beginners, this could be highly convoluting, as these novices strive to forecast the direction of the market. Stock market price forecasting is a complex task even for market experts, let alone novices. The exercise is considered difficult due to its chaotic nature, and the presence of numerous factors that could frequently alter market predictions [3].

Traditionally, most investors rely on some basic tools such as intuition and perception to guide their decision in stock market investing. More informed investors rely on scientific strategies such as fundamental and technical analysis to make decisions. Fundamental analysis evaluates stocks by attempting to measure their intrinsic value, studying everything from the overall economy and industry conditions to the financial strength and management of an individual company's earnings, expenses, assets, and liabilities [2]. On the other hand, technical analysis is focused on examining statistical trends, such as movements in a stock's price and volume, with the assumption that all known fundamentals are already factored into the price, and therefore should not affect investment decisions [2]. These differences are due to the basic principle from which the two schools of thought emanate. Technical analysts consider all external factors instantly reflected in the share price, as opposed to fundamental analysts, who believe that it takes some time for it to happen [4]. Therefore, fundamental analysts believe that there is an opportunity to take advantage of the market and make profits at a time when the price has still not reflected every available company-related information [4], while technical analysts simply do not subscribe to that notion.

Fundamental and technical analysis differ in terms of their approaches and purposes. Technical analysis is primarily used for trading, while fundamental analysis is used for investment. Investors typically use fundamental analysis to buy and hold

[1] Capital.com (https://capital.com/) is an online trading platform that provides several services including investment education, market trends, and news analysis. According to Capital.com, the following provides the summary of what the organization is: "Capital.com has group entities authorized and regulated locally by the Financial Conduct Authority ("FCA"), the Australian Securities and Investments Commission ("ASIC"), the Cyprus Securities and Exchange Commission ("CySEC"), the Financial Services Authority of Seychelles (FSA) and the Securities Commission of The Bahamas ("SCB")"

stocks for an extended period, while traders use technical analysis to make short-term profits. Although they may seem similar, they are essentially different schools of thought with distinct approaches. Fundamental analysts rely on financial statements to evaluate a stock's intrinsic value, whereas technical analysts rely mainly on price movement or time series forecasting, which has gained much attention from researchers [5]. While fundamental analysts analyze complex information beyond financial statements, technical analysts believe all the necessary information can be obtained from charts, which are the trends. For fundamental analysts, if a stock is trading below its estimated intrinsic value, it is considered a good investment. Technical analysts would prefer to chart out the trend before making such a conclusion. There are several other methods for forecasting stock market movements, which could be associated with either fundamental or technical analysis schools of thought. Omar et al. [6] used random forest and deep neural network models; Challa et al. [7], used the Auto-Regressive Integrated Moving Average (ARIMA) model to predict the variation in returns of S&P and other stock exchanges. Sable et al. [8] used the genetic algorithm to detect the direction of the market.

Traditional fundamental and technical approaches for stock forecasting for investment decision-making are sufficient for beginners. The method that a novice investor chooses will depend on the intention and purpose of the investor. If the focus of the investor is to short the market or engage in momentum investing to make quick profits, the investor should consider using the technical approach, while the fundamental method should be engaged if the investor plans to buy and hold to appropriate the potential value growth in the stock [1].

4. The benefits of using stocks as investment vehicles

Experts from financial institutions and the academic community generally agree that several benefits exist in stock market investment. The Royal Bank of Canada [9] posited that stocks can be a valuable part of an investor's investment portfolio and that owning stocks in different companies can help the investor to build savings, protect their money from inflation and taxes, and maximize income from their investments. Investment in stocks has the potential to generate long-term returns that can significantly outperform other types of investments [10]. Stocks also offer a great way for investors to diversify their portfolios and reduce the risk associated with other types of investments.

In addition, investing in stocks is a great way to build wealth over time and create a passive income stream. Furthermore, stock market investing provides opportunities for investors to be part of a company's growth and success. Investors have the potential to profit when a stock price goes up. Finally, investing in stocks could enhance an investor's propensity to learn or be educated about current events and trends in the market. This is because by keeping an eye on the news and tracking the performance of companies, an investor could stay up to date with the latest developments in the market and potentially capitalize on opportunities.

5. Avoiding investment pitfalls, while taking advantage of opportunities

It is generally a fact that investing in stocks could potentially provide investors with opportunities to make money from the stock market. However, it could also result in a loss of funds. It's important to be aware of common mistakes that investors make and try to avoid those mistakes, as they could increase the chances of investment loss.

One of the most common mistakes is buying stocks without prior research. It's important for an investor to understand the risks associated with investing in stocks and have adequate information about a company's fundamentals before making investment decisions. A proper understanding of the fundamentals of a stock and the company would enable an investor to make an informed decision. Another common mistake is buying stocks on the margin. Buying stocks on margin involves borrowing money from a broker to purchase stocks. This can be a risky strategy and should only be used by experienced investors. Beginners should avoid margin purchases no matter how appealing such transactions might be, until such a time that they have a better understanding of stock market trading or investments.

Furthermore, beginners should avoid emotional purchases or buying stocks on the spot or under the pressure of sentiments. Sometimes, it's easy to get caught up in the excitement of buying and selling stocks, but a novice investor should always make an investment plan and keep to the plan to avoid making rash decisions [10]. It is also important for novice investors to begin investing with an amount of money that they can afford to lose without inflicting a major negative change to their lives. This is the concept of little money investing. There are several ways to start investing with a little money. One way is to open a no-fee brokerage account. This kind of account allows the novice investor to invest without paying a commission. Another way to start investing with little money is to buy fractional shares. Fractional shares allow investors to buy a portion of a stock, thereby enabling the investors to diversify their portfolio without having to invest a large amount of money [11].

Little money investing can help investors to own different stocks, thereby enhancing diversification, and reducing portfolio risk. It can also help investors to participate in different investment options in addition to stocks. Such investment options could include bonds, mutual funds, and Exchange Traded Funds [12]. While stock purchases represent ownership in a company, bonds are debt instruments, because the buyer of bonds is basically a lender to the issuing company (SEC, Undated). Mutual funds and ETFs are collections of stocks and bonds. This investment vehicle allows novice investors to invest in diversified portfolios.

Finally, an inexperienced investor should avoid a one-time large-chunk investment and instead engage in regular little investments spread over a period. This is the concept of dollar-cost averaging. This strategy involves investing a set amount of money on a regular basis, which can be a great way to build a portfolio over time without having to invest a large amount of money upfront. By using dollar-cost averaging, investors may lower their average cost per share and reduce the impact of volatility on their portfolios [11]. This helps to minimize the challenges associated with investment timing. The strategy eliminates the effort required to attempt to time the market to buy at the best prices [11].

6. Technology: the revolution for stock market investments

Technology has transformed the financial market, revolutionizing the way investors handle their portfolios. This change has been fueled by advancements in areas like artificial intelligence, big data, analytics, and machine learning [13]. As a result, financial markets have become more efficient and accessible than ever before.

While automated trading systems and real-time market data have been around for decades, the recent availability of data and sophisticated algorithms have enabled investors to make quicker and more informed decisions [13]. There are now numerous online tools and applications that make it easier than ever to invest in stocks. There are also numerous platforms offering various resources for investment in the stock markets. Applications such as Robinhood and Acorns allow investors to buy and sell stocks with just a few taps on their phones [4]. In addition, there are now several robo-advisors that help investors to invest in stocks without having to do research [13]. Technology is making it easier to track investment performance. There are several websites and applications that allow investors to track their portfolios and monitor the performance of their investments. With the help of technology, a growing number of investors can make informed decisions and have better control of their investments.

The evolution of technology has brought about a fresh wave of investment opportunities, revolutionizing the way investors invest. This has resulted in a more efficient, transparent, and accessible investing era. Besides, the advancement in technology has given rise to digital assets and cryptocurrencies, which have opened doors for investors to diversify their portfolios [13]. Consequently, financial markets are now accessible to more investors, including those who previously found them complex and hard to penetrate due to high entry barriers.

As technology advances, the financial markets are also expected to undergo significant changes. Investors who leverage these advancements to their advantage will benefit from the new investment landscape. It is highly likely that the financial markets of the future will be quite different from what we are familiar with today, with technology driving these changes [13]. The potential of these advancements in the financial markets is enormous, and they are expected to continue to disrupt and transform the investment landscape. Technologies such as blockchain, IoT, and AI are anticipated to gain increasing prominence in the financial markets, potentially revolutionizing the way investors manage their portfolios and make investment decisions [14].

It is crucial for investors to remain up to date with the latest technological advancements to stay ahead in the financial landscape. By keeping themselves informed about the opportunities presented by innovation, they can make the most of their investments and benefit from the ever-evolving financial markets [13]. Technology is leading the way and investors who are adaptable and flexible are likely to reap the benefits of new opportunities. Staying informed and connected with the technology-enabled financial markets is essential for investors who want to stay ahead of the game [13].

7. Conclusion

For beginners, investing in stocks can be a daunting process. It's critical for novices to understand the basics of investing and do a bit of research before they get started. It is also crucial that they create a plan that outlines their goals and risk tolerance, and those must be compatible with their overall financial situation [15]. In addition, it is important that they understand the different types of stocks, the terminology associated with the stocks, and the different strategies they can use to invest in the stock market. The stock market can be very volatile, due to its random walk behavior.

It is largely unpredictable and so it's important for investors to be prepared for both short-term and long-term fluctuations. This can be very disorienting and catastrophic for beginners. To minimize this impact, novice investors should consider engaging professional brokers for their investment needs, at least for some time.

Author details

Steven Tairu Bello
Ray and Young School of Business, Louisiana Christian University, Pineville, LA, United States

*Address all correspondence to: steven.bello@lcuniversity.edu

References

[1] Kehinde TO, Chan FT, Chung SH. Scientometric review and analysis of recent approaches to stock market forecasting: Two decades survey. Science Direct Journal. 2023;**213**:119299-119301. DOI: 10.1016/j.eswa.2022.119299

[2] Majaski C. Fundamental vs. technical analysis: What's the difference? Investopedia. 2022. Available from: https://www.investopedia.com/ask/answers/difference-between-fundamental-and-technical-analysis

[3] Zhang X, Qu S, Huang J, Fang B, Yu P. Stock market prediction via multi-source multiple instance learning. IEEE Access. 2018;**6**:50720-50728. DOI: 10.1109/ACCESS.2018.2869735

[4] Petrusheva N, Jordanoski I. Comparative analysis between the fundamental and technical analysis of stocks. Journal of Process Management New Technologies. 2016;**4**(2):26-31. DOI: 10.5937/JPMNT1602026P

[5] Jackson C, PrassannaQuadir J, Sivakumar MV. Stock market analysis and prediction using time series analysis. Materials Today: Proceedings. 2021. DOI: 10.1016/j.matpr.2020.11.364 Available from: https://www.sciencedirect.com/science/article/pii/S2214785320389823

[6] Omar A, Huang S, Salame A, Khurram H, Fareed M. Stock market forecasting using the random forest and deep neural network models before and during the COVID-19 period. Frontier in Environmental Science. 2022;**10**:1-10. DOI: 10.3389/fenvs.2022.917047

[7] Challa ML, Malepati V, Kolusu SNR. S&P BSE sensex and S&P BSE IT return forecasting using ARIMA. Finance Innovation. 2020;**6**(1):47. DOI: 10.1186/s40854-020-00201-5

[8] Sable S, Porwal A, Singh U. Stock price prediction using genetic algorithms and evolution strategies. In: Proceeding of the 2017 International Conference of Electronics, Communication and Aerospace Technology (ICECA). Piscataway, New Jersey: IEEE; 2017. pp. 549-553. DOI: 10.1109/iceca.2017.8212724. Available from: https://search.worldcat.org/title/1021857714

[9] Royal Bank of Canada. Key benefits of investing in stocks. 2023. Available from: https://www6.royalbank.com/en/di/hubs/investing-academy/chapter/key-benefits-of-investing-in-stocks/jv7atg13/jv7atg1j

[10] Dierking D. Benefits of holding stocks for the long-term. 2022. Available from: https://www.investopedia.com/articles/investing/052216/4-benefits-holding-stocks-long-term.asp

[11] Hayes A. Dollar-cost averaging (DCA) explained with examples and considerations. Investopedia. 2023. Available from: https://www.investopedia.com/terms/d/dollarcostaveraging.asp

[12] Chen J. Exchange Traded Funds (ETFs) explanation with pros and cons. Investopedia. 2023. Available from: https://www.investopedia.com/terms/e/etf.asp

[13] Majbour B. How technology is transforming the investment landscape. Forbes 2023. Available from: https://www.forbes.com/sites/forbesbusinesscouncil/2023/02/14/how-technology-is-transforming-the-investment-landscape/?sh=2d8bf26412e4

[14] Kumar S, Lim WM, Sivarajah U, et al. Artificial intelligence and blockchain integration in business: Trends from a bibliometric-content analysis. Information Systems Frontiers. 2023;**25**:871-896. DOI: 10.1007/s10796-022-10279-0

[15] Langager C. How to invest in stocks: A beginner's guide. Investopedia. 2023. Available from: https://www.investopedia.com/articles/basics/06/invest1000.asp

Chapter 8

Assessing the Effect of Financial Management Practices on Financial Performance and the Moderating Role of Farm and Farmers' Socioeconomic Characteristics on Dairy Enterprises

Joanita Kataike, Margret Asiimwe, Robert Mawenu and Willy Rwamparagi Kagarura

Abstract

Financial management practices can positively affect the finance performance, but this relationship is also influenced by the farm and farmer characteristics, which moderates the effect size. Thus, this research investigates the effect financial management practices on financial performance and the moderating role of farm and farmers' socioeconomic characteristics of dairy enterprises. Based on existing researches, four financial management practices were considered and financial performance we considered profitability, liquidity, and solvency. The variables considered for moderation are; respondents' age, education, and enterprise age. A hierarchical multiple regression with primary data was used to test for the moderating effect. The results revealed that financial management practices and firm and farmer characteristics significantly interact better with financial performance among dairy farm enterprise. Thus, the effect of financial management practices on financial performance depends on the firm and farmers' characteristics such as age and education of the farmers, as well as the number of years the dairy enterprise exist. Implying that if dairy enterprises manage their capital structures, working capital, budget, and financial records this will ultimately increase profitability, liquidity, and solvency while incorporating more farm and farmers' characteristics.

Keywords: financial management, performance, firm characteristics, dairy enterprises, Uganda

1. Introduction

In the contemporary world, financial management practices are desirous for all business enterprises. Finance is an integral part of modern economic life and occupies an important place in all economic activities. In this regard, financial management is a goal, as well as a measure of a good performing enterprise. The degree of success or failure over a period of time can be tested on the basis of profitability in an enterprise [1]. In other words, an enterprise may be deemed as sick should it fail to be profitable, implying that not having liquidity its survival is at stake [2]. Appropriate management of working capital, record-keeping, capital structure, and budgeting and budgeting controls for everyday firm operations matters.

In emerging economies, farmers face several challenges among which is financial stress. According to [3] 78.22%, dairy farmer in Nagpur face financial constraints, and this has a negative influence on the financial performance of their farm due to milk payment delay from the cooperative. The financial management framework postulates that firm and socioeconomic characteristics affect the financial decisions made by the farm investors [4, 5]. More so, extant literature shows that demographic factors in the context of personal and socioeconomic factors moderate the relationship between financial management practices and financial performance [6–8]. Furthermore other scholarly work show that financial management is positively related to financial performance and firm characteristics such as firm size, leverage, firm age, income, and firm age [7, 9].

Ironically, Uganda's economy is projected to grow by 2.9% in the 2019/2020 fiscal year, with GDP standing at US$35 billion (at 2016/2017 prices) [10]. The dairy industry contributes significantly to Uganda's GDP value as one of the largest foreign exchange earners, with exports valued at more than US$120.74 million as of 2019 [11]. Furthermore, dairy production has the potential to significantly reduce hunger, malnutrition, rural poverty, improve rural livelihoods, promote food security and nutrition, create employment opportunities, promote gender equality, and contribute to Uganda's overall economic development [12, 13]. According to the most recent statistics, Uganda's annual milk production is 2.04 million tons [10], obtained from an estimated 4.14 million milked cows. Each cow was estimated to produce 492.8 liters of milk per lactation [11]. Out of the total milk produced, 80.2% is marketed for an estimated US$835.9 million (2019), while the remaining 19.8% is consumed on farms and in households. 34% of marketed milk is processed into a variety of products such as powdered milk, cheese, butter, UHT, yogurt, and ice cream, whereas the remaining 66% is sold raw [14, 15].

In terms of dairy product export and import, Uganda exported 0.16 million tons worth over US$120.74 million in 2019, while importing 412 tons worth US$1.69 million [11]. The high proportion of dairy exports to imports indicates a low reliance on and expenditure on imported dairy products, indicating the industry's growth. The increased value of Uganda's dairy exports can be attributed to improved compliance of Uganda's dairy products with regional and international market standards, as well as an annual increase in dairy processing capacities market standards and the annual increase in dairy processing capacities [15].

Despite these developments, studies assessing the effect of financial management on financial performance and the moderating role of farm and farmers' socioeconomic characteristics of dairy enterprises in the Rwenzori region are still scanty. Therefore, the current study seeks to build on the work of earlier researchers elsewhere to explore the influence of financial management on financial performance and the moderating role of farm and farmers' socioeconomic characteristics of dairy enterprises, given the economic viability of the dairy industry.

As for the rest of the book chapter, the outline is as follows: In Section 2, we present the literature of previous research. In Section 3, we present methodology, we used to conduct the study. In Section 4, highlights the empirical results and discusses the link of the study findings with extant literature. In Section 5, we go over the conclusions and the study implications.

2. Literature review

A variety of definitions have been offered to characterize financial management, for instance [16] describes financial management as the acquisition and use of financial resources and protection of equity capital from various sources of risk. Beside, financial management in the agriculture is defined as the economic study of the acquisition and use of capital in agriculture [17]. The overall task of the financial management is to improve financial performance by ensuring that the capital structure, budgeting and budgetary control, working capital management, and financial record keeping; all these components are important for all enterprises to be powerful financially [17–19].

Other scholars suggest that financial management consists of the four processes of budget-making, budget implementation, accounting, and audit, which contribute to financial performance and divide into processes for target-setting and processes for measuring performance [20]. On the other hand, financial management literature suggests that optimal application and commitment toward financial management practices, such as internal systems, (financial record keeping) result in an increased company's performance [21]. The financially well-managed companies are operationally efficient. This stands as a positive sign for investors and farmers' farm performance. In this context, the primary desire by the dairy farmers is to earn more profits and enhance the income of the farmers which is attributed to socioeconomic and farm characteristics [22].

More so, financial performance is a way to satisfy farm owners and can be represented by profitability, growth, and market value. Ref. [23] supported this argument by emphasizing that profitability is an important issue to various stakeholders who have a direct or indirect interest in the entity. In spite of these critical roles that profit plays in the going concern of manufacturing firms, the profitability position of most manufacturing enterprises operating in relation to firm age, firm size, firm growth, loss ratio, liquidity, and leverage of the firm have not drawn much consideration of researchers in the area of finance performance [24]. Nevertheless, financial performance measurement, on the other hand, mostly focuses on the types of financial ratios attained from the financial statements of an enterprise. These measures comprise of profitability ratios, liquidity ratios, activity ratios, and debt ratios [25].

In this regard, the assertion that financial management and financial performance with moderating effect on farm and farmers' socioeconomic characteristics is gaining considerable attention. In pioneering research, [26] published their work on the multinational corporations and domestic corporation financial performance and characteristics. In the process, their results indicated that firm size does not a significant relate the financial performance in any of the cases. Precisely a greater aggressive working capital strategy that has low investment in working capital is related with a higher return and risk, whereas a conservative strategy, which deals with high investment in working capital, has lower return and risk [26, 27].

More so, between 2004 and 2011, a study on working capital management (a measure of financial management) and its effect on profitability was conducted in Ghana by [28]. They used the working capital cycle (WCC) and the gross operating profit (GOP) to calculate profitability. Their research found a negative but significant relationship between working capital and profitability. Furthermore, their research discovered a negative relationship between individual elements of the cash conversion cycle, including inventory turnover period, and profitability. Lastly, their research found a significant negative relationship between leverage and profitability, whereas liquidity measures such as interest cover and the current ratio produced significant positive relationships with profitability.

Investigated the effect of working capital management on profitability in 69 South African listed manufacturing firms from 2007 to 2016 using panel data. According to his research, average collection period and average payment period have a negative but significant effect on profitability, implying that firms that manage their accounts receivable efficiently and pay their creditors on time outperform those that do not. In addition, [29] a positive statistically significant relationship between the number of days in inventory and profitability was found, implying that firms that stock-up and maintain their inventory levels experience fewer stock-outs and have fewer difficulties obtaining financing when needed. This improves operational efficiency and ensures long-term profitability. Because evidence to support this premise was lacking, it was impossible to determine whether a shorter or longer cash conversion cycle improves firm profitability. However, it was discovered that manufacturing firms, on average, carry a significant amount of debt in their capital structures.

It is widely assumed that financial record keeping has a significant impact on the enterprise's financial performance. According to Abdul-Rahamon and Adejare [30], financial record keeping provides significant information about an enterprise's financial strength and current performance, and thus managers find those records useful in making decisions. Financial record keeping and financial transparency are inextricably linked according to Refs. [31–33]. On the other hand, emphasizes that keeping good records makes any business partner or investor more aware of what is going on in their businesses and saves them from loss of money. Similarly [34], discovered a link between record keeping and financial performance of Nairobi County Savings and Credit Cooperatives (SACCOs). According to Chelimo and Sopia [35], approximately 60% of small businesses fail within the first 3 years due to management inefficiencies caused by poor record keeping. This is consistent with the findings of Ademola et al. [36] who found that poor records can lead to financial inefficiency in small and medium-sized businesses, resulting in poor organizational performance.

As investigated by Mwebesa et al. [37], another construct of financial management is capital structure, this is a highly sensitive indicator in financial management research because it influences financial performance. Thus, variable items such as short-term debt, long-term debt, total debt, debt-equity ratio, and firm size and financial performance as measured by return on equity/profitability (ROE) and return on assets (ROA). It was hypothesized that these factors have no significant relationship with firm profitability. The main finding indicated that total debt has a significant negative impact on ROE and ROA, whereas sales size has a significant negative impact only on ROE of American firms [37].

A ten (10) year study on the budgetary control and financial performance of government ministries in Boston, Massachusetts was conducted by Nickson and Mears [38]. The researcher used secondary data (panel data) to conduct a ten-year analysis; the regression model was used to analyze the data, and they discovered that there was a positive relationship between budgetary control and financial performance. Equally, [39] conducted a study to determine the relationship between budget and performance in remittance companies in Mogadishu, Somalia. The target population consisted of seven (7) Somali remittance companies. The researcher chose a sample of 103 people using the judgmental sampling technique of non-probability sampling. The methods used by the researcher included descriptive statistics, standard deviation, and correlation analysis. The study concluded that a moderate relationship existed between budgeting and the performance of remittance companies [39].

Numerous studies on financial management practices and financial performance in Africa has been conducted in West and Southern Africa, with only a few studies being conducted in East Africa [37]. Unfortunately, they also measure a single proxy of financial management and financial performance, excluding the socioeconomic characteristics of the firm owner and the enterprise and other financial management practices. It is against this background that the researchers were motivated to investigate the effect of financial management practices on financial performance with a moderating role of farm and farmers' socioeconomic characteristics of dairy enterprises in Uganda.

3. Methodology

3.1 Sample size determination

In the study, the effect of financial management practices on financial performance with the moderating role of socioeconomic characteristics is analyzed using primary data collected from 162 dairy farmers in the Rwenzori region. In this context, the sample size was determined by a simplified formula as provided by Yamane [40]. In calculating the sample size, a 95% confidence level and level of precision of 5% were assumed. The level of precision is also termed a sampling error. This is the range in which the true value of the population is assumed to be [40]. Based on the formula by Yamane, the sample size for the study included 162 dairy farmers because the target population was 275. However, 156 responses were coded for analysis with a response rate of 96.2% meaning that six questionnaires were discarded.

$$n = \frac{N}{1 + N(e)^2} \tag{1}$$

Where n = sample size.
N = population.
e^2 = level of precision

$$n = \frac{275}{1 + 275(0.05)^2} \tag{2}$$

n = 275/1 + 275(0.0025).
n = 275/1 + 0.6875.
n = 275/1.6875.
n = 162.

3.2 Study design and sampling techniques

This study used a cross-sectional study design to obtain quantitative data. To collect qualitative data, the researchers employed survey questionnaire in every study district. The dairy farm enterprises in the Rwenzori region were from the districts of Kabarole, Kamwenge, and Kyegegwa. The three districts were prioritized because they are important sources of dairy farming and they also participated in the training needs assessment, where financial management was one of the needs required [41]. Also, farmers from these districts are embracing the commercialization of the dairy farming business [41]. Within these districts, particular cooperative groups were selected namely:- Mpanga Dairy Cooperative in Kamwenge, Toro Dairy Cooperative, and KYOFNET in Kabarole and Mirembe Dairy Cooperative in Kyegegwa Districts. Furthermore, the study used both probability and non-probability sampling techniques. In particular, stratified and simple random sampling were used in the context of probability sampling, whereas purposive sampling techniques were preferred for non-probability sampling techniques to collect data from key informants [42].

3.3 Measurement of variable

The financial management practices were the study's independent variable, measured by four indicators, which are working capital management [26–29], capital structure [37], financial record keeping [30, 31, 33], and budget and budgetary control [38, 39], Financial performance was the dependent variable, which was determined by an increase in income, increased profits, and debt collection. The Likert scale with five options was used to assess these variables: 5. Agree, 4. Agree, 3. Neutral, 2. Disagree, and 1. Agree [43]. A mean of 3.5 or higher indicated that the majority of respondents agreed, while a mean of less than 3.5 indicated that the majority of respondents disagreed [44]. The validity and reliability of the instruments were ensured by pre-testing them on a separate sample to determine the reliability of the coefficients. The information from the sample was tested for accuracy and compared to conventional financial management and financial performance instruments. The study also tested for moderation effect using age of the respondents, education level, and years in dairy business/experience.

3.4 Data analysis and hierarchical multiple regression model

Primary data was edited and entered into SPSS© version 25 Software. There were three levels of analysis: descriptive statistics with frequency tables and figures for descriptive analyses and correlation analysis with cross tabulations for relationships between the dependent and independent variables. Finally, we conducted a hierarchical multiple regression to show if our variables of interest explain a statistically significant amount of variance in the dependent variable after accounting for farmer and farm characteristics moderating effect.

3.4.1 Hierarchical multiple regression model

The study examined the moderating effect of firm and farmers' characteristics on the relationship between financial management practices and financial performance of dairy farm enterprises. In pursuance of the above objective, the study set a research

	Model 1 Beta	Model 2 Beta	Model 3 Beta
Constant	0.25	1.45	4.43
Financial management practices	0.35**	0.13**	0.27
Firm & farmers characteristics		0.60**	1.09**
FinMgtP * FP&FXtics			0.89**
R	0.35	0.51	0.6
R Square	**0.12**	**0.26**	**0.37**
Adjusted R square	0.11	0.25	0.35
R Square change	—	0.14	0.1
Sig. (ANOVA)	0.001	0.001	0.001

*Note: **p < .01, N = 394, Dependent variable: Financial performance.*
*FinMgtP * FP&FXtics = Interaction term.*
Source: Primary data.

Table 1.
Hierarchical multiple regression results for a moderation effect.

question that was to be answered. The study carried out a hierarchical multiple regression analysis, intending to establish the predictive power of each explanatory variable. The researcher preferred the hierarchical regression method because of its strength in pointing out the contribution of each predictor at different stages in the regression model [45]. Consequently, the following hierarchical regression model was specified:

We assume our multiple regression model is

$$Y_i = \beta_0 + \beta_1 X_{1i} + \beta_2 X_{2i} + \beta_3 X_{3i} + \beta_{i.} \quad (3)$$

Where Y is the dependent variable (financial performance), β_0 is the constant (intercept), and β_1 to β_3 are coefficients estimated along x1 to x3, whereas x1 is financial management practices, x2 is the firm and farmer characteristics, and x3 is the interaction term. The regression results are provided in the **Table 1** above.

4. Empirical results

Table 2 describes the statistics of the sample respondents based on the farmer and farm characteristics. Most of the respondents were male (78%) and female (22%). In terms of age, 40% were over 60, implying that the majority of dairy farmers are retired and have returned to dairy farming. The sample's education level is dominated by certificate holders (29%) and the number of years in business is dominated by those who have been in business for more than 16 years (48%).

The **Table 3** below demonstrates the reliability and validity of each construct. The capital structure with reliability of 0.8 measured by five items, and working capital management has reliability of 0.7; there are six items, and the Cronbach alpha of budget and budgetary control is 0.8, measured with six items. In addition, financial record-keeping reliability is 0.7, (items 9). Lastly, financial performance scored a reliability of 0.7 (items 5).

Gender	Frequency	Percentage
Male	121	77.6
Female	35	22.4
Total	156	100
Age		
Below 30	18	11.5
40–49	37	23.7
50–59	39	25.0
60 and above	62	39.7
Total	**156**	**100**
Education		
Primary	22	14.1
Secondary	35	22.4
Certificate	45	28.8
Diploma	29	18.6
Bachelors	19	12.2
Masters	6	3.8
Total	**156**	**100**
Years in business		
Below 5 Years	19	12.2
5–10 Years	30	19.2
11–15 Years	32	20.5
16–20 Years	75	48.1
Total	**156**	**100**
Source: Primary data; n = 156.		

Table 2.
Frequency and percentage of farmer and farm characteristics.

Variables	Code	Measurement scale item No.	Cronbach's α
Capital structure	CS	5	0.8
Working capital management	WCM	6	0.7
Budget and budgeting control	BBC	6	0.8
Financial record keeping	FRK	9	0.7
Financial performance	FP	5	0.7
Source: Primary data.			

Table 3.
Reliability of measurement items.

Table 4 reports the correlations among the variables. As expected, financial management practices (FMP) are significantly and positively correlated with financial performance (FP).

Variables	FMP	FRK	CS	BBC	WCM	FP
FMP	1					
FRK	0.81**	1				
CS	0.82**	0.60**	1			
BBC	0.86**	0.62**	0.63**	1		
WCM	0.69**	0.66**	0.62**	0.55**	1	
FP	0.35**	0.27**	0.28**	0.20**	0.20**	1

**$P < 0.01$ *level (1-tailed), n = 156.*

Table 4.
Correlation matric analysis.

Overall, most of the correlation coefficients among the key variables are relatively low, indicating that concerns about multicollinearity are not serious as suggested by Refs. [46–48]. In addition, the correlation analysis results in the table above revealed a positive and significant relationship between financial management practices and financial performance of dairy farm enterprises in the Rwenzori region ($r = 35$, $p < 0.01$). This means that an improvement in financial management practices in terms of improved record-keeping, budgeting, working capital management, and optimal capital is positively associated with an improvement in financial performance.

Furthermore, the results indicated that capital structure (CS) has the highest correlation coefficient ($r = 28$, $P < 0.01$) followed by financial record keeping (FRK) ($r = 0.27$, $p < 0.01$), budgeting (BBC) and working capital management (WCM) ($r = 0.20$, $p < 0.01$), respectively. This implies that farmers should prioritize an optimum capital structure (a balance of debt and equity) to minimize the cost of capital. They should also keep proper record for decision-making as they control their budgets and working capital to improve their financial performance. The findings of FRK and FP are in accordance with the [21, 31–34] who also discovered that financial record keeping boosts financial performance of several enterprises. On the other hand, results of WCM and FM contradict with the studies of [28, 29] whose research revealed a negative relationship between the two variables.

The main objective of this book chapter was to gain a better understanding of the moderating role of dairy farmers, and farm enterprise characteristics on the relationship between financial management practices and financial performance are presented in **Table 1** above. The empirical results suggest that in Model 1, financial management practices accounted for 12% of the variance in financial performance ($R^2 = 0.12$, $p < 0.01$) and caused a positive statistically significant standardized coefficient of ($\beta = 0.35$, $p < 0.01$), where a unit change in financial management practices increases financial performance by 0.35 units. Similarly, the study conducted by Zalaghi et al. [2] showed that firm size affects the relation between working capital management and financial performance measured as return of assets. On the contrary, [49] concluded that financial management measured as working capital management has a negative and significant relationship with profitability and that payables accounts and profitability have a negative relationship.

In Model 2, the introduction of the firm and farmers' characteristics in the equation yielded an additional 14% (R^2 – change = 0.14, $P < 0.01$) to the explanatory power of the model. This implies that firm and farmers' characteristics accounted for the additional 14% of the variance of financial performance and caused a statistically significant coefficient ($\beta = 0.60$, $P < 0.01$), thus improving the predictive power of the model from 12% to 2 6% ($R^2 = 0.26$, $P < 0.01$). This further implies that a unit change in the firm and farmers' characteristics would increase the financial performance of the dairy farmer enterprises by 0.60 units. Beside the inclusion of the interactive term (firm and farmer characteristics), Model 3 increased the predictive power of the main effects of financial management practices and firm and farm characteristics by 10% (R^2 –change = 0.1, $P < 0.01$) from 26 to 37% ($R^2 = 0.37$, $P < 0.01$). Likewise, studies by Refs. [7, 9, 18, 21] concluded that financial management and financial performance. Since the interactive term (financial management practices firm and farmer characteristics) significantly added an extra 10%, it means that the interactive term boosts the explanatory power of the main effects, thereby causing better results than what the main effects would have registered. This means that firm and farmers' characteristics moderate the relationship between financial management practices and financial performance of the dairy farm enterprises in the Rwenzori region.

5. Conclusions

The aim for this manuscript was to explore the moderating role farm and farm characteristics on the influence of financial management practices and financial performance for the dairy farmers in the Rwenzori Region. The results further signify that financial management practices and firm and farmer characteristics significantly interact or fuse to cause better financial performance among dairy farm enterprises. Thus, the effect of financial management practices on financial performance depends on the firm and farmers' characteristics such as age and education of the farmers, as well as the number of years the dairy enterprise has been in existence. Additionally, the nonsignificant effect of financial management practices in Model 3 after including the interaction term means a full moderation of firm and farmer characteristics. This means that financial management practices cannot work sufficiently in isolation to influence the financial performance of dairy farm enterprises in the Rwenzori region. Finally, on the basis of the analyses above the results can be further strengthened if the dairy enterprises manage their financial practices in more efficient ways. Management of capital structures, working capital, budget, and financial records will ultimately increase profitability, liquidity, and solvency while incorporating more farm and farmers' characteristics.

Acknowledgements

Special thanks to the Mountains of the Moon University in particular Faculty of Business and Management Sciences and Makerere University – college of Business and Management Sciences for giving us all the necessary support as we worked on this book chapter. Lastly, we thank our families for all the moral, financial, and spiritual support accorded to the team.

Author details

Joanita Kataike[1]*, Margret Asiimwe[2], Robert Mawenu[2]
and Willy Rwamparagi Kagarura[3]

1 Department of Management Sciences, Faculty of Business and Management Sciences, Mountains of the Moon University, Uganda

2 Department of Banking and Finance, Faculty of Business and Management Sciences, Mountains of the Moon University, Uganda

3 Department of Economics, College of Business and Management Sciences, Uganda

*Address all correspondence to: joanitakat@mmu.ac.ug

References

[1] Sharma FC, Mittal R. Financial Management. India: SBPD Publications; 2023

[2] Zalaghi H, Godini M, Mansouri K. The moderating role of firms characteristics on the relationship between working capital management and financial performance. Advances in Mathematical Finance and Applications. 2019;**4**(1):71-88

[3] Patil AP, Gawande SH, Nande MP, Gobade MR. Constraints faced by the dairy farmers in Nagpur district while adopting animal management practices. Veterinary World. 2009;**2**(3):111

[4] Kourtidis D, Šević Ž, Chatzoglou P. Investors' trading activity: A behavioral perspective and empirical results. The Journal of Socioeconomic. 2011;**40**(5):548-557

[5] Sewell M. Behavioral Finance. 2007. Available from: www.behaviouralfinance.net/behavioural-finance.pdf [Accessed: August 18, 2023]

[6] Manocha S, Bhullar PS, Sachdeva T. Factors determining the investment behaviour of farmers – The moderating role of socioeconomic demographics. Journal of Indian Business Research. 2023;**15**(3):301-317

[7] Gloy BA, LaDue EL. Financial management practices and farm profitability. Agricultural Finance Review. 2003;**63**(2):157-174

[8] Perdue G, Wooten K. Investment management and personality type. Financial Services Review. 2008;**17**(3):219-237

[9] Mahfoudh IO. Effect of Selected Firm Characteristics on Financial Performance of Firms Listed in the Agricultural Sector at the Nairobi Securities Exchange (Doctoral dissertation). Nairobi, Kenya: University of Nairobi; 2013

[10] Uganda Bureau of Statistics (UBOS). Statistical Abstract, Uganda Bureau of Statistics. Republic of Uganda: Ministry of Health Knowledge Management Portal; 2020. p. 2020

[11] Food and Agriculture Organization of the United Nations Data. FAOSTAT. Food and Agriculture Organization of the United Nations Data. 2021. Available from: http://www.fao.org/faostat/en/#data. [Accessed: July 21, 2023]

[12] Food and Agriculture Organization. The Future of Livestock in Uganda. Opportunities and Challenges in the Face of Uncertainty. Rome, Italy: Food and Agriculture Organization; 2019

[13] Waiswa D, Jolly A. Implications of gender discrimination for household food security among small holder dairy farmers in Nakaloke, Mbale District, Uganda. Research Journal of Agriculture and Forestry Sciences. 2021;**2320**:6063

[14] Waiswa D, Günlü A. Economic analysis of dairy production in Uganda, a case study on the performance of dairy cattle enterprises in southwestern Uganda. Asian Journal of Agriculture. 2022;**6**(2):61-67

[15] Dairy Development Authority (DDA). Dairy Development Authority Annual Performance Report FY 2019/20. 2020. Available from: https://dda.go.ug/assets/files/ANNUAL Performance Report FY2019-20.pdf [Accessed: July 20, 2023]

[16] Barry PJ, Ellinger PN, Baker CB, Hopkin JA. Financial Management

in Agriculture. 5th ed. Danville, IL: Interstate Publishers; 1995

[17] Sayari N, Marcum B. Corporate governance and financial performance in the emerging markets: Do ADRs perform any better than non-cross-listed firms? Financial Management from an Emerging Market Perspective. 2017:149-175

[18] Evci S, Şak N. The effect of working capital management on profitability in emerging countries: Evidence from Turkey. Financial Management from an Emerging Market Perspective. 2018;**10**

[19] Raheman A, Nasr M. Working capital management and profitability case of Pakistani firms. International Review of Business Research Papers. 2007;**3**:279-300

[20] Pollitt C. Integrating financial management and performance management. Organization for Economic Co-Operation and Development. 2001;**1**:7-37

[21] Hunjra AI, Butt BZ, Rehman KU. Financial management practices and their impact on organizational performance. World Applied Sciences Journal. 2010;**9**(9):997-1002

[22] Shabbir MS, Wisdom O. The relationship between corporate social responsibility, environmental investments and financial performance: Evidence from manufacturing companies. Environmental Science and Pollution Research. 2020;**27**:39946-39957

[23] Fatihudin D. How measuring financial performance. International Journal of Civil Engineering and Technology (IJCIET). 2018;**9**(6):553-557

[24] Alhassan AF, Bajaher MS, Alshehri AM. Corporate governance, firm attributes and financial performance of Saudi listed banks. Corporate Governance. 2015;**5**(3):282-295

[25] Mabandla NZ, Makoni PL. Working capital management and financial performance: Evidence from listed food and beverage companies in South Africa. Academy of Accounting and Financial Studies Journal. 2019;**23**(2):1-0

[26] Michel A, Shaked I. Multinational corporations vs. domestic corporations: Financial performance and characteristics. Journal of International Business Studies. 1986;**17**:89-100

[27] Gitman LJ, Zutter CJ. Principles of Managerial Finance. Pearson: South Africa; 2014

[28] Korankye T, Adarquah RS. Empirical analysis of working capital management and its impact on the profitability of listed manufacturing firms in Ghana. Research Journal of Finance and Accounting. 2013;**4**(1):124-131

[29] Kasozi J. The effect of working capital management on profitability: A case of listed manufacturing firms in South Africa. Investment Management and Financial Innovations. 2017;**14**(2.2):336-346

[30] Abdul-Rahamon OA, Adejare AT. The analysis of the impact of accounting records keeping on the performance of the small scale enterprises. International Journal of Academic Research in Business and Social Sciences. 2014;**4**(1):1-7

[31] Nelson M, Onias M. Accounting practices of SMEs in Zimbabwe: An investigative study of record keeping for performance measurement (A case study of Bindura). Journal of Accounting and Taxation. 2011;**3**(8):158-161

[32] Amoako GK. Accounting practices of SMEs: A case study of Kumasi Metropolis

in Ghana. International Journal of Business and Management. 2013;**8**(24):73

[33] Muchira BW. Record keeping and growth of micro and small enterprises: A case study of Thika municipality in Kenya. Kenyatta University Library. 2012;**15**:11-16

[34] Lesirma DL. The Relationship between Effectiveness of the Accounting Functions and the Financial Performance of Savings and Credit Cooperative Societies in Nairobi County (Doctoral dissertation). Nairobi, Kenya: University of Nairobi; 2014

[35] Chelimo JK, Sopia IO. Effects of bookkeeping on growth of small and medium business enterprises in Kabarnet town, Baringo County, Kenya. International Journal of Science and Research. 2014;**3**(12):432-437

[36] Ademola GO, Samuel OJ, Ifedolapo O. The roles of record keeping in the survival and growth of small scale enterprises in Ijumu local government area of Kogi state. Global Journal of Management and Business Research. 2012;**12**(13):55-66

[37] Mwebesa LC, Kansiime C, Asiimwe BB, Mugambe P, Rwego IB. The effect of financial record keeping on financial performance of development groups in rural areas of Western Uganda. International Journal of Economics and Finance

[38] Nickson J, Mears S. Budgetary control and performance. Journal of Finance. 2012;**7**(3):78-98

[39] Mohamed AI, Ali AY. Relationship between budgeting and performance of remittance companies in Somalia. Educational Research International. 2013;**2**(1):106-115

[40] Yamane T. Statistics, An Introductory Analysis, 1967. USA: New York Harper and Row CO; 1967

[41] Kataike J, Modekurti DP, Butali E, Magumba D, Mugenyi AR, Aine-Omucunguzi A, et al. A parametric test evaluating smallholder farmers' training needs in Uganda: A case of dairy farmers in the Rwenzori region. Journal of Agribusiness in Developing and Emerging Economies. 2018;**8**(3):537-553

[42] Etikan I, Bala K. Sampling and sampling methods. Bio-metrics & Bio-statistics International Journal. 2017;**5**(6):00149

[43] Likert R. A technique for the measurement of attitudes. Archives of Psychology. 1932;**22**(140):55

[44] Warmbrod JR. Reporting and interpreting scores derived from Likert-type scales. Journal of Agricultural Education. 2014;**55**(5):30-47

[45] Field A. Discovering Statistics Using SPSS Using IBM Statistics. UK: Sage; 2013

[46] Wang S, Ji C, He H, Zhang Z, Zhang L. Tourists' waste reduction behavioral intentions at tourist destinations: An integrative research framework. Sustainable Production and Consumption. 2021;**25**:540-550

[47] Xu G, Wang S, Zhao D. Transition to sustainable transport: Understanding the antecedents of consumer's intention to adopt electric vehicles from the emotional research perspective. Environmental Science and Pollution Research. 2021;**28**:20362-20374

[48] Zhang W, Wang S, Wan L, Zhang Z, Zhao D. Information perspective for understanding consumers' perceptions

of electric vehicles and adoption intentions. Transportation Research Part D: Transport and Environment. 2022;**102**:103157

[49] Lazaridis I, Tryfonidis D. Relationship between working capital management and profitability of listed companies in the Athens stock exchange. Journal of Financial Management & Analysis. 2006;**19**(1):1-12

Section 3

Financialization and the Financial Future of the World

Chapter 9

Public Finance in a Digital Economy

Sylvester Onyeoma

Abstract

This chapter deals with the means by which government raises revenue and expenditure profile. Public finance explains the sources of government revenues and the ways in which revenue is allocated to give maximum benefits on the entire society. It cuts across public treasury operations into economic policies on financial transaction of government bothering on revenue, expenditure and public debts. It also attempts to provide the criteria, with the help of the marginal utility analysis, which determine the revenue and expenditure policies of the government. In response to the advances in technology, the author delves into Public finance in a digital economy to highlight the new trends and emerging issues. Areas covered include: (1) Rationale for government public finance; (2) the functions of theory of public finance (3) sources of government revenue (4) items of government expenditure (4) public debt (5) government budget (6) fiscal federalism and economic growth(7) e-government and e-commerce (8) digital economy (9) emerging trend in digital economy and finance. In response to the advances in technology, the work highlighted the new trends and emerging issues on innovative inclination of sharing advances in the economy using new business models based on big data, cloud computing, virtual reality, artificial intelligence, smart city applications, blockchain technology, online/mobile internet banking and third-party payments. The array of topics covered is recommended for rewarding learning experience.

Keywords: budgeting, economy, public expenditure, government revenue, taxes

1. Introduction

Public finance is the aspect of economics that deals with the means by which government raises revenue. This explains the sources of government revenues and the ways in which revenue is allocated to give maximum benefits on the entire society. It cuts across public treasury operations into economic policies on financial transaction of government bothering on revenue, expenditure and public debts. It also attempts to provide the criteria, with the help of the marginal utility analysis, which determine the revenue and expenditure policies of the government.

1.1 Rationale for government public finance

The rationale for government public finance include the following:

- To reduce unearned income
- Promoting a sense of national-cultural cohesion
- Ensuring the integrity of the social organism
- Reduction in class division
- To reduce all forms of unjustifiable inequalities of wealth and of economic opportunities.

Public finance is concerned with the following:

- The theory of public revenue: This has to do with the sources of government revenue and these include tax revenue and other revenues.
- The theory of public expenditure: Often government revenues are expended on general administration, social and economic services (recurrent and capital expenditure).
- Budgetary Management: This entails the management of the finances of government through appropriate budgetary practices. It covers the formulation, legal authorization and appropriation, execution, control and auditing of government budgets.
- Stabilization and Growth: Government in order to steer the economy towards stability and ultimate economic growth, various fiscal policy tools such as import duties, tax holidays and export duties.
- Public or National Debt Management: The government in order to reduce the effect of public debts on the economy adopts different measures. These measures range from debt rescheduling, debt conversion, etc.

1.2 The functions of the theory of public finance

The main functions of the Theory of Public Finance include the following:

- The enhancement of social stability through the maintenance of law and order and up-keep of territorial integrity of the nation.
- The provision of important public services such as education, health, at affordable rates and the management of public utilities such as PHCN, NIPOST, Water Board, are aspects of the economic functions of government.
- Assisting in redistributing income and wealth in the economy through the manipulation of existing tax rates and tax base.
- Through the application of fiscal policy, government ensures that prices, employment and incomes are reasonably stable in the economy.
- Government ensuring that there is adequate boost in investment and appropriate management of some sectors of the economy in addition to the positive contributions highlighted.

DOI: http://dx.doi.org/10.5772/intechopen.1003127

- Provision of purely social services which entails goods with indivisible benefits that is no one can be excluded from enjoying them. Such services include the provision of roads, street lights, etc.

1.3 Sources of government revenue

The main sources of government revenue include the following:

1. Taxation: Taxes are compulsory payment to the governments without leaving the government with a liability to the payer. They may be direct as income taxes or indirect as sales taxes or export duties.

2. Grants and Gifts: Grants are voluntary financial assistance given by the government of a country or international institution to a defined country for a defined purpose. Most often, administrative and technical conditions are tied to such grants. Grants and gifts are not important sources of government in Nigeria.

3. Administrative Revenues: Administrative revenues are receipts which accrue to the public purse functionally as bye-products of government administrative control. These are voluntary payments occasioned by the rights of operation or practice conferred on the payer.

4. Commercial Revenues: Commercial revenues are resources from payment made for the direct receipts of a good or service produced by the government through its agencies/departments or parastatals. Such revenues include payment for water, electricity, education, health services, telephone, amongst others.

5. Profit and Income from government corporations and parastatals e.g. Federal Inland Revenue Service, Nigerian National Petroleum Corporation, Board of Internal Revenue.

6. Borrowing: Loans from both internal and external sources, that is, government and private individual loans.

7. Custom duties, tariffs, and excise duties.

1.4 Items of government expenditure

These include the following:

1. Construction of road and provision of infrastructural facilities.

2. Provision of both internal and external defense e.g. Ministry of Defense.

3. Provision of healthcare services.

4. Provision of social amenities.

5. Provision of education.

6. Provision of courts and judicial justice.

1.5 Public debt

The government borrowing should be used for the purpose for which it is borrowed. It should be so managed in such a way that the incident of debt should not weigh the government down and the focus of paying back the debt should be maintained [1]. The increasing portfolio of public debts, debt service burden and debt overhang create worry and concern in many African economies including Nigeria. The government can borrow for profitable investment purposes but the situation where governments borrow for consumption in many developing countries should be discouraged as this will not improve the economy. Rather this scenario poses prodigious challenge to economic growth and development in spite of mindful effort to resuscitate nation's economy. Conscious efforts should be made to entrench fiscal discipline in governance and public debt management.

1.6 Government budget

Budget can be defined as a financial statement which spells out estimated government revenue and the proposed expenditure for a particular period usually one year. A budget comprises of a package of proposal regarding intended revenue to be generated from different sources and expected expenditure to be incurred on various items.

Balanced Budget: When the expected revenue equals the proposed expenditure.

Budget Deficit: There is budget deficit if the estimated government revenue is less than its proposed expenditure for a given financial year. This implies that the government plans to spend more money than it is likely to generate through taxation and other sources. In this situation, the government has to use part of its former reserves. If there are no reserves, the government may borrow money to finance the deficit.

1.6.1 Importance of a budget deficit

A budget deficit is useful in the following ways:

1. Increase aggregate expenditure (or demand) and thereby reducing unemployment.

2. It is used to finance a national emergency such as war and other natural disasters like flood, earthquake, and coronavirus pandemic.

3. It is also used to finance huge capital projects.

4. It is used to remedy a deflationary trend (or recession) by increasing aggregate demands.

Budget deficit has the effect of enabling the government to increase expenditure on different projects, thereby helping to increase the level of employment. A budget deficit could result in inflation. This is because it may lead to excess money being in circulation, if the level of productivity does not increase in the same magnitude.

1.6.2 Budget surplus

There is budget surplus if estimated government revenue is greater than the proposed expenditure during a fiscal year. The government plans to spend less money than it is likely to get through taxation and other sources [2].

1.6.3 Importance of budget surplus

1. A surplus budget is used to reduce aggregate demand thereby reducing inflationary pressure in the economy.

2. It is sometimes used to meet one of the conditionalities of world financial institutions, like international Monetary Fund for lending money to enable borrowing country to revitalize its economy.

A budget surplus would lead to an increase in government financial reserves but there may be increase in unemployment because of decreased total investment.

1.6.4 Importance of budget in modern economy

1. The budget is a means of raising revenue. This was the original role of the budget. Through it, the government plan to raise adequate or enough money to finance its activities. In the budget, the government sets out how it plans to generate its revenue and how expenditure is to be carried out.

2. It is used to correct depression or a deflationary situation in an economy. This is true of the deficit budget which can be used to stimulate recovery from a trade depression. During this period, the government will spend more money than its revenues and this has the effect of increasing the level of economic activities, thereby increasing aggregate demand and the level of employment.

3. It is also used to control inflation. This is true of surplus budget. The government plans to spend less money than it generates by way of tax and other sources. This reduces the level of aggregate demand in the economy thereby helping to curb inflation.

4. The budget is also a means of protecting the economy and rectifying a balance of payment deficit. In the budget, the government outlines the various forms of import control. It enumerates the measures by which exports can be encouraged.

5. It is a means of enhancing public welfare and reducing income inequality in the country through the budget, the government could plan to increase taxes on the rich and reduce taxes on those with relatively low income. When free social facilities are provided, the welfare of the citizens is further enhanced.

6. The budget is used as a tool for economic planning. Through this medium, areas or sectors that require attention are identified and ways of improving such sectors are enumerated [3].

1.6.5 Qualities of a good budget

1. A good budget gathers all available economic data with a realistic approach to future issues and can be anticipated to affect everybody.

2. A good budget is one that can be changed and which can be foreseen in advance.

3. A good budget must strive to fulfill the desires of a large group of people.

1.6.6 Principles of revenue allocation in Nigeria

Revenue allocation is the redistribution of fiscal capacity between the various levels of. government, or the nature of fiscal responsibilities between the various tiers of government using guided allocation principles [4].

The major principles of revenue allocation in Nigeria include: Derivation principle (**Table 1**).

S/No	Beneficiary	Percentage of revenue allocated
1	National Government	48.5
2	36 States	26.72
3	774 Indigenous governments	20.60
4	Centrally controlled Special Fund	4.18
	Total	100

Source. Authors' tabulation.

Table 1.
Analysis of revenue allocation formula in Nigeria.

Principle of need, Principle of national interest and Principle of independent revenues. Components of Revenue Allocation Formula in Nigeria.

Two main components of the revenue allocation formula commonly used Nigeria are: Vertical Allocation Formula (VAF) and Horizontal Allocation Formula (HAF).

1.7 E-governance and E-commerce

E-government refers to how governments at every level and in every department use the internet and associated technologies to conduct functions, both internally and with external groups including businesses and citizens. For instance, when you file your taxes online instead of sending them through the mail, you are using e-government. When the government sends your tax refund directly to your bank via direct deposit, that is also e-government.

1.7.1 E-commerce

E-commerce (Electronic Commerce) is the buying and selling of goods and services, or the transmitting of funds or data, over the internet to reduce cost and improve the quality of goods and services while increasing the speed of delivery. There are four main types of ecommerce models that can describe almost every transaction that takes place between consumers and businesses. These include the following:

- **Business-to-Consumer (B2C):** The B2C model involves transaction between business organization and customer. The business organization sells its products directly to a consumer. Customer can view the products shown on the website. The customer can choose a product and order the same.

- **Business-to-Business (B2B):** The B2B model involves the transaction between companies/businesses, such as between a manufacturer and a wholesaler or between wholesaler and a retailer. The business/company sells its products to an intermediate buyer who then sells the product to the final customer.

- **Consumer-to-Business (C2B):** The C2B model involves a transaction between a consumer and business organization.

- **Consumer-to-Consumer (C2C):** The C2C model involves transaction between consumers. Here, a consumer sells directly to another consumer. A well-known example is eBay.

1.8 Digital economy

Digital economy uses digital technologies to cover all businesses, economic, social, cultural etc. activities that are supported by the web and other digital communication technologies such as e-business, e-business infrastructure and e-commerce. Recently, there has been tremendous growth of digital platforms and their influence on our lives and the economy.

1.8.1 Merits of digital economy

Digital economy has given rise to many new trends and start-up ideas. Almost all of the biggest companies in the world (Google, Apple, Microsoft, Amazon) are from the digital world. Some important merits of the digital economy include the following:

- Promotes Use of the Internet

- Rise in E-Commerce.

- Digital Goods and Services

- Transparency: The digital economy helps reduce the black money and corruption in the market and make the economy more transparent.

1.8.2 Demerits of digital economy

- Loss in Employment: Advancement of the digital economy could a threat that may lead to the loss of countless jobs.

- Lack of Experts.

- Heavy Investment are required

2. Emerging technological trends in digital economy and finance

The digital economy is undergoing rapid advancements and transformative changes, especially in emerging markets. The digital economy is accelerated by technological innovation such as artificial intelligence (AI) and technology-driven economic innovation Atiquzzaman et al. [5]. Prominent amongst the new emerging trends include the following:

- Online Banking: The world of finance is rapidly evolving, driven by advancements in technology and changing consumer behaviors on apps like Apple Pay, Google Pay Samsung Pay, Digital wallets and contactless payments, embedded finance which is the integration of financial services into software and systems, Robo-advisers and AI-powered financial services.

- New Development Trend of Blockchain: In the era of digital economy, the development trends of blockchain are applied to the real sector to promote the efficiency of the real economy, accelerate the integration with new digital technologies such as big data, the Internet of things, and artificial intelligence [6].

- New Development Trend of Virtual Reality: The development of virtual reality technology has brought new industrial changes and business opportunities like virtual shopping, psychological therapy and rehabilitation, military simulation, industrial designs and other fields in this era of digital economy.

- Innovative Inclination of sharing advances in the economy using new business model based on big data, cloud computing, mobile internet and third-party payment.

- Digital technology has improved transaction process in the form of point-to-point connection, reduce transaction costs, and enable consumers to enjoy the characteristics of productive services. New Advancement and development of the Internet of things has led to a variety of sensors and terminals that can quickly access the network and gather together.

- New Patterns in AI Advancement has improved Digital Economy leading to emerging economic activities and its core elements in data mining cloud computing, network, artificial intelligence, and blockchain technologies leading to the digital transformation of the economy which is a driving force for innovative economic development Li et al. [7].

- Digital Technology in Operation Optimization and Achieves Lean Management, Production has led to intelligent production, supply chain distribution networks, field environmental management, etc.

- New Trend of Smart City Application has improved urban informatization infrastructure construction, Spatial Structure, Social Structure, urban social order, ecological environment, and infrastructure, urban traffic, logistics, energy, environment, and other information in real time [8, 9].

- New Trends in Mobile Medical Applications aids Chronic Disease Prevention and Health Management Based through the electronic medical record database multi-source, fragmented, and unstructured medical data, clinical data comparison, clinical decision support, and remote patient data analysis.

- New Trend of Personalized Education Application promotes the innovation and development of education in digital economy using Educational Artificial Intelligence (EAI).

DOI: http://dx.doi.org/10.5772/intechopen.1003127

Author details

Sylvester Onyeoma
Department of Economics, Igbinedion University, Okada, Edo State, Nigeria

*Address all correspondence to: onyeoma.sylvester@iuokada.edu.ng

References

[1] Ohiomu S. External debt and economic growth Nexus: Empirical evidence from Nigeria. The American Economist: SAGE Journals USA. 2020;**65**(2):330-343

[2] Onyeoma S. Principles of Economics. Nigeria: Brightway Publishers; 2021

[3] Jhingan ML. The Economics of Development and Planning. 38th ed. New Delhi: Vrenda; 2011

[4] Ohiomu S, Oluyemi SA. Resolving revenue allocation challenges in Nigeria: Implications for sustainable National Development. The American Economist: SAGE Journals USA. 2018;**64**(1):1-12

[5] Atiquzzaman M, Yen N, Xu Z. Big data analytics for cyber-physical system in smart city2021. Proceedings of the BDCPS. In: International Conference on Big Data Analytics for Cyber-physical System in Smart City. Shanghai, China; 2020

[6] Einav L, Levin J. Economics in the age of big data. Science. 2014;**346**:6210. DOI: 10.1126/science.1243089.1243089

[7] Li J, Peng Z, Liu A, He L, Zhang Y. Analysis and future challenge of blockchain in civil aviation application. In: Proceedings of the IEEE 6th International Conference on Computer and Communications (ICCC). Chengdu, China; 2020. pp. 1742-1748

[8] Cheng Y, Meng H, Yuan L, Lei Y. Research on edge computing technology of internet of things based on intelligent and environmental protection. In: Proceedings of the IEEE International Conference on Consumer Electronics and Computer Engineering (ICCECE). Guangzhou, China; 2021

[9] Yang Q. The smart city of Changsha, China—Sciencedirect. Smart City Emergence. 2019;**2019**:219-241

Chapter 10

The Role of Reading Economic News in Germany and the UK

Nadine Strauß, Sophie Knowles and Vesile Cinceoglu

Abstract

This chapter argues that the news media play an important factor in educating the public about financial institutions. It presents some novel survey results, exploring the role of economic news use for the perceived understanding of financial institutions in Germany and the UK. Two web-based surveys were conducted: one in the UK in winter 2018 and one in Germany in summer 2019. Findings show that economic news use is positively related with a better perceived understanding of financial institutions in both countries, even after controlling for demographics and financial socialization. We find that the level of perceived understanding of financial institutions is positively related with education and income and negatively related with being female. The need for information significantly impacted the relationship between economic news use and understanding of financial institutions in the UK but not in Germany. Practical implications for economic and financial news journalists are discussed.

Keywords: financial understanding, news media, need for information, comparative research, survey, UK, Germany

1. Introduction

The way the global economy collapsed during the Global Financial Crisis (GFC) 2008, and the recession that ensued afterwards, highlighted the centrality of financial markets and financial institutions for society and democracy more generally. Now, after a pandemic, the economy is marked by global rising inflation [1], growing inequality [2], a cost-of-living crisis [3], and a new focus on sustainable economic growth [4], which emphasizes the importance of understanding the role financial institutions play in society. At the same time, the 21st century has been characterized by a tremendous increase in complexity of the financial markets [5, 6]. Citizens are confronted with a financial system that is increasingly disconnected from the real-world economy [6, 7], while everyday life has become more and more financialized [8]. In addition, global financial and corporate scandals such as the Pandora Papers, or the insolvency of Wirecard in Germany in 2020 [9]—which have all been widely covered in the international financial press—have questioned the authority, functionality, and honesty of financial institutions worldwide.

Following communication scholars [10–12], we argue that the news media play a crucial role in informing citizens about economic issues, actors, and institutions.

However, research on economic news and its relevance for economic understanding, attitudes, or behavior is lacking (e.g., [13–16]). Although there is a body of research in finance and economics that has investigated the influencing factors of financial literacy (e.g., [17, 18]) and, among others, media use [19–22], a theoretical and empirical discussion of the role of financial news use for the understanding of financial institutions has been underrepresented in academic research so far (see for an exception: [20] on monetary knowledge). What is more, numerous studies have consistently and repeatedly shown that financial literacy and financial understanding are unequally spread among the public and in various parts of the world [23], being particularly low among women, younger cohorts, and the less educated public [17, 18]. It has therefore become paramount that we investigate how the news media and economic news use can contribute to a better understanding of financial institutions. In this cross-national survey study, we therefore investigate how economic news use and additional influencing factors are related to the understanding of financial institutions in two Western democracies–Germany and the UK.

2. Theoretical framework and literature review

2.1 Financial literacy, sociodemographic differences, and personal finance management

Most research about financial knowledge refers to financial literacy, which is generally understood as "a combination of awareness, knowledge, skill, attitude and behaviour necessary to make sound financial decisions and ultimately achieve individual financial well-being" ([24], p. 14). Financial literacy is presented by some authors as the gateway to become an active member of the financial markets (e.g., [25]), to make informed financial decisions [26], to manage retirement planning (e.g., [27]), or to be aware of personal debt levels [28]. However, a worldwide survey by Standard and Poor in 2015 has shown that only 33% of adults worldwide are financially literate [29]. Similarly, academic research has repeatedly provided evidence that financial literacy rates are unequally low in different parts of the world [23] and that people also have difficulties in processing and understanding financial information to various degrees [26, 30].

However, financial understanding is not just about knowing how inflation works, how compound interests play out, or how to invest efficiently and safely (cf. financial literacy: [17, 23]). Instead, financial understanding also expands to the knowledge of the functions and roles of various financial institutions within a democracy. Having a good grasp and understanding of the roles and functions of financial institutions in the countries where citizens live is important to cultivate a knowledgeable and critical citizenry that can make decisions and behave in a way that will benefit their individual economic and social well-being. For example, a recent survey by the European Central Bank (ECB) has shown that there is a positive correlation between people who have a better understanding of the ECB's task and their trust in the institution [31]. Previous research has indeed shown that increased economic knowledge leads to public policy support and institutional trust in the ECB (e.g., [32, 33]) or the European Monetary Union (e.g., [34]).

Looking at past research that has shown that citizens are not very well informed about real economic conditions [35], it becomes clear that the level of economic and financial understanding has not changed much over time (e.g., US: [36]). To identify the reasons for these low levels of financial understandings, a plethora of research has investigated the influencing factors of financial literacy, albeit most of such studies focus on demographic characteristics, such as age, gender, ethnicity, education, marital status, or income (e.g., [18, 37, 38]). For example, women and less-educated individuals have been found to score lower on financial literacy than men or highly educated individuals [17, 18]. Referring to ethnicity, Sabri et al. [39] showed that the Chinese student minority within a Malaysian student sample had a lower level of financial literacy. Furthermore, Lusardi and Mitchell [23] showed that there was a U-shape when it comes to age and financial literacy, where the youngest and oldest groups scored lower when compared to middle-aged people. Similarly, Bianchi [37] showed that financial literacy was positively correlated with income, wealth, and education but negatively with being married and female. Hence, based on previous findings on financial literacy and demographic factors, we hypothesize:

H1: Perceived understanding of financial institutions is higher for (a) older, (b) male, (c) higher-earning, (d) highly educated citizens and for those (e) belonging to the ethnic majority.

Previous research has repeatedly confirmed that there is a gender gap when it comes to financial literacy or economic knowledge (e.g., [17, 18, 20]). However, rather than presenting this discrepancy as a gender issue, scholars believe that males and females are socialized in distinct ways that make economic topics more or less relevant to them [38]. For example, a study of US introductory economic textbooks has shown that 90% of the examples of economists, policy makers, or business leaders are male [40]. In fact, research on financial literacy has also identified environmental and social factors to be related to financial literacy. For example, Kovarova-Simecek and Aubram [41] showed that among a small sample in Austria, the preferred source of financial information are family, friends, and colleagues. Furthermore, Kim et al. [42] have shown that the parental and social environment in which young adults grow up can influence their financial behavior. In other words, the way parents teach their children or raise awareness on how to deal with money and financial matters can have a positive impact on adults' financial behavior later in life. Indeed, Loibl and Hira [43] found a medium bivariate positive and significant correlation ($r = 0.24$) between financial management practices and self-directed financial learning. For this reason, we also want to test whether the ability for personal finance management works as an antecedent to the understanding of financial institutions, in both Germany and the UK. The second hypothesis therefore reads:

H2: A better awareness of personal finance management is related to a better understanding of the role and functions of financial institutions.

2.2 Economic news use and financial understanding

Few scholars in communication science have researched the role of economic news for financial knowledge or understanding. Kalogeropoulos et al. [44] are among the few that have analyzed how the consumption of economic news affects economic sophistication in Denmark. Usually, this stream of research can be situated within the economics, finance, or business discipline (e.g., [20, 22]). Yet, only a small number of scholars in these research fields consider news use as one of the main influencing variables for economic knowledge and rather treat news use as a third variable (e.g., [19]). Moreover, economic news use is sometimes not measured in an adequate way and leaves room for measurement error. For example, Kalogeropoulos et al. [44] measured economic news use as a combination of a general media exposure measure and the results of a content analysis of economic news in Danish news (cf. economic consequence frame).

Based on findings of political news and its influence on political knowledge (e.g., [45–49]), scholars agree that the news media (e.g., television, newspaper, radio, the Internet) play a crucial role in mediating financial information to the public (e.g., [21, 50]). Interestingly, the argument that individuals might use the news media to get an idea of the current economic situation or economic forecasts was put forward already, around thirty years ago [51]. In fact, survey findings indicate that the news media are a preferred source to learn about money management (e.g., [52]), and more lately, research has shown that seeking financial information on social media or online can lead to greater levels of financial literacy [53] or increased financial satisfaction [43, 54]. For example, a study among South Korean youth found that use of media for financial information was strongly and positively related to financial literacy [22].

There is also some indication that economic news use could potentially close the financial knowledge gap between high- and low-income earners, as low-income consumers prefer to learn about the economy via media sources [55]. However, the picture is varied and can depend on external events and the national context. A recent study using cognitive mapping has shown that while general news consumption is connected to a lower complex understanding of the Global Financial Crisis 2007–2009 (GFC) among Dutch citizens, news uses specifically dealing with the GFC are related to higher cognitive complexity when making sense about the GFC but only among the less-educated citizens [46]. Conversely, another study conducted in the Netherlands implies that more news consumption is not necessarily correlated with a better understanding of economic indicators, such as inflation [56]. However, it should be noted here that reading popular newspapers does not guarantee that one comes across or actively consumes economic information. Economic news consumption itself can be influenced by additional external factors. For example, Knowles and Schifferes [21] showed that business and economic news have been used more intensively by UK citizens in 2011 (after GFC) when compared to 2005.

Some recent research investigating the link between economic news use and financial literacy indicates that there might indeed be a correlation. For example, Kovarova-Simecek and Aubram [41] have presented initial results from a convenience sample in Austria that show that there is a positive relationship between the use of financial magazines, the Internet, and newspapers and financial literacy. In addition, van Rooij et al. [25] showed that individuals who scored higher on financial literacy mostly relied on formal sources such as newspapers, financial advisors, and the Internet. More recently, Hayo and Neuenkirch [20] have shown that the use of various media channels (e.g., newspapers, TV) for information about the ECB is positively related with subjective and objective knowledge about the ECB. Thus, following the argumentation above and the findings from previous research, we presume:

H3: The more citizens consume economic news, the higher their perceived understanding of the role and functions of financial institutions.

2.3 The moderating effect of need for economic news

We know from previous research that cognitive elaboration, or the need to be informed, is a crucial factor for the positive effect of news on political behavioral or attitudinal variables [48]. However, only recently, research on financial literacy and economic knowledge has been considering further influencing variables, such as interest in a topic [19, 57] or personal involvement [50]. Sohn et al. [22] argue that using the news media for economic information requires a conscious and active information-seeking behavior, hence implying an intrinsic interest in economic topics. Based on their results, they contended that "gaining financial literacy through media sources is indicative of a young person's active effort to seek personal finance information" ([22], 977).

Equally, Hayo and Neuenkirch [20] have shown that the desire to be informed about the ECB is significantly and positively related to information search and knowledge about the ECB. Similar findings have been reported by van der Cruijsen et al. [57] who found that Dutch respondents with a strong desire to be informed about the ECB and who use various media sources more frequently are more knowledgeable about the ECB. Following these findings, the effect of economic news use on the understanding of financial institutions might be moderated by the conscious and cognitive need to obtain financial information from the media. We thus presume:

H4: The relationship between economic news on perceived understanding of the role and functions of financial institutions is moderated by the need to stay informed about the economy such that the relationship is stronger for those with a higher need to stay informed about the economy.

2.4 Germany and the UK: Two cases in Western democracies

Germany is known as one of the strongest economies in the world, based on nominal GDP [58]. Compared to other countries, financial literacy is moderately high (66%), according to the Standard & Poor's report [29]. However, Hayo and Neuenkirch [20] report that both subjective and objective knowledge about monetary policy and the ECB is rather low among Germans and that they generally have a low interest in these topics. Studying perceived understanding of financial institutions among German citizens is particularly interesting, as Germany has not only faced its biggest post-war fraud scandal with Wirecard in 2020 [59], but it was also one of the European countries that was affected the most by a tax fraud scheme, called "cum-ex" or "cum-cum," that deprived the German state's tax offices of €31.8 billion in total [60].

According to the Standard & Poor's Report mentioned above, financial literacy in the UK is in a similar region to Germany (67%) [29]. Nonetheless, financial literacy remains weak across a wide swathe of the UK public, particularly among women and low-income groups [21]. According to a survey conducted at the height of the pandemic [30], more than half of the UK survey respondents were not sure what GDP meant, and nearly half were not sure they understood government borrowing. People were most confident at understanding unemployment, but one-third were not sure about either interest rates or inflation. The lack of financial literacy makes it harder to ensure that all sections of the community can engage in an economic debate. Although the two countries show similarities in terms of citizens' financial literacy, the two countries differ regarding their media systems. While Germany can be situated within the corporatist model with a high newspaper circulation, strong state intervention in the media system, and institutionalized self-regulation, the UK has the characteristics of a liberal media system, being market dominated and having no institutionalized self-regulation [61]. Therefore, we are interested in the following:

RQ1: What are the differences between Germany and the UK regarding the influence of economic news use on the understanding of financial institutions in both countries?

3. Method and data

3.1 Survey design and sample descriptions

To find answers to the research questions and hypotheses, two online surveys were conducted in Germany in June 2019 and the UK in December 2018, with a panel of respondents provided by Qualtrics. The survey has been approved by the Ethics Committee of the MDX Faculty of Arts and Creative Industries at Middlesex University London, and respondents were provided with an appropriate informed consent on the first page of the online survey. In total, 233 people in Germany and 284 people in the UK were recruited through Qualtrics that resembled the national population of German and UK citizens based on a range of socio-demographic variables, including age and gender. The sample in Germany was balanced with 50.6% male and 49.4% female participants, being on average between 35 and 44 years old (M = 3.35/SD = 1.50), earning on average between €20,000 and €29,999 and €30,000 and €49,999 (M = 2.89/SD = 1.65), and having an average education level of Abitur (M = 3.00/SD = 1.80). The UK sample had slightly more female participants (45.4% male; 54.6% female), an average age between 35 and 44 years (M = 3.36/SD = 1.56), an average income between £20,000 and £29,999, and an average education level at the A level (M = 3.06/SD = 1.96). Only regarding the variable ethnicity, both samples are characterized by an over-representation of white participants (Germany: 93.6% white, 6.4% non-white; UK: 91.9% white, 8.1% non-white). The measurements of all key variables per country are described below in detail (see the descriptive of all key variables in **Table 1**).

3.2 Measurements

Perceived understanding of financial institutions was measured by asking "How well do you understand the role and function of the following institutions" (1 = never heard of them; 4 = very well) for six various financial institutions in the respective country (Germany: $\alpha = 0.92$; UK: $\alpha = 0.87$). For the UK, these were (a) Bank of England, (b) HM Treasury, (c) HMRC (Inland Revenue), (d) DWP (Department of Work and Pensions), (e) OBR (Office of Budget Responsibility), and (e) FCA (Financial Conduct Authority). For Germany, these were (a) Bundesbank, (b) Federal Ministry of Finance, (c) Federal Central Tax Office, (d) The Federal Ministry of Labour and Social Affairs, (e) European Central Bank, and (f) Federal Financial Supervisory Authority (Bafin). Following previous research on the understanding of monetary policy [20] and consumer research that consciously distinguishes between

Variables	Germany		UK	
	M	SD	M	SD
Perceived understanding of financial institutions	2.67	0.69	2.61	0.62
Personal finance management	2.34	0.45	3.43	0.53
Economic news use	3.27	0.84	3.10	1.02
Need for economic information	2.24	0.75	2.31	0.73

Table 1.
Descriptive for key variables in the German and UK sample.

objective and subjective knowledge [62], we chose "perceived" understanding because it's indicative for individuals' decision-making processes. See the means of the understanding of the various financial institutions in Germany and the UK in **Figures 1** and 2.

To measure to what extent citizens were aware and knowledgeable about how to manage their personal finances, we used a common measurement for personal finance management [63], consisting of four questions: "Thinking overall about your, and your partner/spouse's finances, how important, if at all, do you think it is to..." (1 = not important; 4 = very important) (1) save money for a rainy day, (2) put aside money for your retirement, (3) keep track of income and expenditure, and (4) shop around in order to make your money go further (reversed). However, due to a low reliability score, we dropped the fourth, reversed question (as proposed by the R-function alpha), which yielded a satisfactory reliability score (Germany: $\alpha = 0.65$; UK: $\alpha = 0.67$).

Economic news use was inquired by posing three questions: (1) "To what extent do you AGREE or DISAGREE with the following statement? 'I regularly read the financial pages in the papers or online'" (1 = disagree; 4 = agree); (2) "Thinking

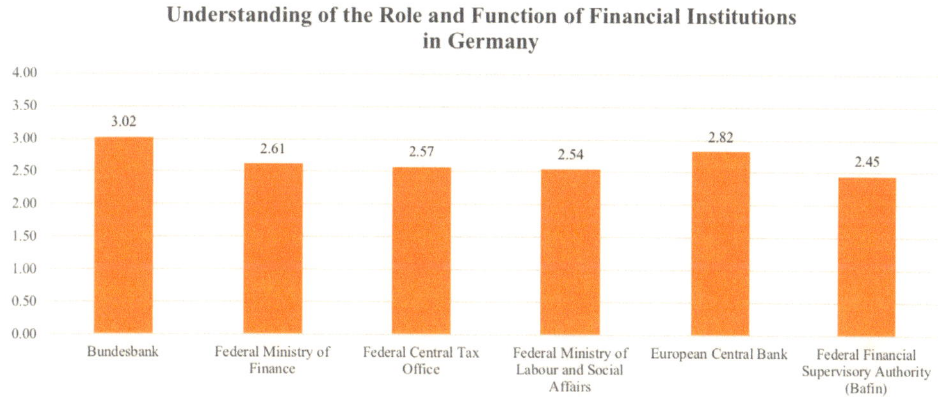

Figure 1.
Means for perceived understanding of the role and function of various financial institutions in Germany.

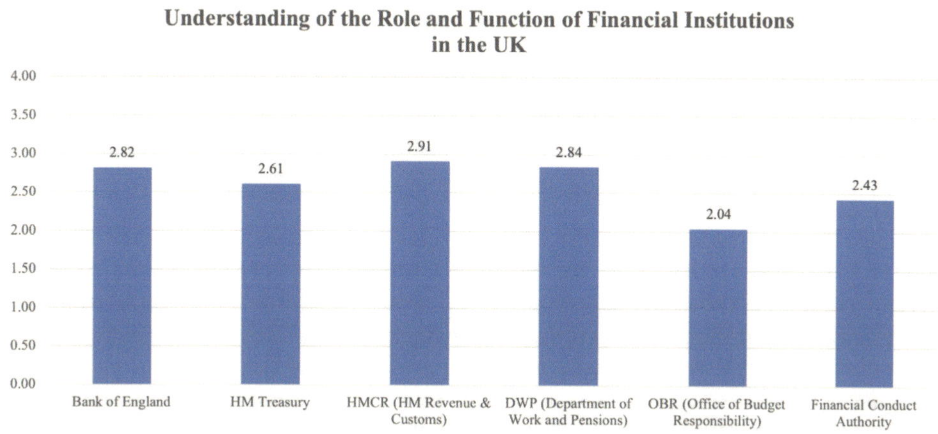

Figure 2.
Means for perceived understanding of the role and function of various financial institutions in the UK.

	Variables	1	2	3	4
1	Perceived understanding of financial institutions	—			
2	Personal finance management	0.21**	—		
3	Economic news use	0.54***	0.22**	—	
4	Need for economic information	0.40***	0.23***	0.48***	—

** $p < 0.01$.
*** $p < 0.001$.

Table 2.
Zero-order correlations among all key variables in the German sample.

	Variables	1	2	3	4
1	Perceived understanding of financial institutions	—			
2	Personal finance management	0.27***	—		
3	Economic news use	0.55***	0.29***	—	
4	Need for economic information	0.36***	0.35***	0.49***	—

** $p < 0.01$.
*** $p < 0.001$.

Table 3.
Zero-order correlations among all key variables in the UK sample.

more generally, how closely have you been following the news about the state of the economy and its future prospects?" (1 = not at all closely; 4 = very closely); and (3) "How frequently do you follow the news about business and the economy?" (1 = I do not follow this type of news, 2 = less than once a month, 3 = once a month, 4 = once a week, 5 = several times a week, 6 = every day). Although we used different wordings and answer scales for this measurement, the reliability score is sufficient (Germany: $\alpha = 0.75$; UK: $\alpha = 0.77$).

The moderator need for economic information was measured by asking a single question: "In your opinion, how important is it for people like you to keep up-to-date with what's happening in financial matters generally such as the economy and your personal finances?" (0 = do not know/no opinion; 1 = not at all important; 3 = very important). The covariate matrix of all key variables for both countries are shown in **Tables 2** and **3**.

3.3 Analysis

To test the hypotheses, we conducted hierarchical regression analysis with listwise deletion in five steps for the German and the UK sample, respectively. In the first block, we only included the sociodemographic variables to predict understanding of financial institutions and test H1. In the second, we added personal finance management to test H2. In the third block, we included economic news use to test H3. In the fourth step, we added need for economic news. To test the moderation effect (H4), we included the interaction effect in the next step. We have checked the regression analysis (excluding the moderation) for robustness and found no indicators that would cause concern for a non-normal, skewed model (e.g., VIF, Cook's distance, Durbin Watson Test).

4. Results

The results (**Table 4**) show that H1 is partly supported for both countries. In all five models for the German sample, we find that men (b) and highly educated (c) and higher earning citizens (d) have a significantly better perceived understanding of financial institutions. Regarding age (a) or ethnicity (e), we do not find any significant relationship. For the UK sample (**Table 5**), only gender seems to be

	Perceived understanding of the role and functions of financial institutions				
	Model 1	**Model 2**	**Model 3**	**Model 4**	**Model 5**
Block 1: Socio-demographics					
Age	0.05 (0.03)	0.08 (0.03)	0.05 (0.02)	0.06 (0.02)	0.07 (0.02)
Gender (1 = Male)	**−0.25*** (0.08)**	**−0.25*** (0.08)**	**−0.16** (0.07)**	**−0.17** (0.07)**	**−0.18** (0.07)**
Education	**0.17** (0.02)**	**0.14* (0.02)**	**0.13* (0.02)**	**0.13* (0.02)**	**0.13* (0.02)**
Income	**0.33*** (0.02)**	**0.32*** (0.02)**	**0.19** (0.02)**	**0.17** (0.02)**	**0.17** (0.02)**
Ethnicity (1 = White)	0.004 (0.16)	0.01 (0.16)	−0.03 (0.14)	−0.02 (0.14)	−0.02 (0.14)
R^2	24.4%				
Block 2: Financial Socialization					
Personal Finance Mng.		**0.17** (0.09)**	0.08 (0.08)	0.06 (0.08)	0.07 (0.08)
R^2		27%			
Block 3: Economic News Use					
Economic News Use			**0.41*** (0.05)**	**0.33*** (0.05)**	0.23 (0.13)
R^2			40.7%		
Block 4: Need for Economic News					
Need for Econ. Info.				**0.19** (0.06)**	0.03 (0.20)
R^2				43.3%	
Block 5: Interaction					
Economic News Use x Need for Economic Information					0.23 (0.06)
Total R^2					43.4%

*$p < 0.05$.
**$p < 0.01$.
***$p < 0.001$.
Notes: Cell entries are final-entry ordinary least squares (OLS) and standardized Beta (β) coefficients; standard errors in parentheses; n = 217 (after listwise deletion); bolded results are within normal confidence intervals based on 5000 bootstraps.

Table 4.
Hierarchical regression analyses predicting the perceived understanding of the role and functions of financial institutions—German sample.

	Perceived understanding of the role and functions of financial institutions				
	Model 1	**Model 2**	**Model 3**	**Model 4**	**Model 5**
Block 1: Socio-demographics					
Age	0.04 (0.03)	−0.04 (0.03)	−0.02 (0.02)	−0.002 (0.02)	0.01 (0.02)
Gender (1 = Male)	**−0.20** (0.08)**	**−0.22** (0.08)**	−0.11 (0.07)	−0.11 (0.07)	−0.11 (0.07)
Education	0.09 (0.02)	0.06 (0.02)	−0.001 (0.02)	−0.003(0.02)	0.01 (0.02)
Income	0.09 (0.03)	0.09 (0.03)	0.05 (0.02)	0.05 (0.02)	0.03 (0.02)
Ethnicity (1 = White)	−0.02 (0.13)	−0.03 (0.13)	−0.06 (0.11)	−0.06 (0.11)	−0.06 (0.11)
R^2	7.1%				
Block 2: Financial Socialization					
Personal Finance Mng.		**0.24*** (0.07)**	**0.12* (0.06)**	0.09 (0.07)	0.08 (0.06)
R^2		12.5%			
Block 3: Economic News Use					
Economic News Use			**0.51*** (0.03)**	**0.47*** (0.04)**	−0.01 (0.11)
R^2			35.3%		
Block 4: Need for Economic News					
Need for Econ. Info.				0.09 (0.06)	−0.27 (0.13)
R^2				35.8%	
Block 5: Interaction					
Economic News Use x Need for Economic Information					**0.75** (0.04)**
Total R^2					38.5%

* *$p < 0.05$.*
** *$p < 0.01$.*
*** *$p < 0.001$.*
Note: Cell entries are final-entry ordinary least squares (OLS) and standardized Beta (β) coefficients; standard errors in parentheses; n = 260 (after listwise deletion); bolded results are within normal confidence intervals based on 5000 bootstraps.

Table 5.
Hierarchical regression analyses predicting the perceived understanding of the role and functions of financial institutions—UK sample.

negatively associated with the outcome variable, as the data show that women have less understanding of financial institutions than men, but this relationship vanishes once the models include economic news use, need for economic information, and the interaction effect. Regarding H2, we find partial support in both the German and the UK sample. For Germany, the relationship only holds in Model 2. For the UK sample, there is a positive, significant relationship between better awareness of personal finance management and the perceived understanding of the role and function of financial institutions, even when including economic news use (Model 3) but not in Model 4–5.

H3 is largely supported in both samples, meaning that the more German and UK citizens consume economic news, the higher their perceived understanding of financial institutions. However, these significant positive relationships disappear once the interaction effects are added to the respective regression models. In the fifth models of the hierarchical regression analyses, we find support for H4 in the UK sample but not in the German sample. Hence, the relationship between economic news use and perceived understanding of financial institutions is significantly and positively moderated by the need for economic information among UK citizens. The plot of the interaction effect (see **Figure 3**), furthermore, shows that citizens with high levels of economic news use and those with a higher need to stay informed about economic news have a better understanding of financial institutions.

By means of the Johnson-Neyman technique, we show at what levels this moderation effect stays significant for the UK sample. **Figure 4** shows that already by scoring higher than one on the question regarding the need for economic information, the

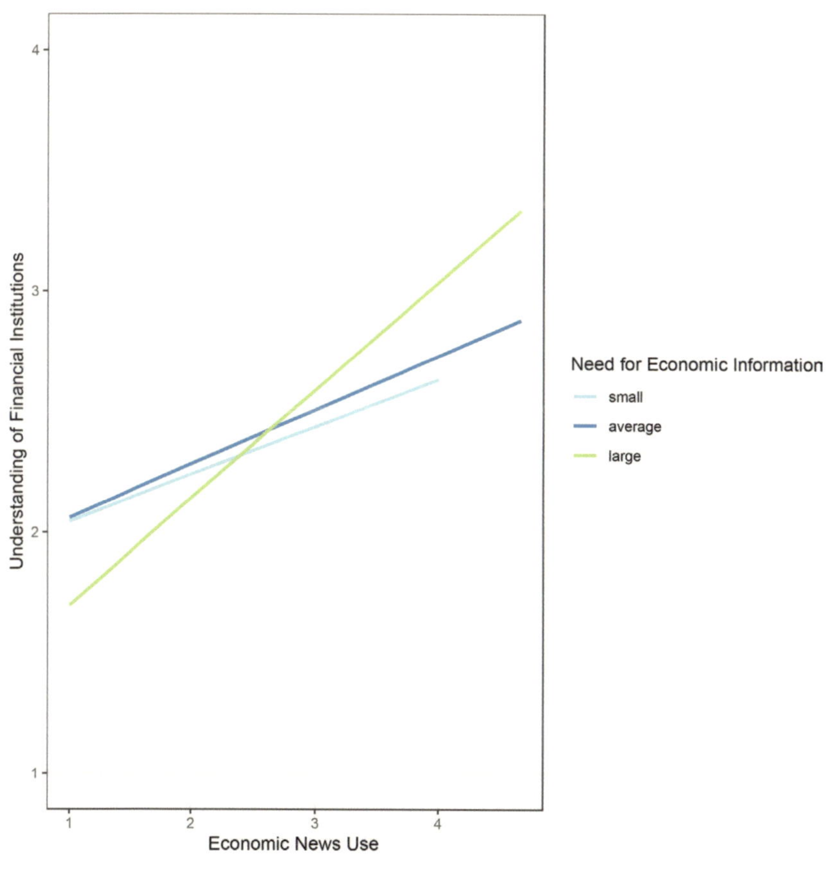

Figure 3.
Conditional plot for interaction effect of economic news use and need for economic information on the perceived understanding of the role and function of financial institutions in the UK sample.

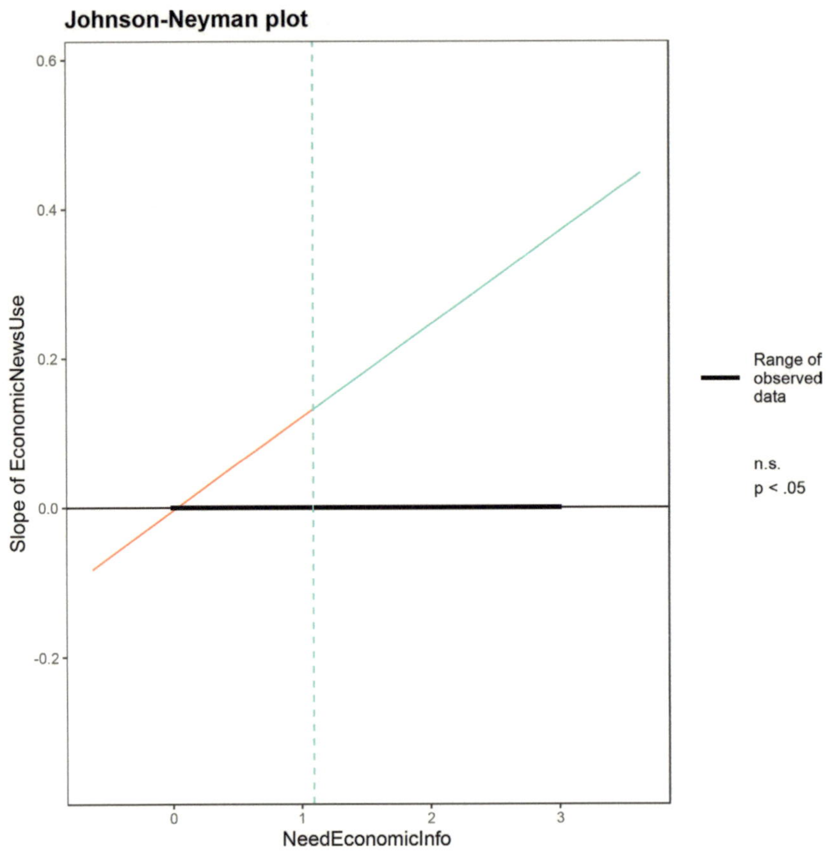

Figure 4.
Johnson-Neyman plot, showing where the conditional slope of economic news use significantly differs from zero.

slope of economic news use becomes positive and significant. Reversely, economic news has no effect on the understanding of financial institutions if the need for economic information is lower than 1.1. We also tested all the regression results and moderation effects for robustness. Bootstrapping results indicate, however, that not all findings are representative of the entire population of German and UK citizens, probably due to the small sample size. The robust coefficients are bolded in **Tables 4** and 5. Hence, generalizations for the German and UK populations need to be considered with caution.

5. Discussion

Understanding the function and role of financial institutions plays a crucial role for a well-functioning democracy. As we argue, only by keeping themselves well-informed about economic topics and institutions, citizens can develop a sound understanding and a critical perspective about the financial system. This enables them to cast deliberative votes and become engaged for a more transparent, just, and sustainable financial system. Scholars in economics, finance, as well as communication science have argued that the news media provide relevant information that contributes to and fosters financial literacy and knowledge [20, 21, 41]. However, only few researchers (e.g., [20]) have also looked at how economic news use can contribute to a better understanding of financial institutions.

In this study, we sought to study how economic news use is related to the perceived understanding of the role and function of financial institutions in Germany and the UK. Our survey results provide clear evidence that there is a significant relationship between economic news use and understanding of financial institutions in both countries. What is more, this study has corroborated previous research on financial literacy [17, 23], showing that the perceived understanding of financial institutions is positively related with education and income and negatively related with being female. However, these findings were more robust and present in the German sample. Similarly, financial socialization or, in other words, the awareness for managing one's personal finances was not a steady influencing factor for the perceived understanding of financial institutions.

Another interesting result of this study was the moderation effect found in the UK sample. Here, it was revealed that the relationship between economic news use and the understanding of financial institutions is stronger for those people who have a higher need to stay informed about the economy. This result does not only support findings on ECB information seeking and knowledge about the ECB [33, 57], it is also in line with findings from political communication where the need for (political) information has repeatedly been shown to play a crucial role in learning from information consumed via the news media (e.g., [47–49]). Hence, rather than providing information in school programs on financial education, teachers should prioritize media literacy and encourage students' curiosity and engagement with financial and economic topics so that they understand the importance of finance in their daily lives. In fact, previous research suggests that merely providing financial information to adolescents is not sufficient to increase financial literacy [18]. Instead, training and workshops should have an attitudinal and practical component to enhance experiential learning that will ultimately lead to better results in financial literacy.

Furthermore, in line with the differences of the media systems in the UK and Germany [61], the findings highlight that the relationship between economic news use and the perceived understanding of financial institutions seems to be higher in the liberal media system in the UK, while in the democratic corporatist model in Germany, sociodemographic data matter more in explaining the understanding of financial institutions in the respective country. It could be possible that the medium newspaper circulation in the liberal model in the UK could be more decisive in explaining the outcome knowledge variable, compared to the democratic corporatist model where newspaper circulation is generally high. What is more, the market-dominated media market in the UK as well as the strong presence of the flagship financial newspaper *Financial Times* in the country might carry more weight in explaining why the relationship between reading economic news and scoring higher on the perceived understanding of financial institutions is stronger for UK citizens than for German citizens—and this despite the fact that the mean value of economic news use was higher in Germany when compared to the UK.

For financial journalism practice, the findings of this study imply several things. First, news media outlets should become more aware of the significance of financial and economic news for their audience. Although the economic news beat is a niche in general news reporting, receiving only limited attention from its audience [64], the findings in this study have shown that economic news use plays an important role in contributing to the perceived understanding of citizens about financial institutions. Second, based on the results from this study, financial journalists should feel more engaged and motivated to make their coverage more attractive to the general audience, especially for women and those on low incomes. For example, a survey study by Knowles and Schifferes [21] revealed that citizens in the UK thought that the financial media should explain economic events in a clearer and easier language and that they should describe better how economic developments affect them as citizens personally. Following the relationships identified in this study, journalists have evidence that their work matters in educating the public on financial topics and institutions. Thus, by making economic news more attractive (e.g., choice of topics or presentation mode), financial journalists have the potential to activate, educate, and engage a broader and more critical audience for economic issues.

Although the regression models were found to be largely robust and most of the results were representative of the population, the study does not come without limitations. First, it would be worthwhile to repeat the survey among a larger representative sample in both countries, given that the bootstrapping results revealed that some estimates were out of the confidence interval bounds. In fact, the survey samples had an over-representation of white respondents in both countries, compared to the national censuses. In addition, some of the measurements should be further developed, added, and improved. For example, the "need for economic information" should not be measured by a single item, and financial socialization could be measured by additional questions [41, 42]. Furthermore, the answer scales of the survey questions should be kept similar across the measurements (cf. economic news use) in future research. In addition, previous research has shown that asking for perceived or subjective knowledge can sometimes lead to overestimations. Hayo and Neuenkirch [20], for example, report that "particularly disinterested men tend to overestimate their own monetary policy knowledge" (p. 19). Hence, rather than only asking for perceived knowledge, objective knowledge questions for the understanding of financial institutions should be composed in a follow-up study.

Despite these shortcomings, this cross-national survey study has provided useful and first-time insights into the influencing variables of the perceived understanding of financial institutions in Germany and the UK. By working out the pivotal role of economic news use consumption, this study has not only shown that the news media should be attributed more relevance in financial education programs, but the study has also formulated directive implications for financial journalism and practice. To sum up, economic journalists need to take a range of socio-demographic factors into account when they write for a broad audience, so that those from lower incomes, who have less education, women, and those with a lower need to stay informed about the economy are not left out of important discussions.

Conflict of interest

The authors report there are no competing interests to declare.

The data set associated with the paper can be requested from the corresponding author.

Author details

Nadine Strauß[1]*, Sophie Knowles[2] and Vesile Cinceoglu[1]

1 Department of Communication and Media Research, University of Zurich, Zurich, Switzerland

2 Department of Media, Middlesex University London, UK

*Address all correspondence to: n.strauss@ikmz.uzh.ch

References

[1] Romei V, Smith A. Global inflation tracker: See how your country compares on rising prices. *Financial Times*. 2023. Available from: https://www.ft.com/content/088d3368-bb8b-4ff3-9df7-a7680d4d81b2

[2] Chancel L. World Inequality Report 2022. Wid World. 2022. Available from: https://wir2022.wid.world/www-site/uploads/2022/01/Summary_WorldInequalityReport2022_English.pdf

[3] Christian A. How the cost-of-living crisis is fuelling job quits. BBC. 2023. Available from: https://www.bbc.com/worklife/article/20230713-how-the-cost-of-living-crisis-is-fuelling-jobquits

[4] Stern LN, Lankes HP, Pierfederici R. These are the 4 steps we need to make economic growth sustainable, resilient and inclusive. WEF. 2022. Available from: https://www.weforum.org/agenda/2022/07/sustainable-resilient-inclusive-economic-growth/

[5] Kyrtsou C, Sornette D, Adcock C. New Facets of Economic Complexity in Modern Financial Markets. New York: Routledge; 2019

[6] Raworth K. Doughnut Economics. Seven Ways to Think like a 21st-Century Economist. London: Penguin Random House; 2017

[7] Mazzucato M. The Value of Everything. Making and Taking in the Global Economy. London: Penguin Random House; 2019

[8] Epstein GA. Financialization and the World Economy. Cheltenham: Edward Elgar Publishing; 2005

[9] Storbeck O. Wirecard: A record of deception, disarray and mismanagement. *Financial Times*. 2021. Available from: https://www.ft.com/content/15bb36e7-54dc-463a-a6d5-70fc38a11c81

[10] Ferree MM, Gamson WA, Gerhards J, Rucht D. Four models of the public sphere in modern democracies. Theory and Society. 2002;**31**(3):289-324

[11] Gans HJ. Democracy and the News. New York: Oxford University Press; 2003

[12] Strömbäck J. In search of a standard: Four models of democracy and their normative implications for journalism. Journalism Studies. 2005;**6**(3):331-345

[13] Davis A. Media effects and the active elite audience: A study of communications in the London stock exchange. European Journal of Communication. 2005;**20**(3):303-326

[14] Greenfield C, Williams P. Financialization, finance rationality and the role of media in Australia. Media, Culture & Society. 2007;**29**(3):415-433

[15] Lee M. A review of communication scholarship on the financial markets and the financial media. International Journal of Communication. 2014;**8**:715-736

[16] Thompson PA. Invested interests? Reflexivity, representation and reporting in financial markets. Journalism. 2013;**14**(2):208-227

[17] Lusardi A, Mitchelli OS. Planning and financial literacy: How do women fare? American Economic Review. 2008;**98**(2):413-417

[18] Lusardi A, Mitchell OS, Curto V. Financial literacy among the young. Journal of Consumer Affairs. 2010;**44**(2):358-380

[19] Förster M, Happ R. The relationship among gender, interest in economic topics, media use, and the economic knowledge of students at vocational schools. Citizenship, Social and Economics Education. 2019;**18**(3):143-157

[20] Hayo B, Neuenkirch E. The influence of media use on layperson monetary policy knowledge in Germany. Scottish Journal of Political Economy. 2018;**65**(1):1-26

[21] Knowles S, Schifferes S. Financial capability, the financial crisis and trust in news media. Journal of Applied Journalism & Media Studies. 2020;**9**(1):61-83

[22] Sohn S-H, Joo S-H, Grable JE, Lee S, Kim M. Adolescents' financial literacy: The role of financial socialization agents, financial experiences, and money attitudes in shaping financial literacy among South Korean youth. Journal of Adolescence. 2012;**35**(4):969-980

[23] Lusardi A, Mitchelli OS. Financial literacy around the world: An overview. Journal of Pension Economics & Finance. 2011;**10**(4):497-508

[24] Atkinson A, Messy F-A. Measuring financial literacy: Results of the OECD/ international network on financial education (INFE) pilot study. OECD Working Papers on Finance, Insurance and Private Pensions. 2012;**15**:1-73

[25] Rooij V, Maarten CJ, Lusardi A, Alessie RJM. Financial literacy, retirement planning and household wealth. The Economic Journal. 2012;**122**(560):449-478

[26] Lusardi A, Mitchelli OS. Financial literacy and retirement preparedness: Evidence and implications for financial education. Business Economics. 2007;**42**(1):35-44

[27] Clark RL, Morrill MS, Allen SG. The role of financial literacy in determining retirement plans. Economic Inquiry. 2012;**50**(4):851-866

[28] Lusardi A, Tufano P. Debt literacy, financial experiences, and overindebtedness. Journal of Pension Economics & Finance. 2015;**14**(4):332-368

[29] Klapper L, Lusardi A, Oudheusden V. Financial Literacy around the World: Insights from the Standard & Poor's Ratings Services Global Financial Literacy Survey. GFLEC (Global Financial Literacy Excellence Center); 2015. Available from: https://gflec.org/initiatives/sp-global-finlit-survey/

[30] Schifferes S, Knowles S. Covid-19, inequality and the media. In: Schifferes S, Knowles S, editors. The Media and Inequality. London: Routledge; 2022. pp. 211-225

[31] Schnabel I. Societal responsibility and central bank independence. European Central Bank. Eurosystem. 2021. Available from: https://www.ecb.europa.eu/press/key/date/2021/html/ecb.sp210527_1~ae50e2be97.en.html

[32] Ehrmann M, Soudan M, Stracca L. Explaining European Union citizens' trust in the European Central Bank in normal and crisis times. The Scandinavian Journal of Economics. 2013;**115**(3):781-807

[33] Hayo B, Neuenkirch E. The German public and its trust in the ECB: The role of knowledge and information search. Journal of International Money and Finance. 2014;**47**:286-303

[34] Hayo B. Knowledge and attitude towards European monetary

union. Journal of Policy Modeling. 1999;**21**(5):641-651

[35] Ranyard R, Missier D, Fabio B, Nicolao D, Summers B. Perceptions and expectations of price changes and inflation: A review and conceptual framework. Journal of Economic Psychology. 2008;**29**(4):378-400

[36] Lusardi A. Financial literacy and the need for financial education: Evidence and implications. Swiss Journal of Economics and Statistics. 2019;**155**(1):1-8

[37] Bianchi M. Financial literacy and portfolio dynamics. The Journal of Finance. 2018;**73**(2):831-859

[38] Driva A, Lührmann M, Winter J. Gender differences and stereotypes in financial literacy: Off to an early start. Economics Letters. 2016;**146**:143-146

[39] Sabri MF, Cook CC, Gudmunson CG. Financial well-being of Malaysian college students. Asian Education and Development Studies. 2012;**1**(2):153-170

[40] Stevenson B, Zlotnik H. Representations of men and women in introductory economics textbooks. AEA Papers and Proceedings. 2018;**108**:180-185

[41] Kovarova-Simecek M, Aubram T. 'Financial literacy, information behavior, and interest in financial news in Austria', social science research. Network. 2018;**2018**:1-34

[42] Kim J, Chatterjee S, Kim J. Outstanding AFCPE® conference paper: Debt burden of young adults in the United States. Journal of Financial Counseling and Planning. 2012;**23**(2):5-67

[43] Loibl C, Hira TK. Self-directed financial learning and financial satisfaction. Journal of Financial Counseling and Planning. 2005;**16**(1):11-21

[44] Kalogeropoulos, Antonios, Albæk, Erik, de Vreese, Claes H., Van Dalen, Arjen (2015), 'The predictors of economic sophistication: Media, interpersonal communication and negative economic experiences', European Journal of Communication 30(4): 385-403.

[45] Beckers K, Aelst V, Peter V, d'Haenens L. What do people learn from following the news? A diary study on the influence of media use on knowledge of current news stories. European Journal of Communication. 2021;**36**(3):254-269

[46] Boukes M, van Esch FAWJ, Snellens JA, Steenman SC, Vliegenthart R. Using cognitive mapping to study the relationship between news exposure and cognitive complexity. Public Opinion Quarterly. 2020;**84**(3):599-628

[47] Boulianne S. Stimulating or reinforcing political interest: Using panel data to examine reciprocal effects between news media and political interest. Political Communication. 2011;**28**(2):147-162

[48] Jr E, William P, Hayes AF, Shah DV, Kwak N. Understanding the relationship between communication and political knowledge: A model comparison approach using panel data. Political Communication. 2005;**22**(4):423-446

[49] Xenos M, Moy P. Direct and differential effects of the internet on political and civic engagement. Journal of Communication. 2007;**57**(4):704-718

[50] Wang S-LA. Financial Communications: Information Processing, Media Integration, and

Ethical Considerations. First ed. New York: Palgrave Macmillan; 2013

[51] MacKuen MB, Erikson RS, Stimson JA. Peasants or bankers? The American electorate and the US economy. American Political Science Review. 1992;**86**(3):597-611

[52] Hilgert MA, Hogarth JM, Beverly SG. Household financial management: The connection between knowledge and behavior. Federal Reserve Bulletin. 2003;**89**:309-322

[53] Sabri MF, Aw EC-X. Financial literacy and related outcomes: The role of financial information sources'. International Journal of Business and Society. 2019;**20**(1):286-298

[54] Cao Y, Liu J. Financial executive orientation, information source, and financial satisfaction of young adults. Journal of Financial Counseling and Planning. 2017;**28**(1):5-19

[55] Rhine SLW, Toussaint-Comeau M. Adult preferences for the delivery of personal finance information. Journal of Financial Counseling and Planning. 2002;**13**(2):11-26

[56] Jansen D-J, Neuenkirch M. Does the media help the general public in understanding inflation? Oxford Bulletin of Economics and Statistics. 2018;**80**(6):1185-1212

[57] van der Cruijsen C, de Haan J, Jansen D-J, Mosch R. Knowledge and opinions about banking supervision: Evidence from a survey of Dutch households. Journal of Financial Stability. 2013;**9**(2):219-229

[58] Worldbank. Gross Domestic Product 2020. World Development Indicators Database. 2020. Available from: https://databank.worldbank.org/data/download/GDP.pdf

[59] Reuters. Timeline: The rise and fall of Wirecard, a German tech champion. *Reuters*. 2021. Available from: https://www.reuters.com/article/us-germany-wirecard-inquiry-timeline-idUSKBN2B811J

[60] Correctiv. The Cumex Files. A Cross-Border Investigation. Correctiv. 2018. Available from: https://correctiv.org/en/top-stories-en/2018/10/18/the-cumex-files/

[61] Hallin DC, Mancini P. Comparing Media Systems. Cambridge: Cambridge University Press; 2004

[62] Moorman C, Diehl K, Brinberg D, Kidwell B. Subjective knowledge, search locations, and consumer choice. Journal of Consumer Research. 2004;**31**(3):673-680

[63] Atkinson A, McKay S, Kempson E, Collard SS. Levels of financial capability in the UK: Results of a baseline survey. Public Money and Management. 2006;**27**(1):29-36

[64] Strauß N. Financial journalism in today's high-frequency news and information era. Journalism. 2019;**20**(2):274-291

Chapter 11

Market Shocks, Financial Literacy, and Net Worth

Ayo Teriba

Abstract

Global shocks typically inflict large persistent contractions on commodity prices compared to small transitory contractions on equity prices. The resulting output headwinds and asset tailwinds set the global income statement and balance sheet on divergent paths. *The cognitive capability* to trace the exposures of income statement transactions and balance sheet portfolios to *global shocks* and the *adaptive capacity* to *take steps to cover exposures* become essential for modulating the pass-through from global shocks to global wealth or net worth. While output-centric literacy remains a crucial determinant of net worth, the realities of smaller and uneven margins along value chains compared to larger capital gains across asset types mean that asset-centric literacy is the most critical determinant of net worth. Each country's performance across three criteria- GDP *growth, FDI stock, and servitization-* should identify her as an *adjuster* who *possesses the cognitive and adaptive capabilities to modulate the pass-through from global shocks to national liquidity, sectoral resilience, and growth,* or as a *non-adjuster* who *needs these capabilities*. We highlight measures of global shocks that global watchdogs must now emphasize, and we offer strategic insights on how country managers can modulate pass-through from global shocks to wealth.

Keywords: global shocks, cycles, trends, commodity prices, equity prices, exports, FDI stocks, patents, trademarks, migrant stock, migrant ratios, services, industry, growth, liquidity, wealth, net worth, literacy, cognitive, adaptive, exposure, liquidity, financing mix, transactions, portfolios, production, innovation, upstream, midstream, downstream, margins, capital gains, adjusters, non-adjusters

1. Introduction

This paper observes that the global shocks since 2008 typically weaken commodity prices and lift equity prices, the market responses are that global experts are stagnating while global FDI stocks are surging. While global exports and FDI stocks were about US$20 trillion in 2010, exports remained less than US$25 trillion by 2020 while FDI stocks climbed above US$41 trillion in 2020.

Section 2 illustrates how the path of wealth creation opportunities from transactions on the income statement is diverging dramatically from the path of wealth creation opportunities on the balance sheet. In Sections 3 and 4, we discuss what this evolving reality portends for the financial literacy required to shield wealth or net worth from unfavorable transaction shocks while seizing vast opportunities from favorable portfolio shocks.

To gauge exposures, in Section 5, we show that each country's performance across three criteria- GDP *growth, FDI stock, and services growth*-should identify her as an *adjuster* who *possesses the cognitive and adaptive capabilities to modulate the pass-through from global shocks to national liquidity, sectoral resilience, and growth,* or as a *non-adjuster* who *needs these capabilities*.

We then highlight measures of global shocks that global watchdogs must now emphasize, and we offer strategic insights on how country managers can modulate pass-through from global shocks to wealth Section 6. We conclude in Section 7.

2. Global market shocks

2.1 Episodes and triggers

We focus on four episodes of market shocks: the first was the well-documented 2008/2009 Global Financial Crisis (GFC), the second was the quiet technological disruptions from 2011 onwards that preceded the third and fourth well-documented shocks, the Pandemic of 2020/2021, and the geopolitical tensions that were triggered by the Russian invasion of Ukraine in March 2022.

i. *Financial Crisis 2008/2009*

- *Financial* Meltdown: Fall in house prices, the crisis in financial institutions/markets.
- *Economic* Meltdown: Low investor/consumer confidence depressed demand.

ii. *Techno-Economic Disruptions of 2011–2016*

Disruptive adoption of breakthroughs in biotechnology, ecological technology, physical technology, and digital technology created global commodity gluts (across crude oil, crops, livestock, and metals) that precipitated a weakening of commodity prices that started from around 2011 and culminated in steep declines in prices from July 2014.

- *Biotechnology* (genetic modification of crops and livestock, and shale)
- *Ecological technology* (renewable energy, energy storage, carbon capture)
- *Physical technology* (nanotechnology, 3D printing, drones, high-speed rail)
- *Digital technology* (hardware, software, internet, cloud, e-platforms, IoT, robotics, AI)

iii. *Pandemic 2020/2021*

- The outbreak of the COVID-19 pandemic and the resort to non-pharmaceutical measures like social distancing and isolation in the absence of pharmaceutical remedies triggered several rounds of global lockdowns until pharmaceutical therapies were eventually developed.

iv. *Geopolitics 2022/2023*

- The outbreak of the Russian-Ukraine war and the imposition of economic and financial sanctions on Russia disrupted global food and energy supplies, shocking food and energy prices, inflation, stock prices, and interest rates.

2.2 Price shocks

The cumulative effects of the four episodes of market shocks since 2008 have been to break the strongly upward trend that commodity global prices enjoyed since the turn of the millennium while lifting equity prices into a sustained upward and resilient trend.

A comparison of the evolution of commodity price and equity price from January 1990 to July 2023 in **Figure 1** reveals that commodity price suffered more severe shocks from each of the four episodes than equity price.

The cyclical swings in commodity price recorded in 2008/2009 gave way to trend breaks from 2011, while the impact of shocks on equity price remained transitory across the four shocks, to make equity price trend steadily upwards since the early 1990s.

Massive surge in the proliferation of innovations in biotechnology, digitization, and renewable energy has increased supply or reduced demand for commodities-including oil, crops, and livestock- enough to depress their prices and weaken the global income statement. In contrast, the rise in the asset values of the various innovations lifts their equity prices and strengthens the global balance sheet.

Widespread resort to government bailouts from 2006/2009, fiscal stimulus, and eventual massive liquidity injections in the form of quantitative easing to cushion advert effects of incomes lost in the various shocks could also explain the resilience of global equity price and the concomitant pass-through to the global balance sheet.

In summary, the opportunities offered in global markets have thus been punctuated by a series of financial, technological, ecological, biological, and geopolitical shocks on four occasions in the last decade and a half. The typical pattern across global

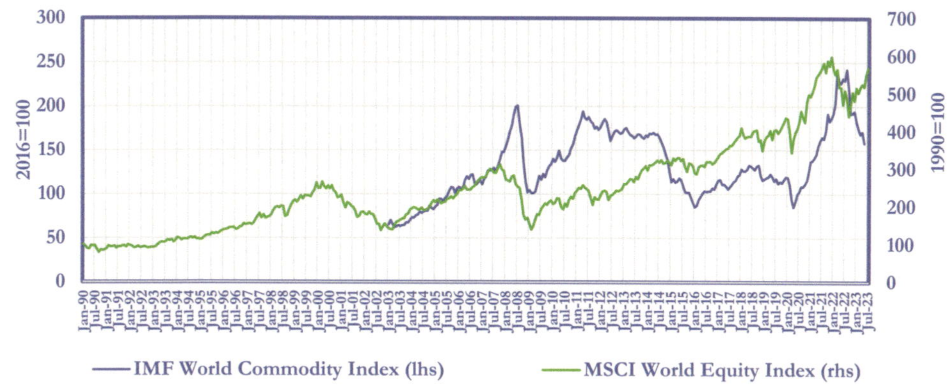

Figure 1.
Global commodity vs. equity index.

shocks is that they inflict larger and longer contractions on commodity prices and more minor and shorter contractions on equity prices.

2.3 Consequences

Since 2008, *global production, and export of industrial, manufactured, agricultural goods, and related commercial services* have decelerated, stagnated, or declined in response to adverse global commodity price developments, while *global asset values, cross-border equity stocks or foreign direct investment (FDI) stocks, and non-commercial services flowing from place-based, space-based, knowledge-based, or skill-based assets* have surged steadily in response to favorable global equity price developments.

These developments have been variously labeled as deindustrialization, servitization, assetization, and/or *financialization. Knowledge, talent, and investment flows are increasingly displacing flows of goods and services as the focal points of global connectedness. There has been a surge in inward* stocks of cross-border equity (a.k.a. foreign direct investment) in search of *four asset clusters-* ideas, skills, physical places, and digital spaces-that could be financialized.

Figure 2 reveals that exports of goods and services that had been the primary focus of global connectedness for centuries have stagnated since 2015 while inward FDI stocks have continued to surge. Consequently, surging global FDI stocks have displaced stagnant global export flows as the of global connectedness and the dominant source of external liquidity.

Figure 3 documents the surge in innovations, **Figure 4** shows the surge in urge in skill migration, **Figure 5** shows the diverging growth paths of services and non-service value-added, and **Figure 6** shows the steady surge in global GDP despite industrial and export stagnation.

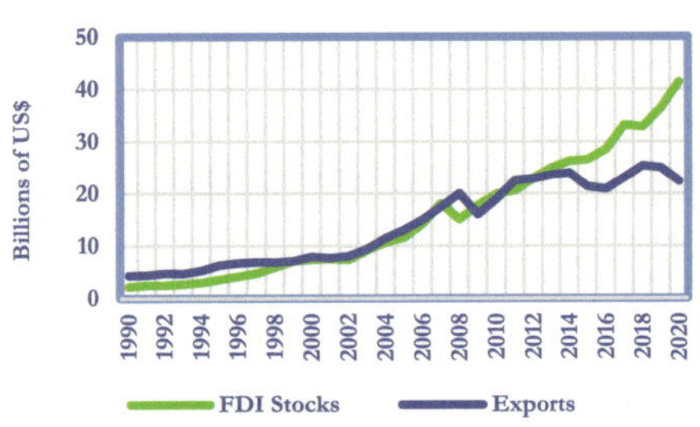

Figure 2.
Global exports vs. FDI stocks.

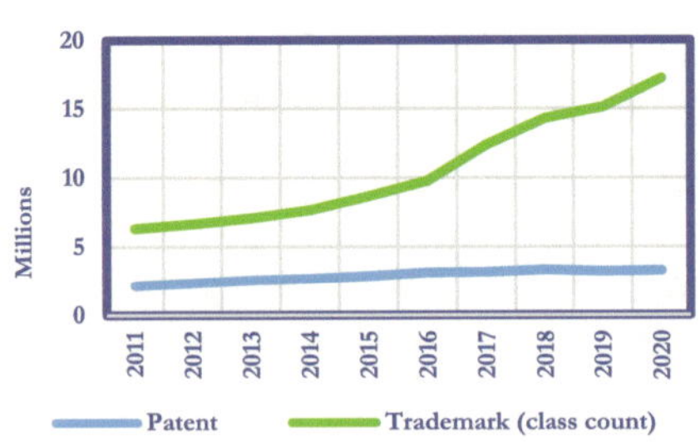

Figure 3.
Global innovations.

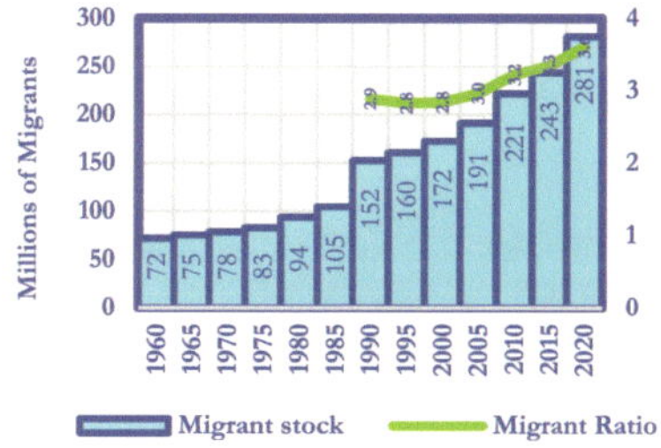

Figure 4.
Global migration trends.

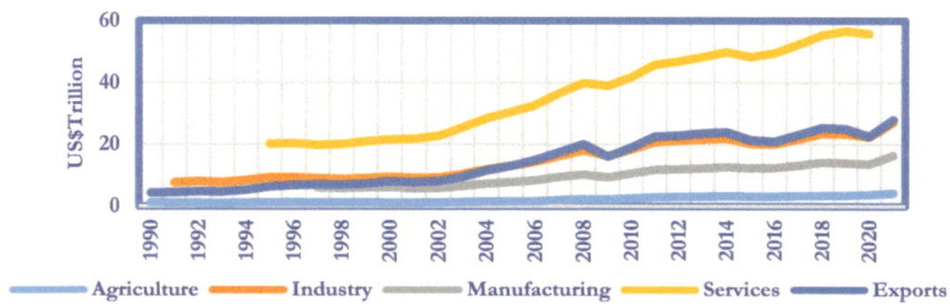

Figure 5.
Global sectoral trends.

Figure 6.
Global GDP trends.

We assess the extent to which selected countries align or misalign with the striking global realities captured in **Figures 2**, **5**, and **6** in Section 5 where we assess the exposures of G7, BRICS, and Next-11 countries to liquidity, growth, and sectoral risks.

Income statement exposures to each of the four episodes of global shocks, using global exports of goods and services as the proxy, have often been larger and protracted than balance sheet exposures, using global FDI Stocks as the proxy, which have often been smaller and fleeting.

Exports have only grown five-fold from US$4.4 trillion to US$22.4 in 1990 by 2020, while foreign direct investment (FDI) stocks that have emerged as the focal point of global connectedness surged nineteen-fold from US$2.2 trillion to US$41.4 trillion over the same period. Global Inward FDI stocks have grown from half the size of annual global exports in 1990 to nearly twice the size of global exports by 2020. Prosperity in today's global markets is fueled more by cross-border equity stocks than cross-border trade flows.

Global shocks typically inflict large persistent contractions on commodity prices compared to small transitory contractions on equity prices.

The resulting output headwinds and asset tailwinds set the global income statement and balance sheet on divergent paths.

3. Financial literacy

Global watchdogs like the IMF, World Bank, and UNCTAD should have the cognitive capability to correctly measure and track all the important dimensions of shocks to global commodity and equity prices, and what they might portend for the outlook of global transactions and global portfolios.

Global, national, sub-national, and corporate decision-makers should be aware of the roles of the two global prices as leading indicators of income statement and balance sheet developments. They should be able to trace the impact points of global price shocks on their income statement and balance sheet. They should have the cognitive capability to assess exposures of income statement transactions and balance sheet portfolios to shocks.

Managers should have the adaptive capability to take steps to reconfigure their participation in relevant value chains to cover their exposures to declining and uneven margins along value chains and have the skills for readjusting their portfolios of assets, equity, and debts to seize opportunities presented by increasing capital gains.

The cognitive capability to trace the exposures of income statement transactions and balance sheet portfolios to *global shocks* and the *adaptive capacity* to *take steps to cover exposures* become essential for modulating the pass-through from global shocks to global net worth.

4. Net worth

Shocks to commodity and equity prices have reduced the roles of income-statements-related flows of goods and commercial services in cross-border transactions and increased the roles of balance-sheet-related ideas, skills, and investment as the current focal points of global connectivity.

Consequently, balance-sheet-based portfolio optimization contributes more to global, national, subnational, and corporate wealth or net worth than income-statement-based transaction optimization. Asset-centrism now contributes more to net worth than output-centrism.

The reality is that activities that enable production, such as innovative placemaking, platform building, knowledge building, and skill building have become more reliable ways for countries, cities, and companies to create economic value and enhance global wealth than the production activities themselves.

Leading countries, cities, and companies increasingly loosen their grip on low-margin segments of their value chains, typically midstream production transactions, by offshoring or outsourcing them, while strengthening their grip on the high-margin segments of the value chains, typically upstream and downstream asset portfolios.

While output-centric literacy remains a crucial determinant of net worth, the realities of smaller and uneven margins along value chains compared to larger capital gains across asset types mean that asset-centric literacy is the most critical determinant of net worth.

5. Country exposures: G7, BRICS, and Next-11

In this section, we assess the extent to which selected countries align or misalign with the striking global realities captured in **Figures 2**, **5**, and Chart to gauge the exposures of G7, BRICS, and Next-11 countries to liquidity risks (**Figures 7–9**), sectoral risks (**Figures 10–12**), and growth risks (**Figures 13–15**).

Each country's performance across three criteria-GDP *growth, FDI stock, and servitization-* should identify her as an *adjuster* who *possesses the cognitive and adaptive capabilities to modulate the pass-through from global shocks to national liquidity, sectoral resilience, and growth,* or as a *non-adjuster* who *needs these capabilities*.

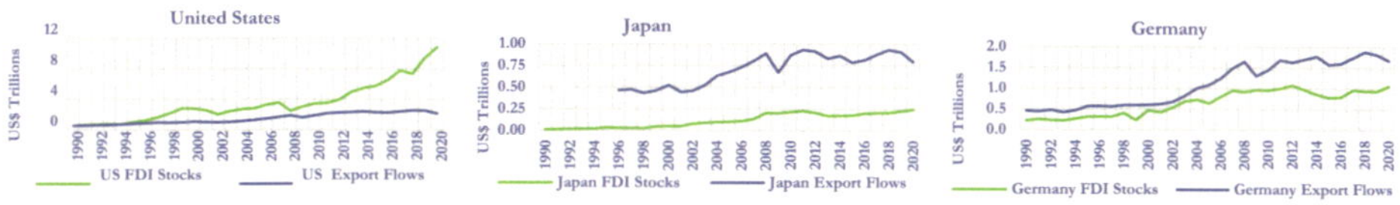

Figure 7.
G7 external financing mix.

Figure 8.
BRICS financing mix.

Figure 9.
Next-11 financing mix.

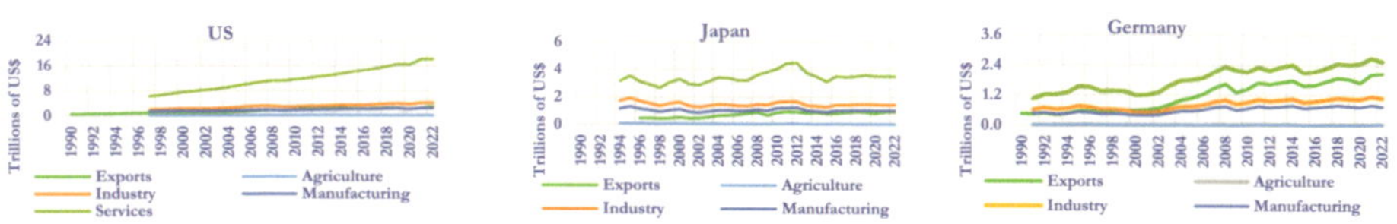

Figure 10.
G7 sectoral dynamics.

Figure 11.
BRICS sectoral dynamics.

Figure 12.
Next-11 sectoral dynamics.

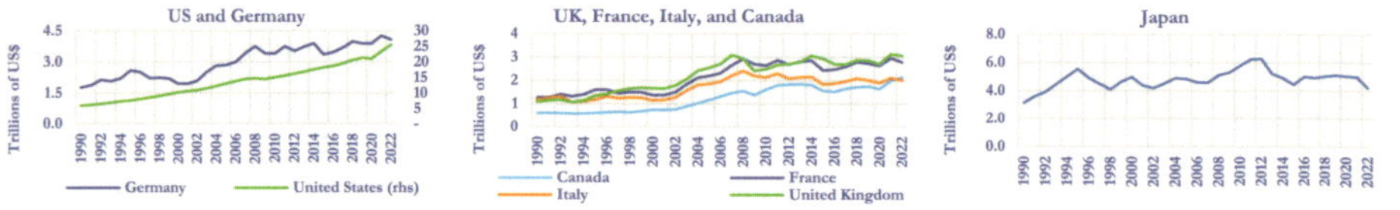

Figure 13.
G7 growth trajectories.

Figure 14.
BRICS growth trajectories.

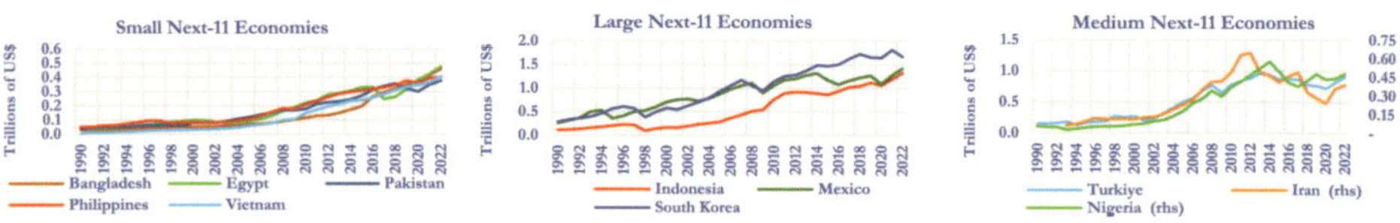

Figure 15.
Next 11 growth trajectories.

5.1 External financing mix

Only countries that align with the evolving global reality of growing inward FDI stocks in the face of sluggish exports as portrayed in **Figure 2** will remain liquid enough to sustain exchange rate stability and diversified GDP growth. Countries with stagnant inward FDI stocks and slow export flows will likely require additional funding to stay liquid enough to support diversified GDP growth.

- Increasingly Liquid Group: The United States from the G7, China, and India from BRICS, Egypt, and the Philippines from N-11 belong to this group of increasingly liquid countries.

- Increasingly Illiquid Group: Japan and Germany from G7, Brazil, Russia, and South Africa from BRICS, and Nigeria from N-11 belong to this group of increasingly illiquid countries.

It is the responsibility of each country, its cities, and its companies to urgently take steps to move from the club of increasingly illiquid nations into the league of increasingly liquid countries.

5.2 Internal sectoral dynamics

Countries must either align with the global reality of stellar growth in services in the face of growth deceleration in other sectors or stagnate. Countries can be classified as servitizers and industrializers.

5.3 GDP trajectories

The *trajectories of gross domestic product (GDP) levels* continue to differ across and within country groupings. This could be due to differences in the external financing mix or internal sectoral dynamics.

Countries across standard groupings can be classified as steady growers and unsteady growers.

- Steady Growers share two attributes in common: inward FDI stocks accelerate, even as exports decelerate, and services accelerate even as other sectors decelerate. Again, the US from the G7, China, India from BRICS, Egypt, Bangladesh, Egypt, Indonesia, Mexico, Pakistan, Philippines, South Korea, and Vietnam from N-11 all fall into the group of steady growers.

- Unsteady growers also share two attributes in common: FDI stocks stagnate, regardless of export performance, although most also face the global reality of stagnant exports and services stagnate along with other sectors. Canada, France, Italy, Japan, Germany, and the United Kingdom from G7, Brazil, Russia, South Africa from BRICS, Iran, Nigeria, and Turkey from N-11 all fall into the group of unsteady growers.

6. Strategic insights

We highlight measures of global shocks that global watchdogs must now emphasize, and we offer strategic insights on how managers can modulate pass-through from global shocks to wealth.

6.1 Global wealth

Global economic watchdogs provide one-sided narratives of global markets.

IMF, World Bank, and UNCTAD only provide comprehensive data and analytical reports on the history and outlook of commodity prices, production, and trade as if only transaction values on the income statement matter. They provide no comprehensive data or analytical reports on the history and outlook of equity prices, assets, and dealmaking as if portfolio values on the balance sheet do not matter.

According to Howells 2020, 'Barely one-fifth of Wall Street's huge gains over recent decades have come from earnings: rising liquidity and investors' appetite for riskier financial assets have propelled stock prices. Similar experiences are shared worldwide, and even in emerging markets, such as India, flat earnings have not deterred waves of foreign money and domestic mutual funds from driving up stock prices [1].'

McKinsey Global Institute (2021) phrased the issue thus,

'Net worth has tripled since 2000, but the increase mainly reflects valuation gains in real assets, especially real estate, rather than investment in productive assets that drive our economies. We have borrowed a page from the corporate world- namely, the balance sheet- to take stock of the underlying health and resilience of the global economy … This view from the balance sheet complements more typical approaches based on GDP, capital investment levels, and other economic flow measures that reflect economic value changes [2].'

International watchdogs must provide data and analytical reports on both sides of the global markets as the world evolves from transaction dominance to portfolio dominance. UNCTAD's World Investment Report provides comprehensive annual data and analytical narratives on all the important dimensions of inward and outward FDI flows but offers no analytical narratives on FDI stocks, providing basic annual data on inward and outward FDI stocks in annex Tables 3 and 4.

The World Bank's World Development Indicators only provide data on FDI flows and offer no data on FDI stocks. The World Bank's Wealth Accounts provides data on the constant US% of human, natural, and produced, and total capital for 146 countries, none for the world, but these were last updated to 2018 on 27 October 2021. None of the global watchdogs provide any data on the prices corresponding to these assets. We used the Morgan Stanley World Equity Index for this study.

6.2 The wealth of nations

The importance of the public sector balance sheet for fiscal liquidity is well articulated in a flurry of recent research at the IMF [3–7]. The IMF's October 2018 Fiscal Monitor, 'It's not just what governments owe, it's what they own.' Gaspar et al. (2018), 'Knowing what a government owns and how they can put their assets to better use matters because they can earn … as much revenue as governments make from corporate income tax receipts' [4]. Harris et al. (2019), 'When governments know what they own, they can better use the assets for the well-being of all their citizens [5].'

Given glaring evidence of large stocks of under-exploited corporate, real estate, and infrastructure assets owned by the Government [8], Nigeria is sitting on a goldmine of assets [9]. The total value of Nigeria's assets, reported to be US$5.6 trillion in 2018 in the World Bank's online *Wealth Accounts*, is eleven times bigger than her GDP, reported to be US$480 billion in 2022 in the World Bank's *World Development Indicators*, and 56 times bigger than her total public debt stock of US$100 billion in 2022 [6].

Yet the country languishes in external, fiscal, and systemic illiquidity as the government keeps trying to rejuvenate export revenue instead of unlocking liquidity from its vast wealth of human, natural, and produced capital by connecting them to the global FDI glut, the way countries like India and Saudi Arabia have been doing in the past decade. The two are among the growing list of countries that now list fundable projects on online platforms to connect them to investable funds around the world.

Saudi Arabia's list of 200 projects in 16 sectors included ARAMCO and football clubs when the list was made public in 2017 as the country sought FDI inflows to the tune of US$200 billion. India Investment Grid currently seeks US$2.28 trillion to fund 15,182 projects in 22 sectors and 78 subsectors that have been originated by 8865 promoters, and 12,265 investors are registered on the platform.

Fiscal conversations in Nigeria should be focused on net worth, not just revenue and debt. We must situate income and debt in the broader context of assets owned by Nigeria and the enormous equity issuance headroom the assets bequeath the country in a post-boom environment in which we are guaranteed to be asset-rich, even when income/revenue shortfalls give little or no debt issuance headroom [10].

Finding new streams of non-tax revenue will be helpful. *Nigeria's debt liabilities are well-known, but her assets are not*. Not knowing what we own adversely affects the assessment of our net worth, as most of our assets do not come into the reckoning in discussions of our solvency. Nigeria should list all assets owned by the government in a *National Asset Register*, *value them*, and *rationalize* them to ensure that *use values* are aligned with *market values* Teriba shows ways of unlocking liquidity from *four types of assets* [11].

7. Conclusion

The cognitive capability to trace the exposures of income statement transactions and balance sheet portfolios to *global shocks* and the *adaptive capacity* to *take steps to cover exposures* are essential for modulating the pass-through from global shocks to net worth.

Global watchdogs must provide data and analytical reports on both sides of the global markets as the world evolves from transaction dominance to portfolio dominance. And country managers must take steps to unlock more liquidity from national assets to fuel growth and diversification.

8. Data sources

Commodity Price Index data is from the IMF's Monthly Global Commodity Price Excel database.

Equity Price Index data is from the online database of Morgan Stanley's *End of the Day Chart*.

Exports, GDP. Agriculture, Industry, Manufacturing, and *Services* from World Bank's *World Development Indicators* (WDI).

Inward FDI Stock data from Annex Table 3 of UNCTAD's World Investment Report.

Patents and Trademark data from the World Intellectual Property Organization (WIPO) database.

Migrants Stock and Migrant Ratio data from the International Migration Office (IMO).

Acknowledgements

I acknowledge helpful insights from class conversations with the 2021, 2022, and 2023 cohorts of scholars who participated in the Economics of Globalization (EOG) course at the National Scholars Program (NSP) of the Nigerian University of Technology and Management (NUTM).

Author details

Ayo Teriba
Economic Associates (EA), Nigeria

*Address all correspondence to: ayo.teriba@econassociates.com

References

[1] Howell MJ. Capital Wars: The Rise of Global Liquidity. 1st ed. Cham: Palgrave Macmillan; Switzerland AG: Springer Nature; 2020

[2] McKinsey Global Institute. The Rise and Rise of the Global Balance Sheet: How Productively Are we Using our Wealth? New York: McKinsey Global Institute (MGI); 2021. Available from: https://www.mckinsey.com/industries/financial-services/our-insights/the-rise-and-rise-of-the-global-balance-sheet-how-productively-are-we-using-our-wealth

[3] Alves M, De Clerck S, Gamboa-Arbelaez J. Public Sector Balance Sheet Database: Overview and Guide for Compilers and Users, IMF Working Paper No. 20/130. Washington, D. C.: International Monetary Fund; 2020. Available from: https://ssrn.com/abstract=3670610

[4] Gaspar V, Harris J, Tieman AF. The Wealth of Nations: Governments Can Better Manage What they Own and Owe. Washington, D. C.: IMF Blog; 2018

[5] Harris J, Senhadji A, Tieman AF. A Global Picture of Public Wealth. Washington, D. C.: IMF Blog; 2019

[6] Yousefi SR. Public Sector Balance Sheet Strength and the Macro Economy, IMF Working Paper No. 19/170. Washington, D. C.: Fiscal Affairs Department, International Monetary Fund; 2019

[7] Detter D, Fölster S. Unlocking Public Wealth: Governments Could Do a Better Job Managing their Assets, Finance and Development. Vol. 55, No. 1. Washington, D. C.: IMF; 2018. Available from: https://www.imf.org/external/pubs/ft/fandd/2018/03/detter.html

[8] Bova E, Dippelsman R, Rideout K, Schaechter A. Another Look at Governments' Balance Sheets: The Role of Nonfinancial Assets' IMF Working Paper, WP/13/95. Washington, D. C.: Fiscal Affairs Department and Statistics Department International Monetary Fund; 2013

[9] Audier A, Bard S, Robeux, L. The Hidden Value in Government Assets. Boston, Massachusetts: BCG Perspectives, Bolton Consulting Group; 2014. Available from: https://bcgperspectives.com

[10] Teriba A. Unlocking Liquidity in Nigeria. 2019. Available from: https://ssrn.com/abstract=3454652

[11] Teriba A. National Financial Strategy and the Wealth of Nigeria. 2020. Available from: https://ssrn.com/abstract=3740787

Chapter 12

Content Analysis of the Financial Literature Over Time in the World

Luisa Anderloni and Ornella Moro

Abstract

The paper offers a conceptualization of the phenomena of financial illiteracy and its relationships with digital skills in a rapidly changing landscape driven by technology. It proposes a bibliometric analysis of the issue from the perspectives of individuals and households, entrepreneurs and firms and financial intermediaries and authorities. The aim of this chapter is to analyse the stream of the worldwide FL literature in order to shed a light on the conceptual structure of the research field, with an emphasis on its evolution over time and its future developments. We are interested in FL themes and in analytical perspectives from different disciplines, and consequently, our focus is more on thematic evolution and approaches than on authors' productivity, authors' influence, networks, research centres and journals.

Keywords: financial literacy, digital literacy, content analysis, bibliometric, vosviewer

1. Introduction

Financial literacy is a topic widely studied in many geographical areas under the light of different disciplines. The aim of this chapter is to analyse the stream of the worldwide FL literature in order to highlight the conceptual structure of the research field, with an emphasis on its trends. We are interested in FL themes and in analytical perspectives from different disciplines, and consequently, we are not adopting the conventional research methods that focus on author productivity, author influence, networks, research centres and journals.

As well known, bibliometrics is a quantitative method which uses scientific literature as data (i.e. citation statistics and number of articles) for its analyses mainly aimed at assessing researchers' productivity and influence through publishing. They provide maps of the state of the art in a given area of scientific knowledge, and they help identify different structures within a research field, hot topics and evolving research frontiers. These tools have been recently used in the domain of financial literacy [1–5] or in specific financial domains such as banking [6, 7], insurance [8], Islamic insurance [9], consumer credit [2], ITC and financial education [10] and green finance [11].

In this paper, we explore the thematic structure of the field of financial literature through the analysis of the occurrences and co-occurrences of authors' keywords. To do this, we move from OECD's definition of financial literacy, as a combination of

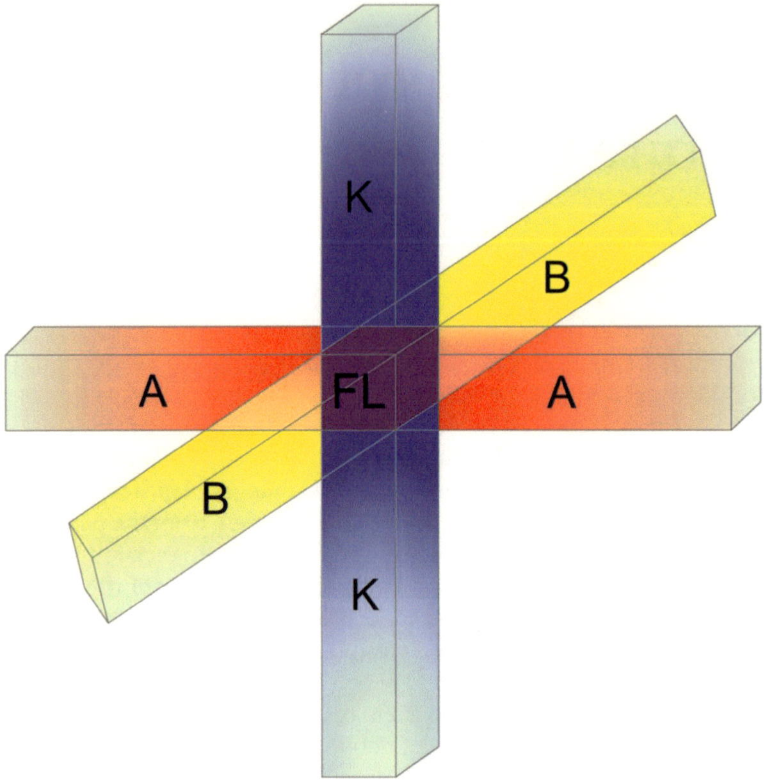

Figure 1.
Financial Literacy: authors' conceptual scheme.

knowledge, attitude and behaviour [12]. These elements are part of a wider wealth of knowledge, abilities and skills, behavioural conducts and habits of individuals. Their specific economic and financial components jointly contribute to determining financial literacy. **Figure 1** graphically shows this concept at the intersection of the three mentioned components.

The structure of the chapter is as follows: Section 2 illustrates the research design and tools, Section 3 discusses the software and methodology used, and Section 4 presents the results considering the keywords used and the related topics, the linkages among subthemes, the interest for the issue (the stream of published papers), the analytical perspective of different disciplines and the geographical research focus. Finally, Section 5 suggests some concluding remarks.

2. Research design and tools

For our cognitive purposes, we first identified the database for the search of publications, selected and refined the search criteria, chose the bibliographic software and performed our analysis selecting some bibliographic representation paths.

In order to create our database, the first step of our analysis was to choose the database for the search of publications that contained the term "financial literacy" in the title, keywords or abstract.

There are different databases for scientific publications (Scopus, Web of Science [WoS], Google Scholar, Dimension, Crossref and Microsoft Academic), with differences in the coverage of the data sources, the completeness and accuracy of citation links and the speed of updating. Our database choice was initially between Web of Science or Scopus, which are the best databases for scientific purposes, have a wide coverage of research publications and are widely used by researchers.

Some authors [13, 14] suggested that WoS and Scopus can be considered complementary databases because they are not "mutually exclusive". Besides other differences [15], the content indexed in Scopus and in WoS is highly overlapping, but the extent of content overlap varies across disciplines with some disciplines covered more extensively than others and others disciplines underrepresented [16]. That is the reason why we decided to use both of them by creating a combined database.

For the merging procedures, we followed the user-friendly three-step procedure suggested by Caputo and Kargina [13], rather than the four-step ones proposed by Echchakoui [14].

In the two above-mentioned databases, the subject areas (social sciences, economics, finance, business, management and accounting and education) were similar but not identical, due to the different categories in the two databases.

As for the time span, we chose the period from 2000 to 2023, since the pre-2000 literature is extremely scanty.

As for the document types, we included articles, books, books chapters, reviews, conference papers and early access.

We had no refinement for the language.

Our search queries initially resulted in 4158 publications in Scopus and 4011 in WoS.[1] Our efforts were aimed at creating one uniform dataset with a unique format with the same criteria for data representation.

The combination process (defined as "the data wrangling") could not be fully automated, as noted by Ullah et al. [18], and it implied a manual work of comparing (using DOI reference and/or titles and/or authors' names) and removing duplicates, checking (i.e. cases with authors' names in a different order or with different or absent abbreviation), unifying and fixing "broken" data (e.g. spelling errors). We then manually checked and evaluated the remaining articles to find the "borderline articles" and to assess if they corresponded to our study focus. In this step, the evaluation of the articles' inclusion/exclusion was based on the article title and abstract. This was the most time- and effort-consuming in the process of literature data gathering.

The final aggregated database was of 3991 publications.

3. The software and methodology

As for software, we used two bibliometric software: Vosviewer [19], which offers a clear thematic network visualisation, with a possible focus on specific clusters, and the open-source web-based interface of the R package, Biblioshiny [20], which provides other processing and visualisations such as lines charts for temporal trend growth, trend topic analysis visualisations and thematic analysis that plots clusters of keywords along two dimensions (density vs. centrality).

[1] Different databases have their own format, with differences in the spectrum of bibliometric data, in the columns ascending order, in writing names (separated or not by commas), in the citation indexes [17].

The same dataset was then expressed in Scopus format for Vosviewer and in WoS format for Biblioshiny as they were the formats more easily uploaded into the two bibliometric software. For Vosviewer we used a simplified database that included only the relevant information for thematic network map visualisation, and we exported them into .csv format, while for Biblioshiny we used, in WoS format (following the process suggested by [13]), a wider spectrum of metadata.

As for methodology, our analysis aimed at shedding light on the conceptual structure of the research field, its evolution and its recent trends; as previously mentioned, it is based on the use of keywords and their connections (occurrences and co-occurrences). We consider keywords as proxies of the issues studied regarding financial literacy in various papers from different disciplines and areas of interest. Financial literacy is indeed a multifaceted, complex topic, and bibliometric techniques allow us to explore this complexity in depth.

As a matter of fact, the two databases which originated our dataset include two categories of keywords: "author keywords," chosen by authors, and keywords suggested by the database providers, named "KeyWord Plus" (in WoS) or "Index Keywords" (in Scopus). However, just the first type of keywords is always present in both databases. Consequently, our methodological choice fell on the author keyword.[2]

In order to test our methodology, we initially set the number of keyword co-occurrences at the minimum level of 1, which produced a large number—equal to 6187—of terms qualified and whose preliminary visualization is given in **Figure 2**.

We noticed that there is a very large number of different words used as keywords which makes the map unreadable and that spelling mistakes or singular/plural for the same terms affect the frequency of co-occurrence of keywords, reducing the efficacy of the network map visualization.[3] The number of authors' keywords was still very high due to the wide number of different synonyms for the same concept. We then increased the minimum number of co-occurrences to 10, in order to reduce the number of keywords in the network and have a better visualization: unfortunately, the map did not help to clearly identify thematic networks in financial literacy. Furthermore, the number of clusters, the number of links and the total links' strengths were not satisfactory for our purpose.

We operated the methodological choice to construct a new thesaurus file by aggregating similar keywords (i.e. same meaning but with a different specification) and also aggregating some terms whose specifications were not providing a useful visualisation (i.e. names of specific research methods). As for countries' names, in general, we aggregated them using their continent name with the exception of India and China, due to their high number of occurrences.

In choosing appropriate and standardized keywords, for some terms, we inspired ourselves with the conceptual framework and keywords proposed by Zaimovic et al. [5] and shown in **Figure 3**.

---

[2] Vosviewer has the option "All keywords" but in our unified dataset it would have not solved the problem Additionally, for duplicate records, the automatic keywords (Keyword Plus or Index Keywords) differ in many cases due to the specific algorithms used by the database's providers.

[3] Spelling errors, singular/plural terms and keywords that had no significance such as abstracts sentences instead of keywords; the term "and" instead of semicolon to distinguish keywords; foreign keywords, and [JEL codes].

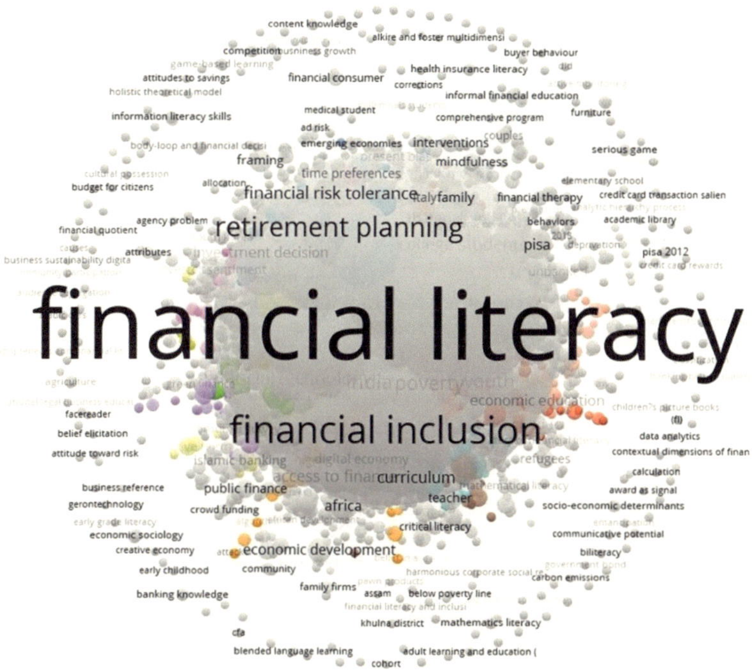

Figure 2.
Vosviewer map visualization using authors' original keywords—1 co-occurrency.

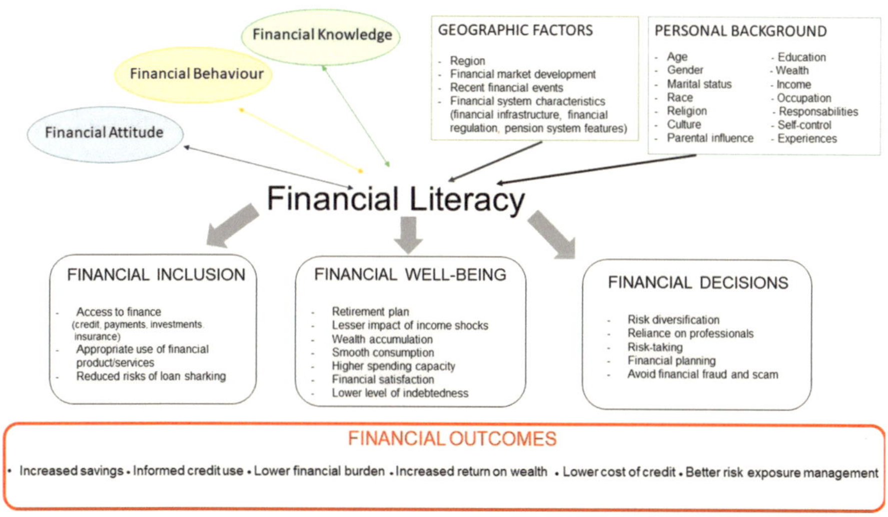

Figure 3.
Financial literacy -conceptual framework (adapted from Zaimovic et al.).

4. The results

The described methodology, sharpened step by step, allowed us to build the final dataset and perform the analysis considering occurrences, co-occurrences and clusters. First of all, our aim is to perform a co-occurrence analysis centered on author keywords. As previously said, our use of co-word analysis is based on the assumption that a paper's keywords adequately and synthetically describe both its content and its connections between issues. The presence of many co-occurrences around the same word may help to identify a research theme central to the studies of different authors.

In a Keyword Co-occurrence Network (KCN) each keyword is represented as a node: the size of the nodes is proportional to the frequency of keyword occurrence (i.e. the number of times that the keyword occurs) [21]. The link between the nodes represents the co-occurrence between keywords in different publications (i.e. keywords that co-occur or occur together). The thickness of the link identifies the occurrence or co-occurrences between keywords (i.e. the number of times that the keywords co-occur or occur together).

Secondarily, in the cluster analysis, keywords/nodes are grouped into clusters. Inside a cluster, the theme's coverage of topics is identified by the cluster's nodes and the relationships between the topics of that theme are identified by the cluster's links [22]. Clusters, in general, are represented in different colours. Each colour identifies a topical cluster.[4]

We chose not to take into account, when building the map, the commonly used keyword "financial literacy" to provide a clearer visualisation of clusters.[5] A preliminary result—setting at 10 the minimum number of co-occurrences to consider—is the map provided in **Figure 4**.

We identified clusters of author keywords co-occurrences using both Vosviewer map and Biblioshiny's factorial analysis map[6] (**Figure 5**). The results, in terms of cluster composition, were quite similar but not identical, and they provided us with food for thought about links among topics. The clusters in the maps, on the contrary, had a different representation. The following remarks, however, will be referred to the Vosviewer map as it enables us to provide useful graphical details.

From a preliminary view of the Vosviewer map emerges the prevailing position, in terms of size of nodes, of keywords such as education, behaviour, followed by financial planning, pensions/retirement, research methods and then attitudes and financial inclusion, entrepreneurs, investments and risk.[7] As previously said, the size of the node shows the relevance of the theme among researchers.

Links and nodes of the same colour define a unique cluster in which the distance among components and the thickness of links derive from the strong or weak association of topics: keywords are close to each other because a large proportion of articles treat them together, as investments and risk (the two blue nodes one next to the other in

---

[4] If there is a high number of clusters, the colour differentiation might be limited only to some of them. Clusters are non-overlapping in Vosviewer, which means that an item may belong to only one clusters. Clusters do not exhaustively cover all items in a map as there also are keywords that do not belong to any clusters.

[5] We opted for the same methodological choice in some of Biblioshiny's graphs, in order to have a better representation in the maps.

[6] Factorial analysis's visual representation is useful to understand the conceptual structures map of Financial Literacy research area. It categorizes author's keywords into groups according to two dimensions: the frequency of use of each term and the joint use of the terms in each document (Dim 1 and Dim 2). Words are distant from each other when only a small fraction of articles uses these words together. The centre of the axes represents the centre of the research fields, showing large shared topics. The parameters used in our analysis were automatic clustering with Multiple Correspondence Analysis (MCA), 100 as the maximum number of terms, a minimum number of documents of 5 for graphic parameters. The keywords are divided into 7 distinct clusters that are highlighted in various colours.

[7] Each word relative to keyword/theme will be written with the initial capital letter.

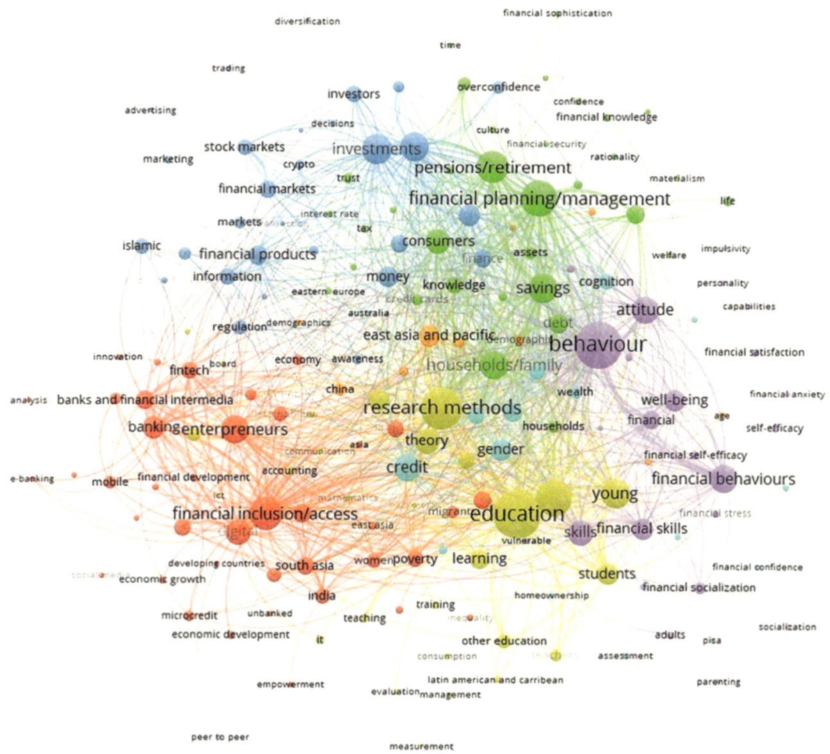

Figure 4.
Vosviewer map of authors' keyword after keyword substitution and without the keyword "financial literacy"—10 co-occurrences.

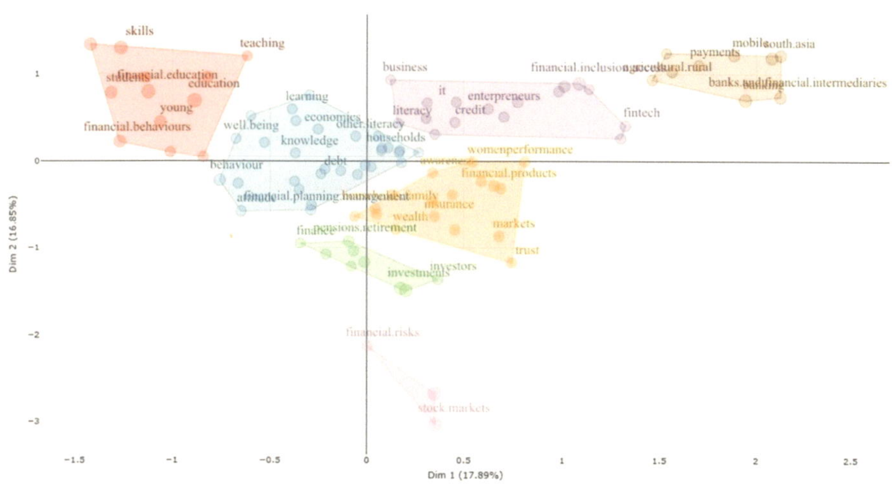

Figure 5.
Clusters in Biblioshiny factorial map.

the upper part of the map in **Figure 4**) or as education and financial education (the two tangent yellow nodes in the lower right part of the map). On the contrary, they are distant from each other when only a small fraction of articles uses these keywords together.

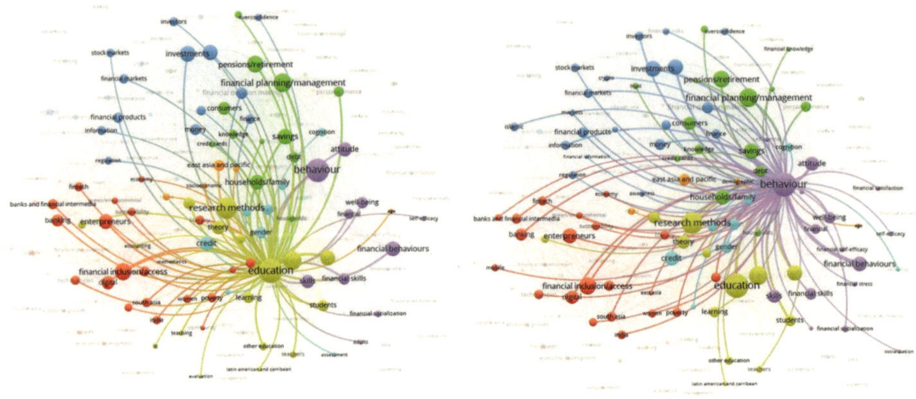

Figure 6.
Vosviewer map: education and behaviors—links with other nodes.

The node of a cluster generally has several links with nodes of other clusters, as further illustrated for education and behaviours (**Figure 6**) where the topic education, in yellow, is connected with many topics of other clusters (expressed in different colours). The same for the topic behaviour (in purple). The wider the spectrum of "external links," as shown for the two keywords in the map, the more the theme is an essential and fundamental cross-cutting theme in the financial literacy research area.

In the red cluster of **Figure 4**, there are three main topics which deserve to be mentioned: financial inclusion, digital and entrepreneurs. Financial inclusion is connected to themes related to poverty, migrants, women, unbanked (**Figure 7**). This node is very near to the nodes digital and technologies and to the nodes Africa and India, attesting to the relevance that researchers give to the use of digital instruments for improving the financial and socioeconomic conditions of disadvantaged people, especially in the poorest areas of the world.

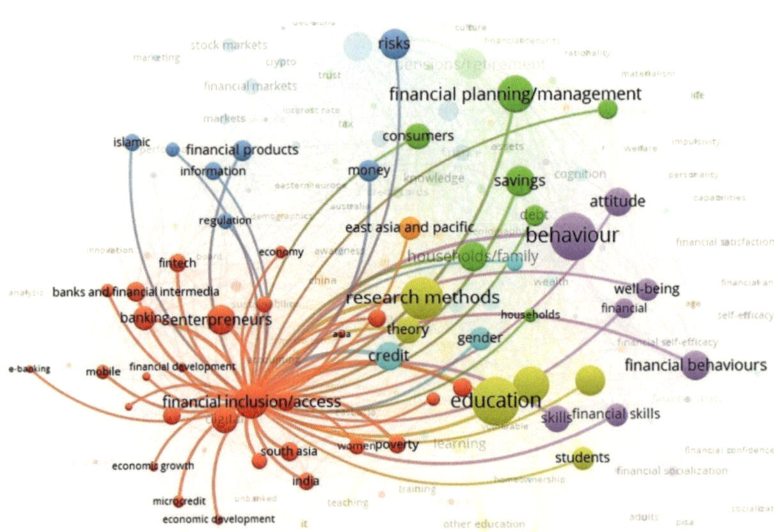

Figure 7.
Vosviewer map: financial inclusion—links with other nodes.

Additionally, the red cluster is home to topics such as digital, fintech, IT, mobile and technologies that demonstrate how the digital world—which has seen advancements like chatbots, mobile technology, peer-to-peer lending and e-banking—is seen as a means of hastening financial inclusion but also may have significant developments in the investments (blue nodes) and the pension/retirement and financial planning/management topics, the green nodes (**Figure 8**).

Entrepreneurs is another topic that deserves some reflections: compared to digital, it has a narrower spectrum of links with other internal and external nodes; it has a natural and close proximity to banking (or banks and financial intermediaries) and to sustainability and green/environment, which, at the moment, are very small nodes. At a longer distance, there is a connection with the financial inclusion node. Financial inclusion might foster the birth and growth of entrepreneurs and vice versa (**Figure 9**).

The blue cluster in **Figure 10** is made of topics such as investments (and investors), risks, finance, financial decision-making, stock markets and financial markets, performance, money, insurance and financial products, information, and critical issues such as overconfidence, emotions, often analysed under psychological or attitudinal perspectives. As mentioned before, the proximity between investment and risk is very strong, while the distance with other themes of the cluster is wider. Two themes external to the cluster are instead very near as strictly connected: pensions/retirements and financial planning/management. Clearly, this cluster is linked, although with a long distance, to education and financial education, behaviour and financial behavior and attitudes.

The green cluster in **Figure 11** aggregates terms related to households or consumers and to the financial activity to grant a better life during retirement years. Keywords with the highest occurrences are financial planning/management and

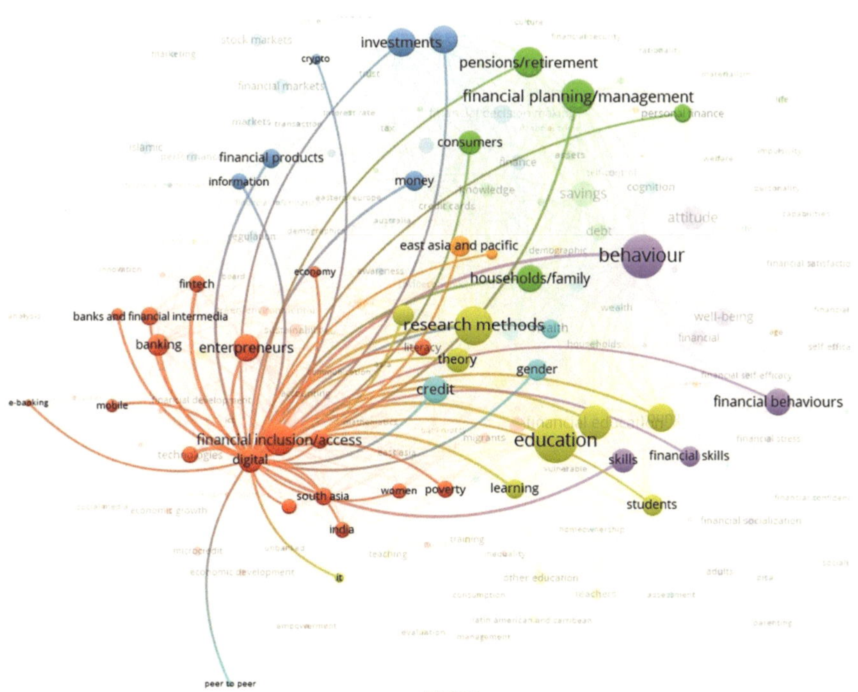

Figure 8.
Vosviewer map: digital—links with other nodes.

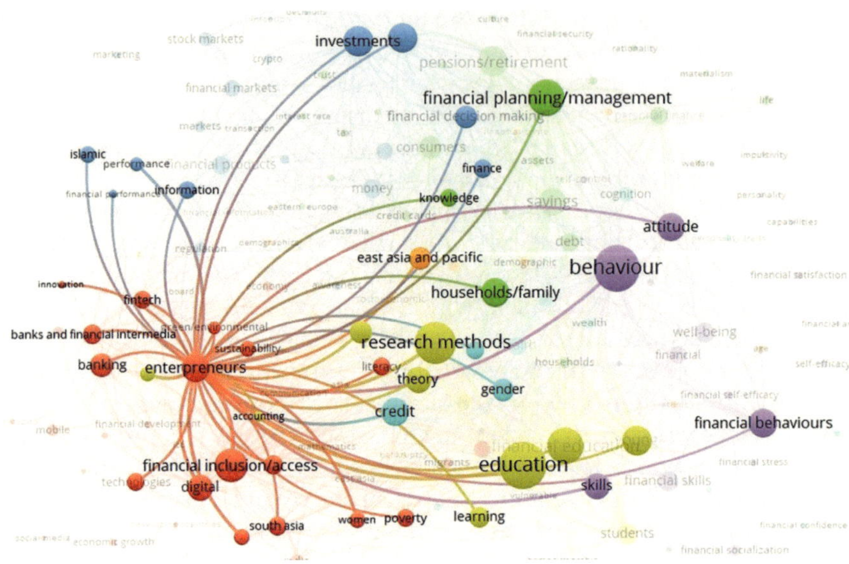

Figure 9.
Vosviewer map: entrepreneurs—links with other nodes.

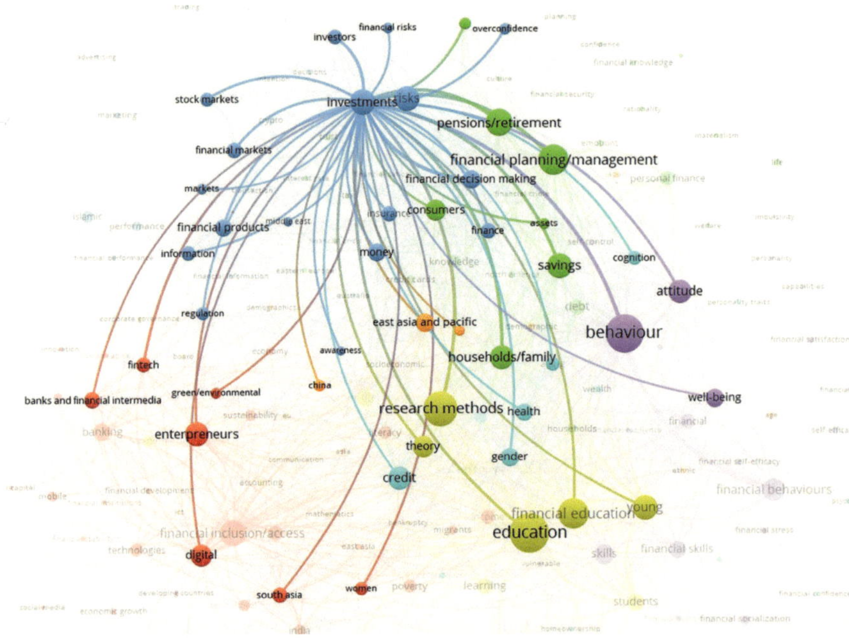

Figure 10.
Vosviewer map: investment—links with other nodes.

pensions/retirement, which share a strict proximity, savings, debt and personal finance. Financial planning/management shares links with some external nodes of the investment cluster, with the behavioural and attitudes cluster and with the education one. There also are links with items of the red cluster, such as financial inclusion, digital and entrepreneurs.

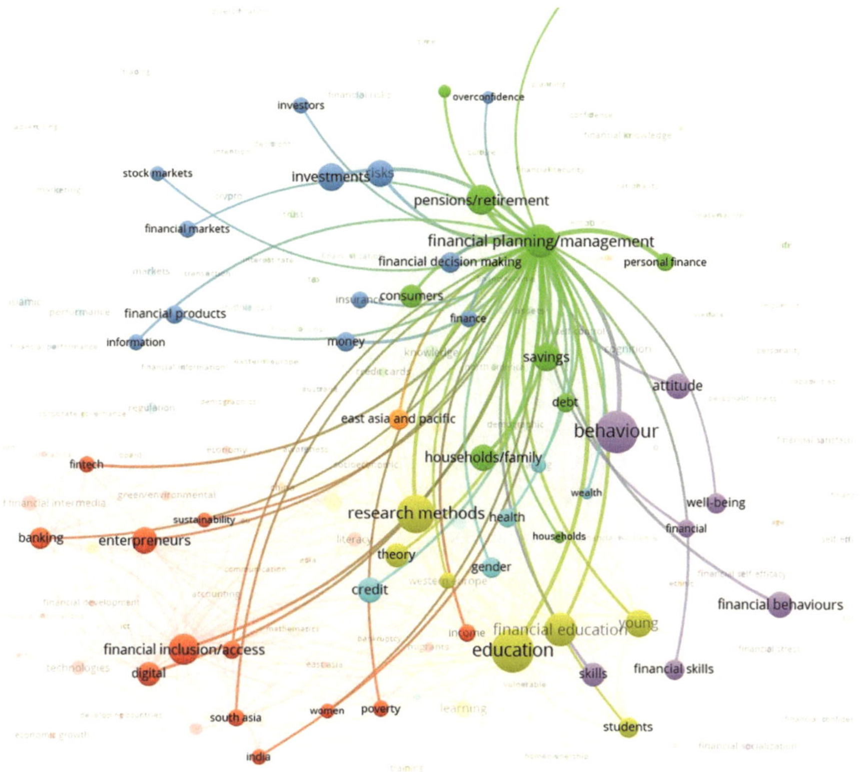

Figure 11.
Vosviewer map: financial planning/management—links with other nodes.

The yellow cluster (in the map on the left side in **Figure 6**) is relative to educational themes, with education, financial education and young as main nodes but also teachers, learning, other literatures, mathematics and training. As previously noted, education has pervasive connections with other clusters' nodes, but in particular, it shows many links with the nodes of the red cluster, from financial inclusion to entrepreneurs, women, poverty, and with nodes of the digital world and geographic areas such as Africa, India and South Asia.

It also deserves to be noted that research methods and theory are important nodes inside this yellow cluster. Research methods is a keyword we introduced to generally define specific statistical/economic/mathematical methods and tools used for obtaining empirical evidence in the researched topics. The large size of this node (**Figure 12**) evidences the pervasive adoption of rigorous research approaches in the financial literacy thematic area.

The purple cluster (**Figure 13**) is relative to behavioural and attitudinal topics with a financial focus or with a general perspective, to skills, to goals such as well-being, financial socialization, financial satisfaction and financial resilience. It also includes topics such as personality, anxiety, vulnerability and stress control. The stricter proximity inside the cluster regards behavior and attitudes. There is also a strict proximity with debt and saving, which belong to other clusters.

The light blue cluster (**Figure 4**), for which we do not provide a detailed visualisation, contains a variety of different topics related to individual issues, such as aging, gender, health, financial fragility and financial keywords related to financial

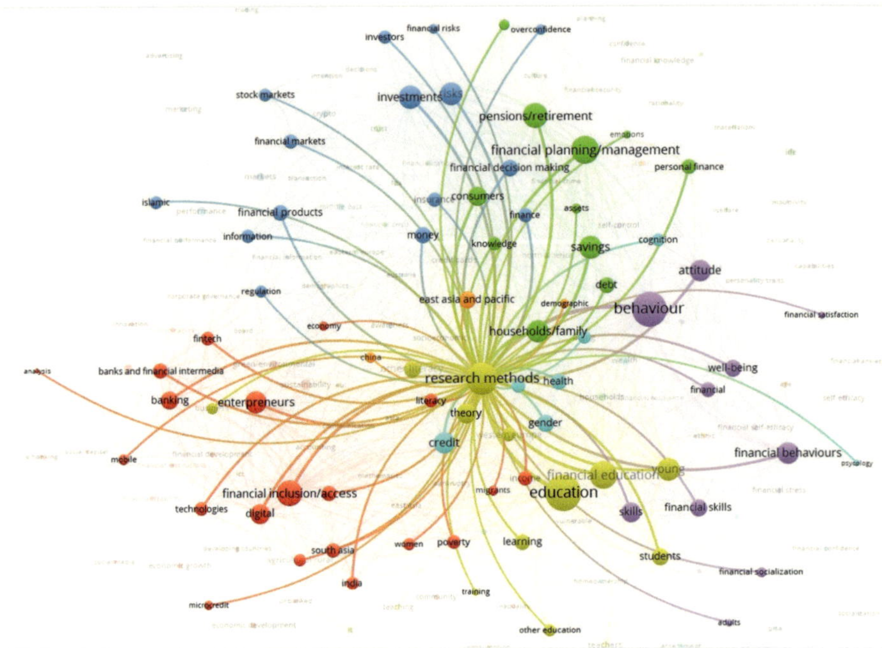

Figure 12.
Vosviewer map: research methods—links with other nodes.

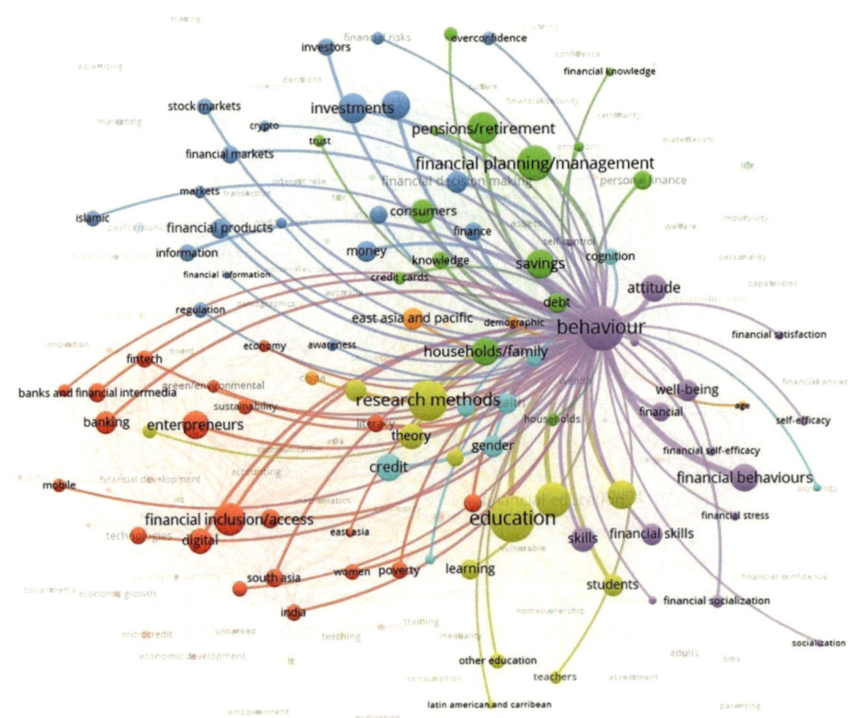

Figure 13.
Vosviewer map: behaviour— links with other nodes.

decisions such as credit, loans, wealth and homeownership. There are also themes which introduce a psychological perspective for the mentioned issues, such as psychology, personality traits, financial confidence, cognition and assessment.

The last cluster, the orange one, is a very small one with few nodes of small sizes, such as demographic, crime (with an external link to digital), financial crime and geographical area of East Asia and Pacific, which has links with a wide spectrum of external nodes.

Vosviewer maps have given us a first idea of the spectrum and composition of subthemes inside the financial literacy research area, but the Biblioshiny software helped us to have other information for deepening our analysis. The following considerations and statements will be then based on the Biblioshiny statistical output.

For a better understanding of topics' relevance and trends, it is useful to start analysing the number of documents published over the years. The higher the scientific production of articles, the higher the researchers' attention to the central themes of research. The scientific production of financial literacy in the time span from 2000 to the beginning of 2023 is shown in **Figure 14**: up to 2015, the production is moderate, while from 2016 to the end of 2022 it increases sharply, with a very steep curve after 2021, evidencing keen attention to financial literacy themes in the very last years.

The quantitative analysis of journals and editors publishing research studies on financial literacy issues provides us with interesting insights connected to the emergence of one theme over others.

The variety of journals publishing researchers' findings demonstrates the multidisciplinary nature of financial literature studies in which financial, behavioural and family counselling issues are involved (**Figure 15**).

The journals that started publishing articles in the field of financial literacy were journals focused on household needs: such as the *Journal of Financial Counseling and Planning*, which in the years has consolidated its position as the more prolific journal for financial literature, followed by the *Journal of Family and Economic Issues* and by *the International Journal of Consumer Studies* (**Figure 16**). After 10 years, journals dealing with economic and financial issues (*Journal of Pension Economics and Finance, International Journal of Bank Marketing*) showed a greater interest in the financial literacy themes. The growing number of publications from journals focused on social/psychological/behavioural issues appeared from 2013 to 2014 and sharply rose just in

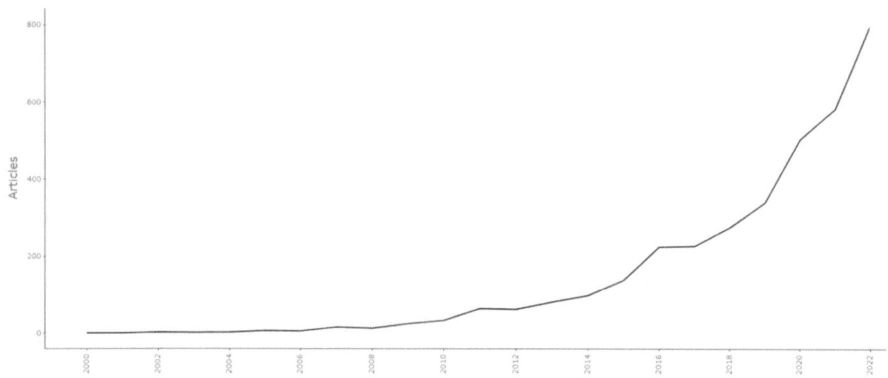

Figure 14.
Cumulative scientific production from 2000 to 2022.

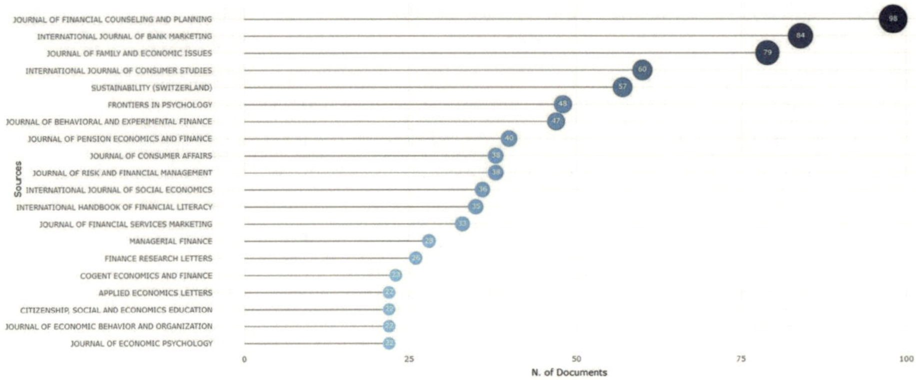

Figure 15.
Most relevant sources (year 2023).

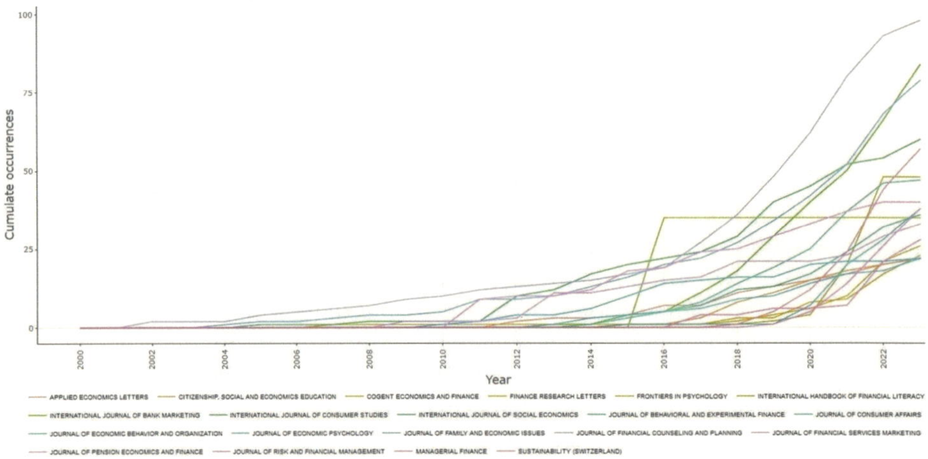

Figure 16.
Sources production over time.

the last years (*Frontiers in Psychology*), and their success sheds light on the quantitative data of keywords such as education and behaviors.

In the recent time span, there has been a widening of financial journals interested in financial literacy themes (*Managerial finance*, *Finance research letters*, *Journal of Risk and Financial Management*), and there is also a bursting activity of the journal *Sustainability* (Switzerland), whose articles cover analysis in a wide number of countries. *The International Handbook of Financial Literacy* is the exception as it limited its publishing activity in a single year.

The visualisation known as the tree field plot (**Figure 17**) shows the statistical links among researchers' countries, topics and sources.[8] Most scientific outputs pertain to the USA, followed by a bunch of Asian countries (India, Malaysia, Indonesia and China). These results are based on statistics from 2023, but they are also corroborated by consistent trends in worldwide output over time.

[8] The number of items in the graph are respectively 15, 15, and 20 (the same number of sources previously analysed).

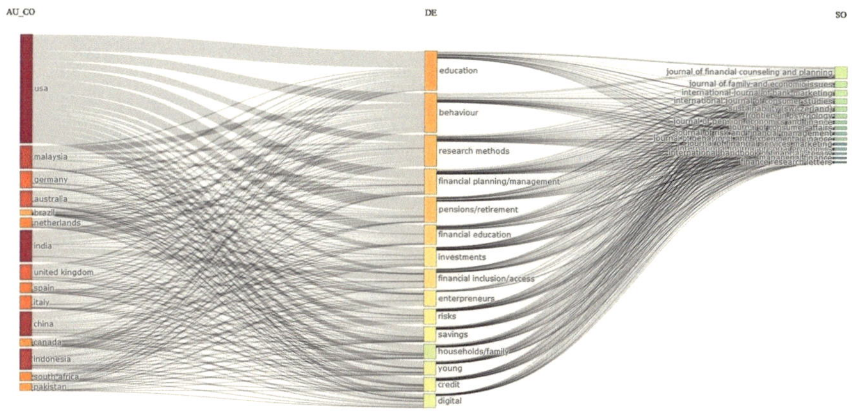

Figure 17.
Three field plots: authors' countries, authors' keywords, sources.

The theme's size in the graph of **Figure 17** reflects the number of occurrences for single topics in 2023, evidencing their relevance inside the financial literacy research area. What is important to point out is the massive production of studies, from the USA, in the fields of education, financial education, pensions/retirement, financial planning/management and behaviour, whereas the commitment of American researchers to the other themes is quantitatively weaker. In the group of Indian studies, there is a relative predominance of those focused on financial inclusion/access followed by those on behaviour and financial planning/management. In Chinese studies, there are not winning themes, but the researches are spread all over the range of financial literacy topics. In Indonesia prevails the interest in behaviours and topics related to entrepreneurship.

If we adjust our point of view from themes towards nations, it emerges that studies on education are produced from all nations, without a specific qualification, whereas other subthemes seem to have distinct patterns of geographical beginning. For instance, the behaviour theme is prominently produced from the USA, Malaysia, India and Indonesia, while pensions/retirement stems prominently from the USA, Australia, Germany and Malaysia; financial inclusion/access has more contributions from India and, with small numbers, from the USA, China, Malaysia, Indonesia and South Africa; digital themes and, with lower occurrences, also entrepreneurs themes stem from both industrialized countries and PVS.

The right side of the graph illustrates what we have already observed regarding the distribution of articles among sources. Biblioshiny does not give us the possibility of analysing the dispersion of themes among sources; however, the already-seen journals' specialization helps to hypothetically identify the themes' publishers.

Another step of analysis concerns the themes most frequently chosen by researchers. The size of the nodes in Vosviewer map has already given us such information, but it is useful to see it with a more effective visual representation.

The graph entitled "Most relevant words" in **Figure 18** shows the cumulated frequency, in the time span 2020–2023, of the author's keywords. Education and behaviour are the most used words over time as well as research methods, pensions/retirement, financial planning/management, financial inclusion/access, investments and entrepreneurs are frequent keywords.

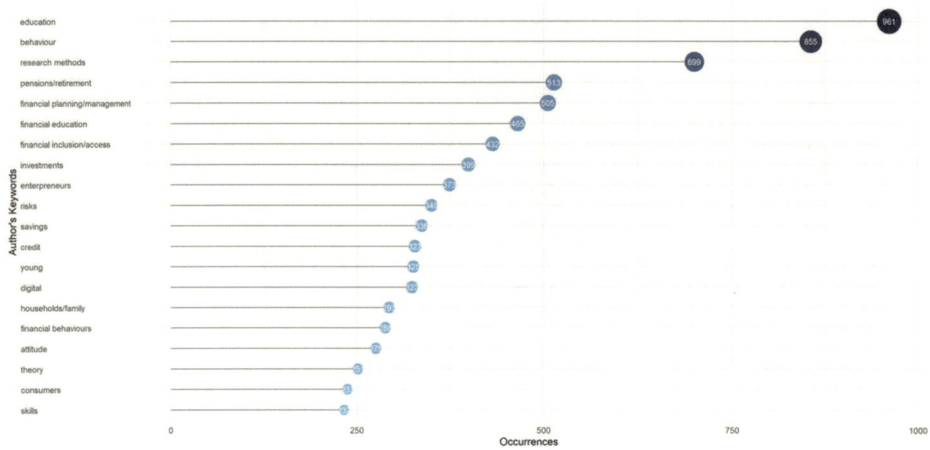

Figure 18.
Most relevant words.

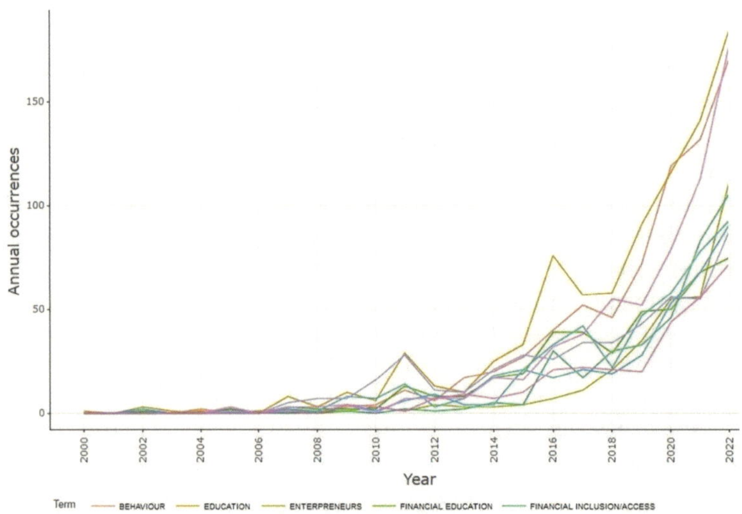

Figure 19.
Word's frequency in every single year.

But it is by analysing the annual frequencies of keywords (we considered the first 20 keywords; **Figure 19**) that it is possible to pinpoint the uneven topics' preferences among authors, starting from 2010s on, with some themes more analysed than others. The two central themes, education and behaviours, became highly popular after 2014, with growing numbers of research studies every year, and this information can be linked with the already-seen trend of psychological journals' production. Other themes had significantly lower popularity with the exceptions, in the last few years, of topics connected to entrepreneurs and financial inclusion/access.

The limited number of 20 for the most used keywords, useful for clear visualisations, does not capture the emergence of new topics which have, necessarily, lower frequencies. For this scope we used another Biblioshiny visualisation, named "Trend topics" (**Figure 20**) which easily shows since when and how long some topics became

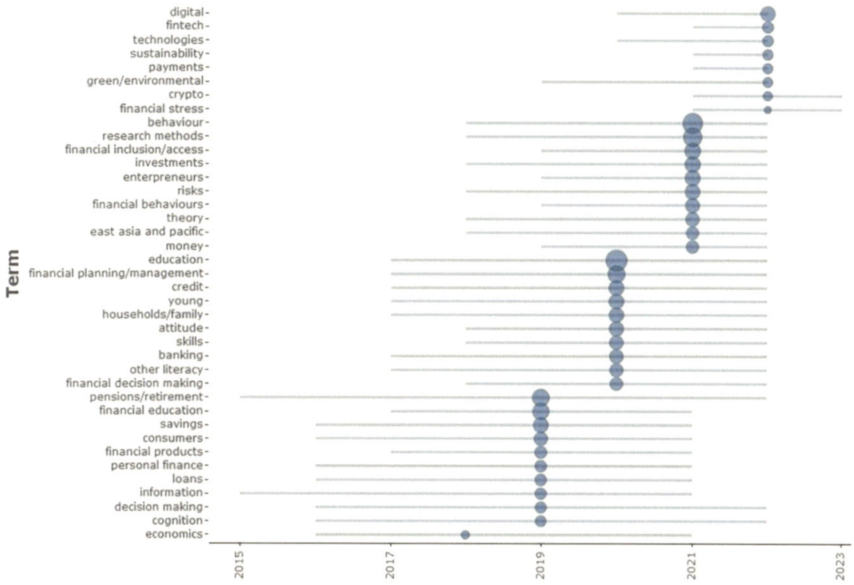

Figure 20.
Trend topics.

more popular and which gives evidence of the emerging themes in the very last years.[9] Consequently, it is possible to say that researchers have focused their attention, since the early years of our time span, on a "stable" group of themes such as pensions/retirement, savings, followed by young, education in general and financial education, credit and financial planning. The focus on behavior, financial behavior, investments, entrepreneurs and financial inclusion/access emerged in more recent years.

New and emerging topics with lower frequencies but growing appealing are: (1) entrepreneurs, sustainability and green/environment and (2) technologies and the digital world, as shown in **Figures 21** and **22**. The former has an increased frequency of contributions in the last few years but has a weaker attraction force compared to those linked to the technologies and the digital world, with the exception of topics linked to the entrepreneurs' perspective. The relation between technology and financial literacy [23] is going to be a strong one both in terms of number of articles published and in terms of subthemes chosen (digital, fintech, technologies, payments, money, crypto).

A closer look at the inter-linkages among the themes separated by various time spans, namely the periods from 2000 to 2010, 2011–2015, 2016–2020 and 2021–2023, underscores the thematic evolution (**Figure 23**)[10] in the domain of financial literacy.

The left side shows some of the themes that were widely used from 2000 to 2010 in which a wide group of subthemes converge. They are financial decision making, pensions/retirement, behaviour, entrepreneurs, banking, education, other literacy,

[9] The parameters set in order to visualise the keywords were: minimum frequency 25 number of words per year.

[10] The time segmentation is based on the subjective judgement of the authors keeping in view the better representation of thematic evolution. The parameters are: field author's keywords; number of keywords 100, minimum cluster frequency (per thousand documents) 5, weight index weighted by word-occurrences minimum weight index 0.1.

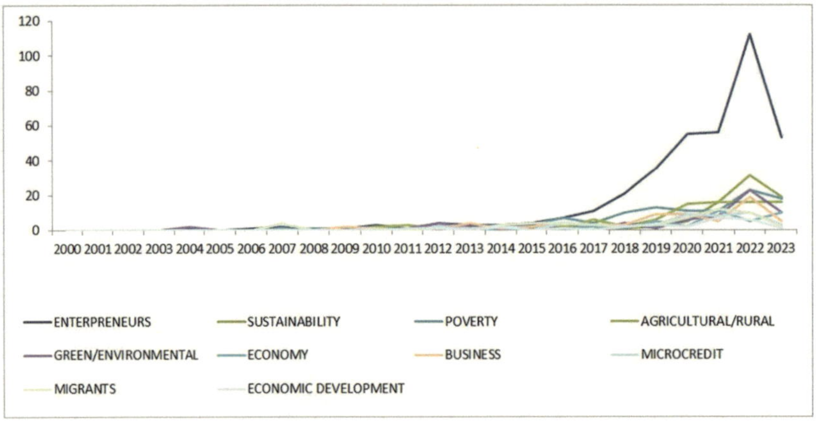

Figure 21.
Entrepreneurs topics in financial literacy over time.

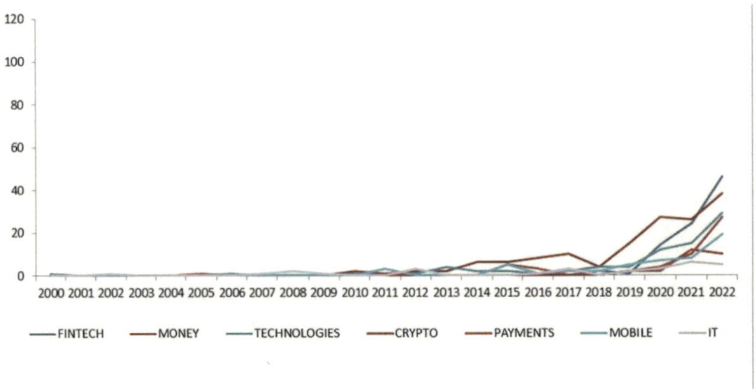

Figure 22.
Digital world topics in financial literature over time.

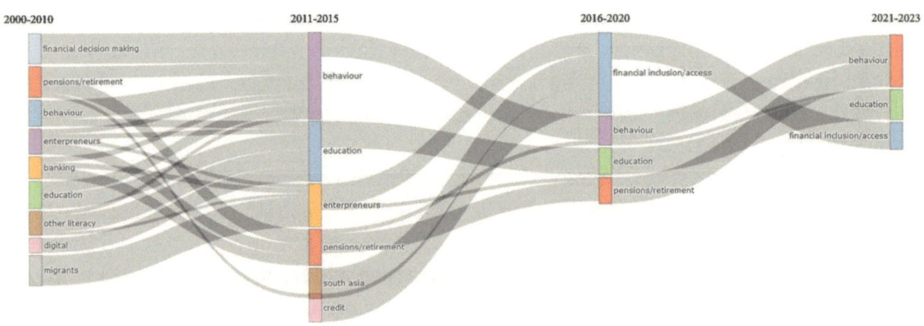

Figure 23.
Thematic evolution.

digital and migrants. The second or middle part shows some of the themes that were widely used from 2011 to 2015. Some of the themes that have emerged during this period are an evolution of the previously used themes and have a connection in their content, but there also is a clear shift in research fields. Education is an extension of previous studies on education, other literacies, digital, entrepreneurs and behaviour. The topic relative to entrepreneurs is a further development of the same theme, but it also attracted studies from migrants, other literacies and banking. The topic of pensions/retirement evolved by attracting studies previously dealing with banking and entrepreneurs. In the behaviour themes many studies previously pertaining to different themes converge. South Asia and credit evidence a new and independent interest in their thematic area of research.

In the subsequent period (2016–2020) in the financial inclusion/access area of research converge studies previously targeted as entrepreneurs, South Asia and credit, while the other thematic areas of research are stable in their development.

5. Conclusions

This study analyses the conceptual structure of the financial literacy research area. We collected our dataset from Scopus and Web of Science, in order to benefit from their differences in disciplines and the contents' coverage. We made a necessary merge among Scopus and WoS data, eliminating duplications and articles not related to our scope of analysis. We also uniformed the data format and created a homogeneous single dataset.

We performed a thematic content analysis focused on authors' keywords, with the assumption that they adequately and synthetically describe both a paper's content and its connections among issues. We operated the methodological choice to construct a new thesaurus file by aggregating similar keywords and also aggregating some terms whose specifications were not providing a useful visualization. In choosing appropriate and standardised keywords, for some terms, we inspired ourselves with the conceptual framework and keywords proposed in other studies on financial literature. In our analysis we did not include the keyword "financial literature," as our dataset was obtained looking for articles on this theme and as we wanted to have a clear visualisation of results pertaining to financial literacy conceptual structure.

We performed a network analysis based on the author keywords occurrences and co-occurrences. We identified thematic clusters, with the help of Vosviewer software, and highlighted internal and external cluster links for specific themes. We also used the automated workflow in Biblioshiny software, focused on prominent journals, countries, themes and evolutionary paths to deepen our analysis and identify possible future developments.

Results show that there has been a quantitative and qualitative evolution of the research domain of financial literacy over a period of time of more than 20 years. There has been a gradual increase in publications over the years with significant growth in the last decade and in particular in the last two years. The growing number of publications is a consequence both of the broadening interest of researchers and journals for the themes of financial literacy and of the entry of new authors, in particular from emerging economies, who contributed to fostering the growth of the financial Literacy domain and to influence its conceptual structure.

Financial Literacy has evolved as an interdisciplinary research field: this observation stems from the gradual emergence of journals with different scopes and perspectives of analysis and from themes and specific topics chosen by authors over time. Initial publications, from sources on consumer and family, services marketing and social psychology domains, have been followed by a growing number of publications in journals dealing with economic and financial issues and, later, in journals dealing with social/psychological/behavioural issues.

The growth of the articles' number and the expanding role of psychological journals paved the path for the journey from a domain-specific approach, initially focused on demographic, economic or financial variables, towards an interdisciplinary approach considering the behaviorual and psychological variables and their influence on financial decision. Behavioural topics gradually attracted greater attention, merged with other themes and became a central and developed theme. Education evolved from mere financial knowledge to its application in various, and in some cases "new," decision-making areas such as the entrepreneurs issues, the digital ones, the ones related to other literacies, the banking ones and, in the very last years, the financial inclusion/access ones. This last theme, highlighted by the growing interest of PVS researchers, is becoming an emergent theme whose borders are gradually broadening to include innovative topics related to entrepreneurs, such as green/environment or sustainability, and digital and technology issues, such as mobile, crypto and peer to peer. Vosviewer detailed node maps on these themes clearly showed the interdisciplinary connections among topics and the proximity of some themes traditionally belonging to different domains.

As for the prospective areas for research, we think that some themes deserve more attention and deeper analysis, such as the links between financial literacy and digital literacy, between financial literacy and entrepreneurs' issues, and financial literacy links with (and effects on) sustainable development goals and inclusion.

Author details

Luisa Anderloni[1*] and Ornella Moro[2]

1 Università di Milano—University of Milan, Italy

2 Università di Sassari—University of Sassari, Italy

*Address all correspondence to: luisa.anderloni@unimi.it

References

[1] Abad-Segura E, González-Zamar MD. Effects of financial education and financial literacy on creative entrepreneurship: A worldwide research. Education Sciences [Internet]. 2019;**9**(3):238. DOI: 10.3390/educsci9030238

[2] Bedi HS, Karn AK, Kaur GP, Duggal R. Financial literacy–A Bibliometric analysis. Our Heritage. 2019;**67**(10):1042-1054

[3] Goyal K, Kumar S. Financial literacy: A systematic review and Bibliometric analysis. International Journal of Consumer Studies. 2020;**14**(1):152. DOI: 10.1111/ijcs.12605

[4] Ingale KK, Paluri RA. Financial literacy and financial behavior: A bibliometric analysis. Review of Behavioral Finance. 2022;**14**(1):130-154. DOI: 10.1108/RBF-06-2020-0141

[5] Zaimovic A, Torlakovic A, Arnaut-Berilo A, Zaimovic T, Dedovic L, Nuhic MM. Mapping financial literacy: A systematic literature review of determinants and recent trends. Sustainability. 2023;**15**:9358. DOI: 10.3390/su15129358

[6] Doku JN, Nabieu GAA. Bank efficiency and competition: Bibliometric analysis of concepts and emerging issues. Journal of Economic Studies. 2023;**October**. DOI: 10.1108/JES-02-2023-0067

[7] Qi B, Marie M, Abdelwahed AS, Khatatbeh IN, Omran M, Fayad AAS. Bank risk literature (1978-2022): A bibliometric analysis and research front mapping. Sustainability. 2023;**15**:4508. DOI: 10.3390/su15054508

[8] Anderloni L, Moro O, Tanda A. Governance and performance in insurance companies: A bibliometric analysis and a meta-analysis. International Journal of Economics and Finance. 2020;**12**(11). DOI: 10.5539/ijefv12n11p1

[9] Khan A, Hassan MK, Paltrinieri A, Dreassi A, Bahoo S. A bibliometric review of takaful literature. International Review of Economics and Finance. 2020;**69**:389-405

[10] Valencia DC, Giraldo MCB, Valencia-Arias J, Palacios-Moya L, Bran-Piedrahita L. Relationship between ICT use and financial education levels in Latin America. International Journal of Innovation, Management and Technology. 2018;**9**(4):174-177

[11] Zhang D, Zhang Z, Managi S. A Bibliometric analysis on green finance: Current status, development, and future directions. Finance Research Letters. 2019;**29**:425-430

[12] OECD-INFE. Financial Education and the Crisis. Policy Paper and Guidance. Paris: OECD; 2009

[13] Caputo A, Kargina M. A user-friendly method to merge Scopus and Web of Science data during bibliometric analysis. Journal of Market Analysis. 2022;**10**:82-88. DOI: 10.1057/s41270-021-00142-7

[14] Echchakoui S. Why and how to merge Scopus and Web of Science during bibliometric analysis: The case of sales force literature from 1912 to 2019. Journal of Marketing Analytics. 2020;**8**:165-184. DOI: 10.1057/s41270-020-00081-9

[15] Joshi A. Comparison between Scopus and ISI web of science. Journal Global Values. 2016;**7**(1):1-11

[16] Visser M, van Eck NJ, Waltman L. Large-scale comparison of bibliographic data sources: Scopus, Web of Science, Dimensions, Crossref, and Microsoft Academic. Quantitative Science Studies. 2021;**2**(1):20-41

[17] Kumpulainen M, Seppänen M. Combining Web of Science and Scopus datasets in citation-based literature study. Scientometrics. 2022;**127**:5613-5631. DOI: 10.1007/s11192-022-04475-

[18] Ullah R, Asghar I, Griffiths MG. An integrated methodology for bibliometric analysis: A case study of internet of things in healthcare applications. Sensors (Basel). 2022;**23**(1):67. DOI: 10.3390/s23010067

[19] van Eck NJ, Waltman L. Software survey: VOSviewer, a computer program for bibliometric mapping. Scientometrics. 2010;**84**(2):523-538

[20] Aria M, Cuccurullo C. Bibliometrix: An R-Tool for Comprehensive Science Mapping Analysis. IdeasRepecOrg; 2017. Available from: https://ideas.repec.org/a/eee/infome/v11y2017i4p959-975.html

[21] Ding Y, Chowdhury G, Foo S. Bibliometric cartography of information retrieval research by using co-word analysis. Information Processing and Management. 2001;**37**(6):817-842. DOI: 10.1016/S0306-4573(00)00051-0

[22] Donthu N, Kumar S, Pattnaik D. Forty-five years of Journal of Business Research: A bibliometric analysis. Journal of Business Research. 2020;**109**(1):1-14

[23] G20/OECD-INFE. Digitalisation and Financial Literacy. Paris: OECD; 2018

Chapter 13

The Future of Finance: Synthesizing CeFi and DeFi for the Benefit of All

Luyao Zhang

Abstract

Decentralized Finance (DeFi) is changing the world of finance with innovative solutions and groundbreaking innovations such as the Automatic Market Maker, Flash Loans, and Initial Coin Offering, fundamentally reshaping financial ecosystems and promoting decentralization and financial inclusion beyond Centralized Finance (CeFi). Nonetheless, this innovation brings forth critical concerns including potential centralization, ethical issues, and questions about inclusivity. In this chapter, we explore the finance literature at the frontier, delving into the definitions, metrics, and quantification used to gauge CeFi and DeFi performance. We emphasize the importance of a human-centric perspective in addressing the shortcomings of financial technology, with the aim of enhancing global financial literacy and bridging the digital divide. Additionally, we address the blockchain trilemma that curtails DeFi's potential positing that an integration of CeFi and DeFi approaches could be the key to overcoming this challenge. Drawing upon insights from ancient Greek philosophy, this chapter concludes by underscoring governance models, be decentralized or centralized, that serve the common good or social welfare, emphasizing that technological progress should distinguish means from ends and be rooted in human values to ensure financial prosperity for all.

Keywords: decentralized finance, centralized finance, financial technology, blockchain, financial inclusion

1. Introduction

Decentralized Finance, or DeFi, is an emerging financial market built on the infrastructure of blockchain technology [1]. Is DeFi the future of finance? By September 8, 2023, DeFi exceeded the market value of 40 billion, supporting various financial services, including payment, exchange, lending, derivatives, and asset management [2]. Furthermore, DeFi introduces brand new financial solutions, such as the Automatic Market Maker [3, 4], Flash Loans [5], and Initial Coin Offering [6]. These innovations have revolutionized the way investors and consumers approach financial systems.

In contrast to Centralized Finance (CeFi), DeFi presents the advantage of liberating financial processes from dependence on centralized intermediaries [7]. Yet, DeFi grapples with the blockchain trilemma: balancing efficiency, security, and decentralization [8]. Recent research indicates potential centralization tendencies in DeFi, attributed to elements such as incentive structures [9–11]. Additionally, challenges in achieving widespread inclusivity in DeFi have been highlighted, possibly due to technical hurdles, despite its foundational aim of fostering inclusiveness [12]. DeFi's complete autonomy serves as a double-edged sword, potentially paving the way for ethical issues such as discrimination [13] and criminal activities [14].

However, it is essential to remember that CeFi has created financial prosperity for hundreds of years, emphasizing the importance of human trust [15]. The question then arises, why "throw the baby with the bathwater?" The debate between decentralization and centralization is not about choosing one over the other but about determining the appropriate balance. As Qin et al. [7] and Wieandt and Heppding [16] suggest, the real value may lie in the interdependence between traditional finance and its decentralized counterpart.

In this chapter, we explore the cutting-edge finance literature, delving into the definitions, metrics, and quantification used to evaluate the performance of CeFi and DeFi. We emphasize the importance of a human-centric perspective in addressing the shortcomings of current financial applications, with the aim of enhancing global financial literacy and bridging the digital divide. Additionally, we consider the promise of a hybrid solution that combines the strengths of both spheres, drawing on insights from economics, law, and technology to envision a progressive future for finance. As illustrated in **Figure 1**, we envision the future of finance for all.

2. The frontier of finance literature

Tables 1 and **2** present a curated selection of literature at the forefront of financial technologies (Fintech), detailing the year and venue of publications, as well as their focus on CeFi, DeFi, or both. Additionally, the methods employed—whether theoretical,

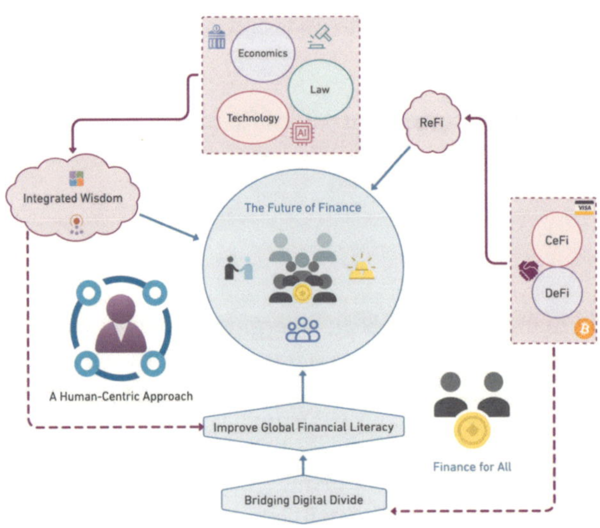

Figure 1.
The future of finance. Note: This figure illustrates a human-centric approach to the future of finance.

Citation (year)	**Venue**	**CeFi**	**DeFi**	**Method**		
				Theoretical	**Empirical**	**Review-based**
[16] (2023)	Journal of Financial Economics	□	■	✓		
[17] (2023)	Production and Operations Management	■	■	✓	✓	
[18] (2023)	Management Science	□	■	✓		
[19] (2023)	Journal of Political Economy	■	□	✓	✓	
[20] (2023)	Management Science	□	■		✓	
[21] (2023)	Management Science	□	■		✓	
[22] (2023)	Journal of Accounting and Economics	□	■		✓	
[23] (2023)	Management Science	□	■		✓	
[24] (2023)	Management Science	□	■		✓	
[25] (2023)	Management Science	■	■		✓	
[26] (2023)	Journal of Finance	□	■	✓		
[27] (2023)	Review of Economic Studies	■	□	✓		
[8] (2022)	Proceedings of the 4th ACM Conference on Advances in Financial Technologies	□	■			✓
[28] (2022)	Journal of Financial Economics	□	■	✓		
[29] (2022)	Journal of Political Economy	■	□	✓		
[30] (2022)	Journal of Financial Economics	□	■	✓		
[31] (2022)	Management Science	□	■		✓	

Note: The symbols in the table have specific meanings.
■: *The topic is the primary focus of the paper.*
□: *The topic is mentioned or discussed but not the main focus.*
✓: *The paper covers the theoretical, empirical, and/or review-based method.*

Table 1.
Literature at the frontier of financial technologies.

Citation (year)	**Venue**	**CeFi**	**DeFi**	**Method**		
				Theoretical	**Empirical**	**Review-based**
[32] (2022)	Journal of Accounting Research	□	■		✓	
[6] (2021)	Management Science	□	■	✓		
[1] (2021)	John Wiley & Sons	□	■			✓
[33] (2021)	Review of Financial Studies	□	■		✓	
[34] (2021)	Financial and Economic Review	■	■			✓
[15] (2021)	Information Systems Research	■	■			✓
[35] (2021)	Management Science	□	■	✓		
[36] (2021)	Crypto Valley Conference on Blockchain Technology (CVCBT)	■	■			✓

Citation (year)	Venue	CeFi	DeFi	Method		
				Theoretical	Empirical	Review-based
[7] (2021)	Financial Cryptography and Data Security	□	■			✓
[37] (2020)	Management Science	□	■	✓	✓	
[38] (2020)	Review of Financial Studies	□	■		✓	
[38] (2020)	Journal of Financial Economics	□	■		✓	
[39] (2020)	Journal of Finance	□	■		✓	
[2] (2020)	Journal of Financial Regulation	□	■			✓
[40] (2019)	Review of Financial Studies	■	■		✓	
[41] (2019)	The Review of Financial Studies	■	■			✓

Note: The symbols in the table have specific meanings.
■*: The topic is the primary focus of the paper.*
□*: The topic is mentioned or discussed but not the main focus.*
✓*: The paper covers the theoretical, empirical, and/or review-based method.*

Table 2.
Literature at the frontier of financial technologies.

empirical, or review-based—are highlighted. Notably, the majority of the literature emphasizes DeFi, while nearly a quarter focuses on CeFi and only a handful on both. The research methodologies are well-distributed among theoretical, empirical, and review-based approaches. However, we observe a conspicuous absence of behavioral and experimental methods, which are central to financial and economic research.

We conducted a preliminary natural language processing analysis on the titles and abstracts of the chosen literature. Those intrigued can find the replicable code on GitHub at: https://github.com/sunshineluyao/finance. The word clouds in **Figures 2** and **3** visually illustrate the most recurrent words in the titles and abstracts from **Tables 1** and **2**, with the size of each word indicating its frequency. Furthermore,

Figure 2.
The word cloud of literature titles. Note: This word cloud provides a visual representation of the most frequently occurring words in the titles of the literature in **Tables 1** *and 2. The size of each word corresponds to its frequency.*

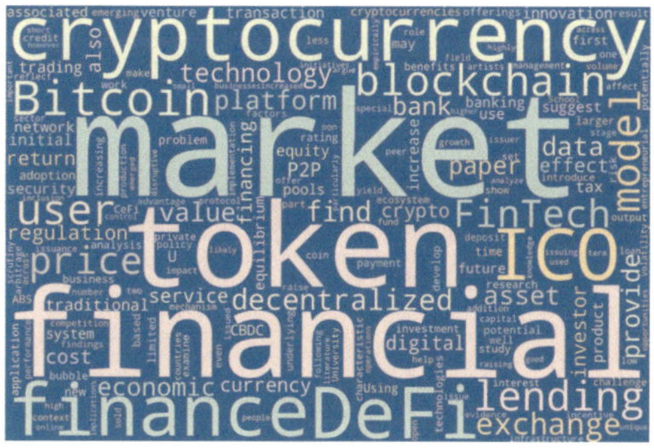

Figure 3.
The word cloud of literature abstract. Note: This word cloud provides a visual representation of the most frequently occurring words in the titles of the literature in ***Tables 1*** *and* ***2****. The size of each word corresponds to its frequency.*

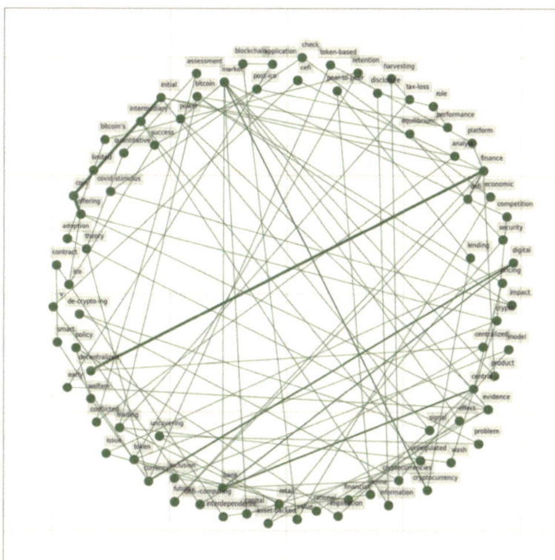

Figure 4.
The bigram of literature title. Note: This figure illustrates the most frequently occurring bigrams (pairs of adjacent words) from the titles of the literature in ***Tables 1*** *and* ***2****. The position, color, or size of each bigram may represent its significance or frequency.*

Figures 4 and **5** display the bigrams derived from the literature's titles and abstracts. These bigrams spotlight prevalent word pairs, with their position, color, or size denoting their significance. **Tables 3** and **4** detail the top 25 bigrams found in the titles and abstracts. The visuals emphasize the dominance of the decentralized finance market. Beyond traditional financial paradigms, there's a marked rise in attention toward DeFi assets such as Bitcoin, cryptocurrency, and tokens, the crypto crowdsourcing phenomenon of initial coin offerings (ICO), and the pivotal role of blockchain infrastructure. While the literature's focus on groundbreaking financial technologies heralds potential advancements, there remains a discernible absence of a human-centric lens that highlights how these technologies can elevate financial literacy, decision-making, and strategy.

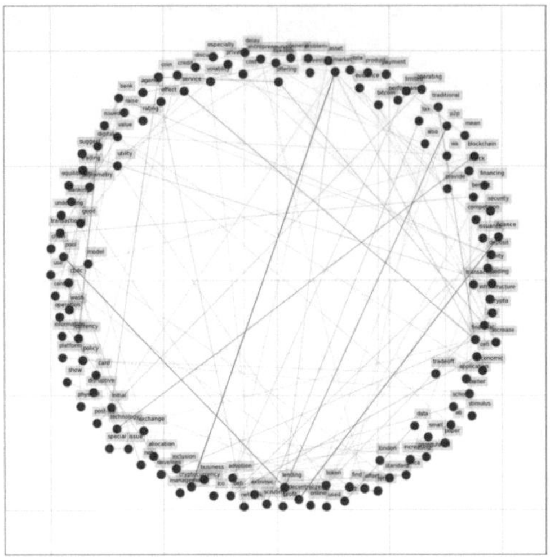

Figure 5.
The bigram of literature abstract. Note: This figure illustrates the most frequently occurring bigrams (pairs of adjacent words) from the abstract of the literature in ***Tables 1*** *and* ***2****. The position, color, or size of each bigram may represent its significance or frequency.*

Bigram	Counts
(decentralized, finance)	5
(coin, offering)	5
(initial, coin)	5
(central, bank)	3
(digital, currency)	3
(cryptocurrency, market)	2
(bank, digital)	2
(finance, defi)	2
(security, equilibrium)	1
(covid-stimulus, check)	1
(asset-backed, security)	1
(evidence, asset-backed)	1
(early, evidence)	1
(application, early)	1
(blockchain, application)	1
(value, blockchain)	1
(economic, value)	1
(check, economic)	1
(retail, trading)	1
(impact, covid-stimulus)	1
(bitcoin, impact)	1

Bigram	Counts
(trading, bitcoin)	1
(bitcoin, pricing)	1
(uncovering, retail)	1
(problem, uncovering)	1

*Note: The table presents frequently occurring bigrams (two adjacent words) extracted from titles of the literature in **Tables 1** and 2. The "counts" column indicates how often each bigram appears across the surveyed literature.*

Table 3.
Bigrams for titles in literature.

Bigram	Counts
(cryptocurrency, market)	11
(decentralized, finance)	9
(p2p, lending)	8
(lending, pool)	8
(digital, currency)	7
(blockchain, technology)	6
(financial, service)	6
(traditional, financial)	5
(coin, offering)	5
(initial, coin)	4
(offering, icos)	4
(tax, scrutiny)	4
(data, set)	4
(cefi, defi)	4
(net, transactional)	3
(special, issue)	3
(value, chain)	3
(cryptocurrency, return)	3
(agency, problem)	3
(business, school)	3
(operating, performance)	3
(post-ico, operating)	3
(bank, deposit)	3
(mean, payment)	3
(cryptocurrency, price)	3

*Note: The table presents frequently occurring bigrams (two adjacent words) extracted from abstracts of the literature in **Tables 1** and 2. The "counts" column indicates how often each bigram appears across the surveyed literature.*

Table 4.
Bigrams for abstracts in literature.

3. DeFi or CeFi: Definition, measurement, and quantification

The first step to philosophizing is to define. Qin et al. [7] first point out the lack of clear definitions to distinguish DeFi from CeFi and provide a CeFi–DeFi Decision Tree with three guiding questions on facets of ownership settlement, transaction execution, and protocol governance:

1. Ownership settlement: Are the financial assets controlled by the user (non-custodial)?

2. Transaction execution: Can someone single-handedly censor a transaction execution?

3. Protocol governance: Can someone single-handedly censor the protocol execution?

As illustrated in **Figure 6**, when adopting a human-centric lens to scrutinize the definition of DeFi, the conclusions drawn can be contentious, especially when viewed without the foundational assumption of a universally high financial literacy level. To delve deeper:

1. *Ownership settlement:* Many DeFi platforms indeed eliminate the need for a trusted third-party custodian for asset management. Yet, this does not unequivocally ensure that financial assets are directly controlled by their users. Implicit in this setup is the expectation that all users possess a uniform level of financial literacy, particularly the expertise to use a cryptocurrency wallet [42]. However, the proficient and safe use of a self-custodial wallet demands a combination of technical acumen and a sustained commitment to security practices. This includes the safeguarding of the wallet's private key, ensuring that the wallet software, associated devices, and networks are secure, and vigilance against potential phishing or fraudulent threats [7].

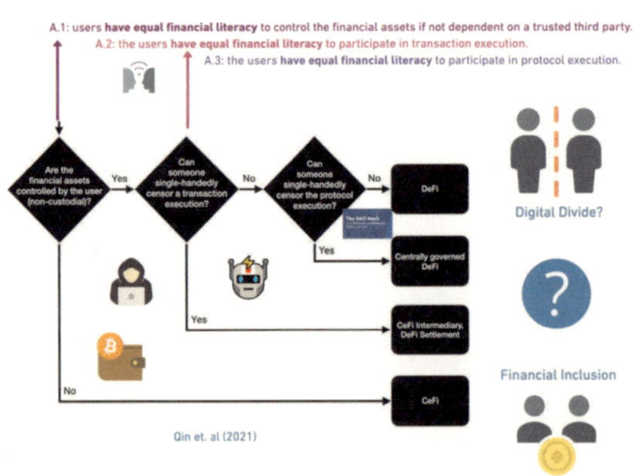

Figure 6.
The definition of CeFi-CeFi. Note: This table expands upon the CeFi-DeFi decision tree as presented in ref. [7]. It delves deeper into the nuanced responses to guiding questions, particularly when factoring in the underlying assumptions about financial literacy levels.

2. *Transaction execution:* While many DeFi platforms are erected upon public blockchains, offering open access for transaction recording, they do not necessarily ensure immunity from individualized transaction censorship. Implicit here is the notion that all participants possess equivalent financial literacy to engage in transaction execution, a presumption that often falls short of reality. The phenomenon of miner extractable value (MEV) exemplifies this, highlighting how dominant entities can disadvantage average users by manipulating transaction inclusions, exclusions, or sequencing. This raises significant ethical quandaries within the DeFi realm [43, 44]. Studies by Wahrstätter et al. [45] and Heimbach et al. [46] further spotlight the centralized tendencies within transaction executions, especially emphasizing the block-creation process of the Proof-of-Stake (PoS) Ethereum blockchain. Additionally, Wahrstätter et al. [47] elaborate on PoS Ethereum's censorship tendencies, noting that nearly 46% of its blocks are produced by censoring entities.

3. *Protocol governance:* Current DeFi systems still grapple with the threat of unilateral censorship during protocol execution. Investigations by Sai et al. [48] highlight the disproportionate influence of core developers and founders of major public blockchains over the protocol's developmental trajectory. Compounding this concern, research by Feichtinger et al. [49] underscores the challenges within decentralized governance structures, such as DAOs in DeFi platforms, pointing to steep participation costs, minimal engagement rates, and a trend leaning toward voting power centralization.

Zhang et al. [9] offer a comprehensive systematization of knowledge pertaining to blockchain decentralization, emphasizing measurement techniques, quantification, and rigorous scientific methodologies. The suite of metrics they introduce—including Shannon entropy, the Gini Coefficient, the Nakamoto Coefficient, and the Herfindahl-Hirschman Index (HHI)—not only gauge blockchain decentralization but can also be applied to assess the decentralization of financial markets. Expanding on this, Ao et al. [10] and Zhang et al. [11] integrate insights from social network analyses, employing network characteristics like the number of components, the giant component size ratio, modularity, standard deviations of degree centrality, the number of cores, and the p-values from the core-peripheral test to quantify transaction decentralization within decentralized banks. Surprisingly, these measures collectively reveal an inclination toward centralization, seemingly at odds with the foundational tenets of decentralized finance. Even more concerning, research by Ao et al. [10] and Zhang et al. [11] pinpoints centralized exchanges as the dominant forces, or "cores," within the network landscape of decentralized banks. This leads to a pressing conundrum: Given the decentralized ethos of DeFi, why is there an observable deviation from its peer-to-peer transaction ideal? The resolution to this may rest in a holistic viewpoint that emphasizes human-centric factors. While the infrastructure for decentralization exists, it requires a well-thought-out incentive design to encourage genuinely decentralized user interactions. Analogously, a distributed transportation system also needs incentives that encourage widespread travel rather than mere clustering around metropolitan hubs.

4. The blockchain trilemma and a synthetic solution

The blockchain trilemma[1], a term initially coined by Vitalik Buterin, the founder of the largest smart contract blockchain Ethereum by market value, posits that when designing a blockchain, developers face a challenging balancing act between three critical pillars: decentralization, security, and scalability. Conventional wisdom asserts that a blockchain can effectively optimize only two of these three factors at any given time. Abadi and Brunnermeier's study [50] offers a robust mathematical substantiation and advancement of the trilemma, demonstrating that any consensus approach, whether centralized or decentralized, inevitably sacrifices one of the key objectives—be it fault-tolerance, resource efficiency, or full transferability. Building on the foundation of blockchain consensus [51–54], DeFi is not exempt from this trilemma. Yet, DeFi indeed contributes beyond CeFi in numerous ways: from the innovative introduction of crypto assets with unique utilities [55–57] and the advent of automated transaction fee models [58, 59], to the development of groundbreaking rule-bound financial management strategies encompassing crypto assets [33, 60–63]. Moreover, DeFi's role in facilitating rule-based monetary policies [64, 65] has bolstered trust in financial systems. The pressing question remains: How can DeFi transcend the trilemma to unlock its full potential?

Current research illustrates the strategies to foster synergies between DeFi and CeFi, enabling them to mutually reinforce each other, especially in scenarios where one might falter [7, 66, 67]. This collaboration aims to enhance the efficiency of financial services by establishing trust for financial data interoperability across diverse systems and entities. It endeavors to offer a dual trust safeguard for digital assets and to protect users from financial crimes and crises. Moreover, it facilitates broader financial user onboarding, effectively expanding the inclusivity of financial ecosystems.

In **Figure** 7, we provide an illustrative comparison between CeFi and DeFi. Let us consider two scenarios: In CeFi, four individuals—B, C, D, and E—hold assets valued at 5, 7, 8, and 10 units, respectively. In DeFi, four different individuals—A, B, C, and D—own assets amounting to 10, 5, 3, and 2 units, respectively. If we arrange individuals in CeFi by ascending financial literacy and those in DeFi by descending financial literacy, Person A could be someone proficient in economics and finance but lacks the technical skills for DeFi. Conversely, Person E might be adept in coding and the blockchain domain but lacks the traditional credentials required to open a bank account in CeFi. In choosing between DeFi and CeFi, one would have to forgo the advantages of the other. However, in an integrated world where both coexist, all five individuals can equally possess assets of 10 units, leading to a more inclusive economic landscape.

We then calculate the Gini coefficient, a widely used statistical measure of income and wealth distribution in a population, used by economists and policymakers to gauge economic inequality [68][2]. In the realm of DeFi, CeFi, and their combined

---

[1] https://coinmarketcap.com/alexandria/glossary/blockchain-trilemma

[2] The Gini coefficient, denoted as G, is a measure of statistical dispersion representing the inequality in a distribution. It ranges between 0 and 1, where 0 represents perfect equality (everyone has the same income) and 1 represents perfect inequality (one person has all the income, and all others have none). Given a population with n individuals and their incomes sorted in non-decreasing order $x_1, x_2, \ldots, x_n$, the Gini coefficient is defined as: $G = \frac{\sum_{i=1}^{n}(2i-n-1)x_i}{n\sum_{i=1}^{n}x_i}$. However, it's important to note that this formula assumes non-negative and nonzero values for x_i, and the incomes are sorted in non-decreasing order.

DOI: http://dx.doi.org/10.5772/intechopen.1003042

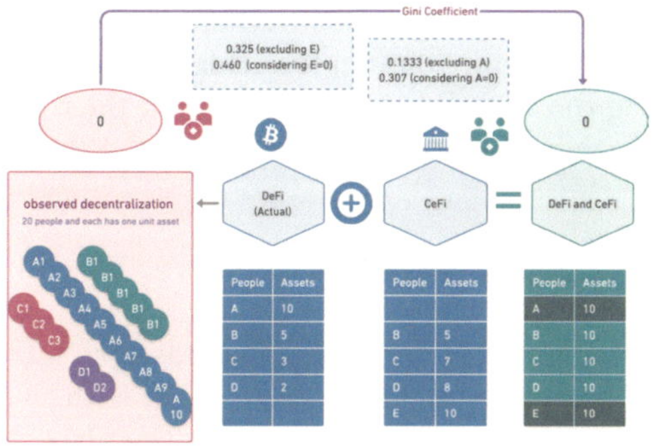

Figure 7.
Financial equality and inclusion: Comparing DeFi, CeFi, and their integration. Note: This illustration provides a concrete example of how an integrated approach, combining both DeFi and CeFi, might enhance financial equality and inclusion, as opposed to opting exclusively for one or the other. Inclusion than choosing one over the other.

scenarios, the respective Gini coefficients ranging from most to least unequal are as follows[3]:

- For DeFi: 0.325, or 0.460 when accounting for individuals with 0 units of assets.
- For CeFi: 0.1333, or 0.307 when considering individuals with no assets.
- For the combined scenario: 0.

It's worth noting a unique challenge in DeFi: Due to its inherent decentralized anonymity, perceived equality may surpass actual levels. For instance, individuals A, B, C, and D might distribute their assets across 10, 5, 3, and 2 crypto wallets, respectively. This distribution would yield an observed Gini coefficient of 0, masking the actual coefficient of 0.325. Consequently, DeFi's drift toward centralization might be more pronounced than it appears.

Our example reinforces the imperative of adopting a human-centric approach, emphasizing that the optimal financial system hinges on individuals' specific financial literacy levels.

- Ideally, if everyone possesses equal and high literacy in both CeFi and DeFi, either system would achieve maximum inclusion and equality.
- In an extreme scenario where the populace has profound literacy in CeFi but minimal familiarity with DeFi, CeFi emerges as the preferred choice to serve the collective interest.
- Conversely, in a situation where individuals are well-versed in DeFi but lack proficiency in CeFi, DeFi stands out as the best system for universal benefit.

[3] The replicable code for calculating Gini coefficient is on GitHub at: https://github.com/sunshineluyao/finance.

In practice, given the varying expertise levels among people, a hybrid solution promises to cater to a larger demographic, fostering both equality and inclusion. Furthermore, bolstering the overall financial literacy of the public emerges as the ultimate pathway to shared prosperity, irrespective of the chosen governance model.

5. Conclusions

DeFi marks a significant shift in the financial landscape, introducing groundbreaking solutions that have redefined our relationship with financial systems. With its rapid growth and innovation, it's undeniable that DeFi has carved a prominent space in today's financial ecosystem. However, as with any new technology, it comes with its set of challenges, from concerns of centralization drift to questions about broader inclusivity. CeFi has anchored global economies for centuries, emphasizing the inalienable value of human trust. After a deep dive into the definition, measurement, and quantification of DeFi, we find that improving global financial literacy is crucial to fulfilling the underlying assumption for DeFi to achieve its core goal of decentralization. Otherwise, the name of DeFi might be merely a pretentious marketing that "justifies and veil decisions of a ruling dictatorship behind the facade of a community [49]".

We contend further that neither decentralization nor centralization is the ultimate goal in themselves, but rather tools to achieve the common good or social welfare [41]. This perspective echoes ancient Greek philosophy, as depicted in **Figure 8**. Ancient Greek philosophers evaluated the merit of a government based on whether it acted for the collective benefit of the community or favored select groups or individuals at the cost of justice. By this standard, we can discern both commendable and flawed governance models across varying degrees of centralization. For a decentralized system to promote the common good, it demands a higher level of civic maturity from its citizens, where autonomy becomes preferable to paternalism in such settings, as discussed in Ref. [69].[4] At its best, the most decentralized governance can epitomize true democracy when complemented by a highly civilized citizenry; at its worst, it risks degenerating into ochlocracy. Conversely, centralized governance can lead to an ideal monarchy or aristocracy when led by benevolent rulers, but it might also devolve into tyranny or oligarchy, subscribing to the adage that absolute power can corrupt absolutely. This same principle extends to financial governance. To harness the potential of decentralized governance for the common good, it's imperative to adopt a human-centric approach that enhances global financial literacy, empowering individuals to actively participate in digital-age financial governance. Such decentralization can be realized through the collaborative efforts of DeFi, leveraging advanced technology, disintermediation, and cross-border engagements, and CeFi, utilizing judicious oversight, networking hubs, and a gold standard of efficiency [2].

To wrap up, instead of framing the ascent of DeFi as a threat rendering traditional finance redundant, it's more insightful to envision it as a collaborative frontier. Marrying the trust and solidity of CeFi with the dynamism and inclusivity of DeFi can herald a composite financial paradigm. Such a system would not only elevate global financial literacy but also pave the way for an inclusive financial future for all. As we

[4] For example, if all citizens can securely safeguard the private keys to their financial assets, they would not need to depend on custodial institutions for recovery when their keys are lost or stolen due to financial crimes.

DOI: http://dx.doi.org/10.5772/intechopen.1003042

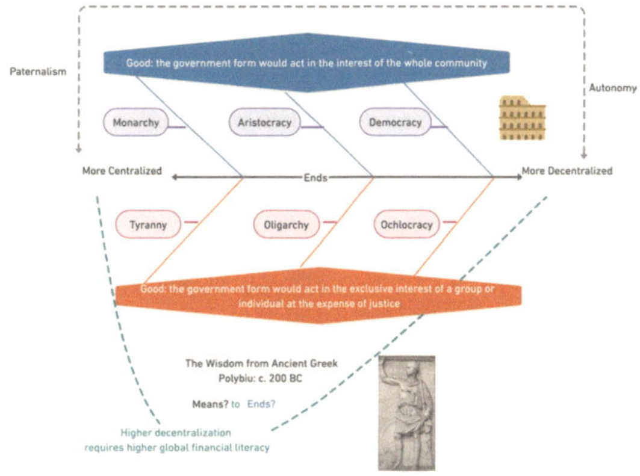

Figure 8.
The future of financial governance: Ends or means? Note: This figure illustrates the distinction between centralized and decentralized approaches in governance design. It highlights the ultimate goal of achieving common goods, drawing upon insights from ancient Greek philosophy.

move forward, it's imperative to ensure that our pursuit of technological innovation remains anchored in human-centric values, embracing the best of both worlds to achieve financial prosperity for everyone.

Acknowledgements

Luyao Zhang is supported by the National Science Foundation China on the project entitled "Trust Mechanism Design on Blockchain: An Interdisciplinary Approach of Game Theory, Reinforcement Learning, and Human-AI Interactions (Grant No. 12201266)."

Notes/thanks/other declarations

I would like to acknowledge the pioneering scholars in financial technologies, including Profs. Campbell Harvey, Lin William Cong, and Hanna Halaburda, for their invaluable inspiration.

Author details

Luyao Zhang
Duke Kunshan University, Suzhou, China

*Address all correspondence to: lz183@duke.edu

References

[1] Harvey CR, Ramachandran A, Santoro J. DeFi and the Future of Finance. Hoboken, NJ: John Wiley & Sons; 2021. Available from: https://www.wiley.com/en-us/about

[2] Zetzsche DA, Arner DW, Buckley RP. Decentralized finance (defi). Journal of Financial Regulation. 2020;**6**:172-203

[3] Mohan V. Automated market makers and decentralized exchanges: A DeFi primer. Financial Innovation. 2022; **8**(1):20

[4] Xu J, Paruch K, Cousaert S, Feng Y. Sok: Decentralized exchanges (dex) with automated market maker (amm) protocols. ACM Computing Surveys. 2023;**55**(11):1-50

[5] Wang D, Wu S, Lin Z, Wu L, Yuan X, Zhou Y, et al. Towards a first step to understand flash loan and its applications in defi ecosystem. In: Proceedings of the Ninth International Workshop on Security in Blockchain and Cloud Computing. ACM. 2021. pp. 23-28. Available from: https://dl.acm.org/doi/proceedings/10.1145/3133956

[6] Chod J, Lyandres E. A theory of ICOs: Diversification, agency, and information asymmetry. Management Science. 2021; **67**(10):5969-5989

[7] Qin K, Zhou L, Afonin Y, Lazzaretti L, Gervais A. CeFi vs. DeFi–Comparing centralized to decentralized finance. In: Presented at the 2021 Crypto Valley Conference on Blockchain Technology (CVCBT). Zug, Switzerland; October 28 – November 5 2021. Available from: https://arxiv.org/abs/2106.08157

[8] Werner S, Perez D, Gudgeon L, Klages-Mundt A, Harz D, Knottenbelt W. Sok: Decentralized finance (defi). In: Proceedings of the 4th ACM Conference on Advances in Financial Technologies. Association for Computing Machinery (ACM). 2022. pp. 30-46. Available from: https://dl.acm.org/doi/proceedings/10.1145/3133956

[9] Zhang L, Ma X, Liu Y. SoK: Blockchain decentralization. arXiv preprint arXiv:220504256. 2022

[10] Ao Z, Horvath G, Zhang L. Is decentralized finance actually decentralized? A social network analysis of the Aave protocol on the Ethereum blockchain; 2023

[11] Zhang Y, Chen Z, Sun Y, Liu Y, Zhang L. Blockchain network analysis: A comparative study of decentralized banks. In: Science and Information Conference. Berlin, Germany: Springer; 2023. pp. 1022-1042

[12] Cong LW, Tang K, Wang Y, Zhao X. Inclusion and Democratization through web3 and Defi? Initial Evidence from the Ethereum Ecosystem. Cambridge, MA, USA: National Bureau of Economic Research; 2023

[13] Zhang L, Sun Y, Quan Y, Cao J, Tong X. On the mechanics of NFT valuation: AI ethics and social media. arXiv preprint arXiv:230710201. 2023

[14] Trozze A, Kamps J, Akartuna EA, Hetzel FJ, Kleinberg B, Davies T, et al. Cryptocurrencies and future financial crime. Crime Science. 2022;**11**:1-35

[15] Hendershott T, Zhang X, Zhao JL, Zheng Z. FinTech as a game changer: Overview of research frontiers. Information Systems Research. 2021; **32**(1):1-17

[16] Chod J, Lyandres E. Product market competition with crypto tokens and smart contracts. Journal of Financial Economics. 2023;**149**(1):73-91

[17] Chung S, Kim K, Lee CH, Oh W. Interdependence between online peer-to-peer lending and cryptocurrency markets and its effects on financial inclusion. Production and Operations Management. 2023;**32**:1939-1957. DOI: 10.1111/poms.13950

[18] Sockin M, Xiong W. A model of cryptocurrencies. Management Science. 2023

[19] Chiu J, Davoodalhosseini SM, Jiang J, Zhu Y. Bank market power and central bank digital currency: Theory and quantitative assessment. Journal of Political Economy. 2023;**131**(5): 1213-1248

[20] Barth A, Andreas J, Laturnus R, Mansouri S, Wagner A. Conflicted analysts and initial coin offerings. Management Science. 2023 forthcoming

[21] Cong LW, Li X, Tang K, Yang Y. Crypto wash trading. 2023

[22] Cong LW, Landsman W, Maydew E, Rabetti D. Tax-loss harvesting with cryptocurrencies. Journal of Accounting and Economics. 2023:101607

[23] Davydiuk T, Gupta D, Rosen S. De-crypto-ing signals in initial coin offerings: Evidence of rational token retention. Management Science. 2023

[24] Divakaruni A, Zimmerman P. Uncovering retail trading in bitcoin: The impact of COVID-19 stimulus checks. Management Science. 2023

[25] Chen X, Cheng Q, Luo T. The economic value of blockchain applications: Early evidence from asset-backed securities. Management Science. 2023

[26] Biais B, Bisiere C, Bouvard M, Casamatta C, Menkveld AJ. Equilibrium bitcoin pricing. The Journal of Finance. 2023;**78**(2):967-1014

[27] Keister T, Sanches D. Should central banks issue digital currency? The Review of Economic Studies. 2023;**90**(1): 404-431

[28] Hinzen FJ, John K, Saleh F. Bitcoin's limited adoption problem. Journal of Financial Economics. 2022;**144**(2): 347-369

[29] Williamson S. Central bank digital currency: Welfare and policy implications. Journal of Political Economy. 2022;**130**(11):2829-2861

[30] Cong LW, Li Y, Wang N. Token-based platform finance. Journal of Financial Economics. 2022;**144**(3): 972-991

[31] Lyandres E, Palazzo B, Rabetti D. Initial coin offering (ico) success and post-ico performance. Management Science. 2022;**68**(12):8658-8679

[32] Bourveau T, De George ET, Ellahie A, Macciocchi D. The role of disclosure and information intermediaries in an unregulated capital market: Evidence from initial coin offerings. Journal of Accounting Research. 2022;**60**(1):129-167

[33] Liu Y, Tsyvinski A. Risks and returns of cryptocurrency. The Review of Financial Studies. 2021;**34**(6):2689-2727

[34] Katona T. Decentralized finance: The possibilities of a blockchain "money lego" system. Financial and Economic Review. 2021;**20**(1):74-102

[35] Wei Y, Dukes A. Cryptocurrency adoption with speculative price bubbles. Marketing Science. 2021;**40**(2):241-260

[36] Bartoletti M, Chiang JH, Lafuente AL. SoK: Lending pools in decentralized finance. In: Financial Cryptography and Data Security. FC 2021 International Workshops: CoDecFin, DeFi, VOTING, and WTSC, Virtual Event. Berlin, Germany: Springer; March 5, 2021. Revised Selected Papers 25, 2021. pp. 553-578

[37] Whitaker A, Kräussl R. Fractional equity, blockchain, and the future of creative work. Management Science. 2020;**66**(10):4594-4611

[38] Howell ST, Niessner M, Yermack D. Initial coin offerings: Financing growth with cryptocurrency token sales. The Review of Financial Studies. 2020;**33**(9): 3925-3974

[39] Griffin JM, Shams A. Is bitcoin really untethered? The Journal of Finance. 2020;**75**(4):1913-1964

[40] Chen MA, Wu Q, Yang B. How valuable is FinTech innovation? The Review of Financial Studies. 2019;**32**(5): 2062-2106

[41] Goldstein I, Jiang W, Karolyi GA. To FinTech and beyond. The Review of Financial Studies. 2019;**32**(5):1647-1661

[42] Suratkar S, Shirole M, Bhirud S. Cryptocurrency wallet: A review. In: 2020 4th International Conference on Computer, Communication and Signal Processing (ICCCSP). Vol. 2020. New York City, United States: IEEE; 2020. pp. 1-7. Available from: https://www.ieee.org/conferences/publishing/index.html

[43] Daian P, Goldfeder S, Kell T, Li Y, Zhao X, Bentov I, et al. Flash boys 2.0: Frontrunning in decentralized exchanges, miner extractable value, and consensus instability. In: 2020 IEEE Symposium on Security and Privacy (SP). New York, NY: IEEE; 2020. pp. 910-927

[44] Fu Y, Zhuang Z, Zhang L. Ai ethics on blockchain: Topic analysis on twitter data for blockchain security. In: Science and Information Conference. Springer; 2023. pp. 82-100

[45] Wahrstätter A, Zhou L, Qin K, Svetinovic D, Gervais A. Time to Bribe: Measuring block construction market. arXiv preprint arXiv:230516468. 2023

[46] Heimbach L, Kiffer L, Torres CF, Wattenhofer R. Ethereum's proposer-builder separation: Promises and realities. arXiv preprint arXiv: 230519037. 2023

[47] Wahrstätter A, Ernstberger J, Yaish A, Zhou L, Qin K, Tsuchiya T, et al. Blockchain censorship. arXiv preprint arXiv:230518545. 2023

[48] Sai AR, Buckley J, Fitzgerald B, Le Gear A. Taxonomy of centralization in public blockchain systems: A systematic literature review. Information Processing & Management. 2021;**58**(4): 102584

[49] Feichtinger R, Fritsch R, Vonlanthen Y, Wattenhofer R. The hidden shortcomings of (D) AOs–An empirical study of on-chain governance. arXiv preprint arXiv:230212125. 2023

[50] Abadi J, Brunnermeier M. Blockchain Economics. Cambridge, MA, USA: National Bureau of Economic Research; 2018

[51] Bamakan SMH, Motavali A, Bondarti AB. A survey of blockchain

consensus algorithms performance evaluation criteria. Expert Systems with Applications. Amsterdam, Netherlands: Elsevier; 2020;**154**:113385

[52] Lashkari B, Musilek P. A comprehensive review of blockchain consensus mechanisms. IEEE Access. 2021;**9**:43620-43652

[53] Bano S, Sonnino A, Al-Bassam M, Azouvi S, McCorry P, Meiklejohn S, et al. SoK: Consensus in the age of blockchains. In: Proceedings of the 1st ACM Conference on Advances in Financial Technologies. ACM. 2019. pp. 183-198. Available from: https://dl.acm.org/doi/proceedings/10.1145/3133956

[54] Zhang L, Tian X. On blockchain we cooperate: An evolutionary game perspective. arXiv preprint arXiv: 221205357. 2022

[55] Catalini C, Gans JS. Initial Coin Offerings and the Value of Crypto Tokens. Cambridge, MA, USA: National Bureau of Economic Research; 2018

[56] Yu H, Sun Y, Liu Y, Zhang L. Bitcoin Gold, Litecoin Silver: An Introduction to Cryptocurrency's Valuation and Trading Strategy. arXiv preprint arXiv: 230800013. 2023

[57] Liu Y, Zhang L, Zhao Y. Deciphering bitcoin blockchain data by cohort analysis. Scientific Data. 2022;**9**(1):136

[58] Liu Y, Lu Y, Nayak K, Zhang F, Zhang L, Zhao Y. Empirical analysis of eip-1559: Transaction fees, waiting times, and consensus security. In: Proceedings of the 2022 ACM SIGSAC Conference on Computer and Communications Security. ACM. 2022. pp. 2099-2113. Available from: https://dl.acm.org/doi/proceedings/10.1145/3133956

[59] Zhang L, Zhang F. Understand waiting time in transaction fee mechanism: An interdisciplinary perspective. arXiv preprint arXiv: 230502552. 2023

[60] Liu Y, Zhang L. Cryptocurrency valuation: An explainable AI approach. In: Science and Information Conference. Berlin, Germany: Springer; 2023. pp. 785-807

[61] Zhang L, Wu T, Lahrichi S, Salas-Flores CG, Li J. A data science pipeline for algorithmic trading: A comparative study of applications for finance and cryptoeconomics. In: 2022 IEEE International Conference on Blockchain (Blockchain). New York, NY: IEEE; 2022. pp. 298-303

[62] Zhu J, Zhang L. Educational game on cryptocurrency investment: Using microeconomic decision-making to understand macroeconomics principles. Eastern Economic Journal. 2023;**49**(2): 262-272

[63] Jiang Z, Liang J. Cryptocurrency portfolio management with deep reinforcement learning. In: 2017 Intelligent Systems Conference (IntelliSys). New York, NY: IEEE; 2017. pp. 905-913

[64] Pernice IG, Henningsen S, Proskalovich R, Florian M, Elendner H, Scheuermann B. Monetary stabilization in cryptocurrencies–design approaches and open questions. In: 2019 Crypto Valley Conference on Blockchain Technology (Cvcbt). New York, NY: IEEE; 2019. pp. 47-59

[65] Zhang L, Liu Y. Optimal algorithmic monetary policy. arXiv preprint arXiv: 210407888. 2021

[66] Wieandt A, Heppding L. Centralized and decentralized finance: Coexistence

or convergence? In: The Fintech Disruption: How Financial Innovation Is Transforming the Banking Industry. Berlin, Germany: Springer; 2023. pp. 11-51

[67] Zhang S. The design principle of blockchain: An initiative for the sok of soks. arXiv preprint arXiv:230100479. 2023

[68] Dorfman R. A formula for the Gini coefficient. The Review of Economics and Statistics. 1979;**61**(1):146-149. DOI: 10.2307/1924845. Available from: https://www.jstor.org/stable/1924845

[69] Dworkin G. Paternalism. In: Zalta EN, editor. The Stanford Encyclopedia of Philosophy. Fall 2020 ed. Stanford, CA: Metaphysics Research Lab, Stanford University; 2020